WITHDRAWN

THE BRITANNICA GUIDE TO

POLITICAL AND SOCIAL MOVEMENTS

THAT CHANGED THE MODERN WORLD

TURNING POINTS IN HISTORY

THE BRITANNICA GUIDE TO

POLITICAL AND SOCIAL MOVEMENTS

THAT CHANGED THE MODERN WORLD

EDITED BY HEATHER M. CAMPBELL, SENIOR EDITOR, GEOGRAPHY AND HISTORY

Britannica®
Educational Publishing

IN ASSOCIATION WITH

ROSEN
EDUCATIONAL SERVICES

Published in 2010 by Britannica Educational Publishing
(a trademark of Encyclopædia Britannica, Inc.)
in association with Rosen Educational Services, LLC
29 East 21st Street, New York, NY 10010.

First Edition

Britannica Educational Publishing
Michael I. Levy: Executive Editor
Marilyn L. Barton: Senior Coordinator, Production Control
Steven Bosco: Director, Editorial Technologies
Lisa S. Braucher: Senior Producer and Data Editor
Yvette Charboneau: Senior Copy Editor
Kathy Nakamura: Manager, Media Acquisition
Heather M. Campbell: Senior Editor, Geography and History

Rosen Educational Services
Jeanne Nagle: Senior Editor
Laura Cummings: Editor
Nelson Sá: Art Director
Matthew Cauli: Designer
Introduction by Jeri Freedman

Library of Congress Cataloging-in-Publication Data

The Britannica guide to political and social movements that changed the modern world /
edited by Heather M. Campbell.—1st ed.
    p. cm.—(Turning points in history)
"In association with Britannica Educational Publishing, Rosen Educational Services."
ISBN 978-1-61530-016-7 (library binding)
1. History, Modern. 2. Liberalism—History. 3. Conservatism—History. 4. Socialism—
History. 5. Communism—History. 6. Fascism—History. 7. Anarchism—History. 8.
Democracy—History. 9. Nationalism—History. 10. Social movements—History. I.
Campbell, Heather M.
D208.B68 2010
322.4—dc22

                                                                    2009037443

On the cover: Prague residents resist approaching Soviet tanks during 1968's Prague
Spring reform movement. Change brought about by political and social movements is
often met with opposition, from heated debate to physical violence. *LIBOR HAJSKY/
AFP/Getty Images*

CONTENTS

108

147

295

301

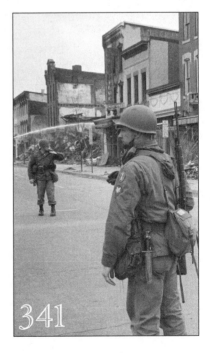

Introduction

There is strength in numbers, which is why efforts to effect change that have plenty of support and high participation rates are the most likely to succeed. Such movements are formed when people organize with the goal of putting ideas into action, often in an attempt to bring about political or social change. As many successful political and social movements through the ages have demonstrated, groups with a well-thought-out agenda and clear goals can raise civilizations to new heights or bring them down, create empires or destroy them. They can radically alter the course of a nation and the lives of its citizens.

The history and foundations of the most influential political and social movements in the world form the basis of this book. A selection of movements is covered, including a number of political philosophies—democracy, socialism, communism, fascism—that seek to define the way that people should be ruled. These are the organized concepts and beliefs that, once put into practice by dedicated interest groups, have changed the world—sometimes for the better, sometimes not.

By their very nature, political and social movements deal with two main questions: How should society be organized, and what is the best way to bring about a reorganization, if necessary? Naturally, the former question implies that the present arrangement of society is less than ideal—at least according to those people who wish to improve their lot. Methods of reorganizing society include persuasion and coercion. Persuasion involves appeals designed to sway people's minds and attitudes through the dissemination of information. Coercion, on the other hand, involves the concrete use or threat of violence. This can be organized force such as military conquest or internal revolution, or guerrilla tactics such as those used by terrorists.

Throughout history, certain political movements have become so powerful that they were able to overthrow a country's existing government through revolution, which is the near-perfect melding of persuasion and coercion. Spurred (and persuaded) by the eloquence of fervent individuals, ordinary citizens have risen up and fought for the right to determine how they were governed. For instance, the leaders of the American and French revolutions were heavily influenced by ideas expressed in the writings of men such as John Locke, Thomas Hobbes, Jean-Jacques Rousseau, and Charles-Louis de Secondat, Baron de La Brède et de Montesquieu. The concepts popularized by these writers, which form the basis of classical liberalism, support the idea that people have the right to take action to improve the conditions under which they live, and that the authority of government over individuals should be limited. The spread of their ideas compelled people to take up arms against what they deemed an oppressive regime. The result of both revolutions was a move from monarchy to democracy.

Another political movement that effected radical governmental change through revolution was the form of socialism called communism. Based on ideas proposed by a philosopher, Karl Marx, communism was formulated to address the problem of class struggle, whereby the upper class has most of the wealth while the lower classes do most of the work. The supporters of communism believed that they could better the lives of everyone if all people could be made to act for the common, rather than the individual, good. In the 20th century both Russia and China overthrew imperial regimes and ultimately instituted communist forms of government.

In contrast to the authoritarian rule of the communists, social democracy, which was adopted in countries such as the UK, provides a balance between the overarching individual freedom of classical liberalism and the rigidly structured form of communism seen in the Soviet Union and China. Under this form of socialism, the government maintains control of the distribution of some resources to the populace, such as national health care, so that everyone has access to them. However, the people retain their individual freedoms and right to self-rule.

Fascism, which had flourished throughout Europe between 1919 and 1945, gives all authority to a central government. The ruling party believes in rule by an elite group—themselves—and disdains democracy and liberal principles. National pride is a guiding principle of fascism. National fascism gave rise to groups such as Adolf Hitler's Nazi Party.

National fascism is an extreme form of nationalism, loyalty to one's country above all others. Positive change can come about in this type of atmosphere, as citizens of a country exert their right to self-determinism—making their own laws and ruling themselves. This happened when colonies ruled by European powers rebelled and became independent nations.

Yet another type of political movement is based on religious beliefs. Some religio-political movements are designed to directly promote the tenets of a particular faith. Among these movements are Christian and Islamic fundamentalism. Both of these movements seek to change the laws and behaviours of society to follow the rules of the faith. An example of such a movement is the rule of the Taliban in modern Afghanistan, which forced all citizens to conform to its interpretation of Islam.

However, conversion is not always the goal of religious political movements. Some political movements use religion as a tool to achieve political ends—for example, to recruit members for holy wars and violent uprisings against those they consider to be their enemies. An example of such movements is Hezbollah, an Islamic organization that has employed violence to achieve political ends.

Not all organized movements are aimed at regime change or political upheaval, however. Social movements are designed to encourage change by influencing the attitudes of individuals in society. Such movements may use political means to improve the conditions of particular groups within society, by enacting legislation that promotes social change. Within the past 150 years, several important social movements have greatly influenced the political climates of countries around the world. Others have great potential to make significant political changes for years to come.

The abolition movement was a reaction to the cruelty and inhumanity of the African slave trade. In the mid-1700s, protests arose that questioned the practice of slavery. Abolitionists in Europe and the United States met with initial success. However, slavery was an integral part of the highly profitable agricultural economy in the southern United States. The right to own slaves was one of the main issues that led to the conflict between the pro-slavery South and abolitionist North known as the American Civil War.

After Pres. Abraham Lincoln's Emancipation Proclamation (1863), which freed slaves in the United States, the abolitionist movement quickly gained momentum in other nations, and slavery was eventually stamped out for good. The end of slavery, however, did not yet guarantee African Americans equality. Even though most states had laws regarding the equal treatment of whites and blacks, blacks were often denied certain constitutional rights. The separation of whites and blacks, known as segregation, became common. It was not until the civil rights movement, which began in the 1950s and picked up steam in the 1960s, that American blacks gained more rights.

Civil rights leaders have pursued political and economic avenues to bring about social change. In the early 1950s, the National Association for the Advancement of Colored People (NAACP) brought the fight against segregation to the U.S. Supreme Court. The 1954 case of *Brown* v. *Board of Education of Topeka* made segregation unconstitutional. The Alabama bus boycott, instigated after the arrest of Rosa Parks and led by the charismatic Rev. Martin Luther King, Jr., was a nonviolent yet reasonably effective means of steering the existing social and political system toward greater equality.

Race is not the only motivating force behind groups that have organized to gain some measure of equality. Sexual orientation and gender have also been the subjects of social movements around the world. Gay men and lesbians have faced many of the same issues as African Americans in the 1960s with regard to oppressive laws and social stigmas; in fact, many in the gay rights movement frequently draw comparisons between their struggle and the civil rights movement. The women's rights movement, also called the feminist movement, emerged in the 19th century, with suffrage as the main goal. The movement weakened after women achieved the right to vote but experienced an American resurgence in the 1960s, focusing on fairness in the workplace. Today the feminist movement rallies support for women in developing nations and countries with tyrannical religious or governmental rules.

There also are groups that believe rights are not exclusive to human beings. Animal rights activists believe animals have ethical and moral rights. Some consider the animal rights movement the first social reform movement started by philosophers. In 1972, Australian philosopher Peter Singer wrote *Animal Liberation*, one of the movement's most important documents. Singer and other philosophers argued that since animals can suffer, it is a moral duty to keep them from harm. Increasing reports of animal brutality at factory farms and research facilities have resulted in the formation of numerous animal rights organizations. Perhaps the most notable group today is the People for the Ethical Treatment of Animals (PETA). Today, groups like PETA have multimillion-dollar budgets and millions of members. Their persistent fight has helped to initiate widespread reforms and regulations against animal cruelty.

The political and ethical movement called environmentalism strives to protect and improve the natural environment. Environmentalists hope to change harmful human activities through political, social, and economic ways. The first environmentalists advocated the efficient use of Earth's resources, known as conservation. Some fought to have large areas of wilderness protected by government legislation.

In the 1960s, activists began to advocate "green" living. Many groups focused on nonviolent protests and increased education. Others resorted to criminal activities called ecoterrorism. In Europe, political parties collectively known as the Greens have become larger and more vocal since the early 1970s. The success of these groups may have helped to draw attention to the growing environmental problems around the world. International environmental groups such as Greenpeace are dedicated to protecting the environment through direct, nonviolent actions.

Pacifism is an ethical movement against the use of war and violence to settle disputes. Since wars are instigated and carried out by national ruling bodies, pacifists are often at odds with governments, national laws, and militaries. While all pacifists have a similar goal—an end to war and violence—various groups go about achieving this goal in different ways. Some choose to educate the population about the inherent evils of war. Others choose to stage public demonstrations and protests. The Women's International League for Peace and Freedom (WILPF), founded by Jane Addams, is the oldest continuously active peace organization in the United States.

Through this book, readers should be better able to garner an understanding of the nature of the various political and social movements that have shaped the world in the past, have created the issues we are dealing with today, and will continue to influence our world in the future.

Chapter 1: Liberalism

Liberalism is one of the most enduring political doctrines in human history, fostering the rise of representative democracy throughout the world. It takes protecting and enhancing the freedom of the individual to be the central problem of politics. Liberals typically believe that government is necessary to protect individuals from being harmed by others, but they also recognize that government itself can pose a threat to liberty. As the revolutionary American pamphleteer Thomas Paine expressed it in "Common Sense" (1776), government is at best "a necessary evil." Laws, judges, and police are needed to secure the individual's life and liberty, but their coercive power may also be turned against him. The problem, then, is to devise a system that gives government the power necessary to protect individual liberty but also prevents those who govern from abusing that power.

The problem is compounded when one asks whether this is all that government can or should do on behalf of individual freedom. Some liberals—the so-called neoclassical liberals, or libertarians—answer that it is. Since the late 19th century, however, most liberals have insisted that the powers of government can promote as well as protect the freedom of the individual. According to modern liberalism, the chief task of government is to remove obstacles that prevent individuals from living freely or from fully realizing their potential. Such obstacles include poverty, disease, discrimination, and ignorance. The disagreement among liberals over whether government should promote individual freedom rather than merely protect it is reflected to some extent in the different prevailing conceptions of liberalism in the United States and Europe since the late 20th century. In the United States liberalism

*Part of Franklin Roosevelt's New Deal program involved creating jobs
for those who had become unemployed during the Great Depression. The
program is considered a prime example of liberalism in action.* New York
Times Co./Hulton Archive/Getty Images

is associated with the welfare-state policies of the New
Deal program of the Democratic administration of Pres.
Franklin D. Roosevelt, whereas in Europe it is more
commonly associated with a commitment to limited government and laissez-faire economic policies.

CLASSICAL LIBERALISM

Although liberal ideas were not noticeable in European
politics until the early 16th century, liberalism has a considerable "prehistory" reaching back to the Middle Ages
and even earlier. In the Middle Ages the rights and responsibilities of the individual were determined by his place in
a hierarchical social system that placed great stress upon
acquiescence and conformity. Under the impact of the
slow commercialization and urbanization of Europe in

the later Middle Ages, the intellectual ferment of the Renaissance, and the spread of Protestantism in the 16th century, the old feudal stratification of society gradually began to dissolve, leading to a fear of instability so powerful that monarchical absolutism was viewed as the only remedy to civil dissension.

The ambitions of national rulers and the requirements of expanding industry and commerce led gradually to the adoption of economic policies based on mercantilism, a school of thought that advocated government intervention in a country's economy to increase state wealth and power. However, as such intervention increasingly served established interests and inhibited enterprise, it was challenged by members of the newly emerging middle class. This challenge was a significant factor in the great revolutions that rocked England and France in the 17th and 18th centuries — most notably the English Civil Wars (1642–51), the Glorious Revolution (1688–89), the American Revolution (1775–83), and the French Revolution (1789). Classical liberalism as an articulated creed is a result of those great collisions.

In the English Civil Wars, the absolutist king Charles I was defeated by the forces of Parliament and eventually executed. The Glorious Revolution resulted in the abdication and exile of James II and the establishment of a complex form of balanced government in which power was divided between the king, his ministers, and Parliament. In time this system would become a model for liberal political movements in other countries. The political ideas that helped to inspire these revolts were given formal expression in the work of the English philosophers Thomas Hobbes and John Locke. In *Leviathan* (1651), Hobbes argued that the absolute power of the sovereign was ultimately justified by the consent of the governed, who agreed, in a hypothetical social contract, to obey the

THOMAS HOBBES

(b. April 5, 1588, Westport, Wiltshire, Eng. — d. Dec. 4, 1679,
Hardwick Hall, Derbyshire)

Thomas Hobbes was an influential English philosopher
and political theorist whose works are considered important statements of the nascent ideas of liberalism. The son
of a vicar who abandoned his family, Hobbes was raised by
his uncle. After graduating from the University of Oxford
he became a tutor and traveled with his pupil in Europe,
where he engaged Galileo in philosophical discussions on
the nature of motion. He later turned to political theory,
but his support for absolutism put him at odds with the
rising antiroyalist sentiment of the time. He fled to Paris
in 1640, where he tutored the future King Charles II of
England. In Paris he wrote his best-known work, *Leviathan*
(1651), in which he attempted to justify the absolute power
of the sovereign on the basis of a hypothetical social contract in which individuals seek to protect themselves from
one another by agreeing to obey the sovereign in all matters. Hobbes returned to Britain in 1651 after the death of
Charles I.

sovereign in all matters in exchange for a guarantee of
peace and security.

Locke also held a social-contract theory of government, but he maintained that the parties to the contract
could not reasonably place themselves under the absolute
power of a ruler. Absolute rule, he argued, is at odds with
the point and justification of political authority, which is
that it is necessary to protect the person and property of
individuals and to guarantee their natural rights to freedom of thought, speech, and worship. Significantly, Locke

JOHN LOCKE
(b. Aug. 29, 1632, Wrington, Somerset, Eng.—d. Oct. 28, 1704, Oates, Essex)

John Locke was an English philosopher integral to the development of liberalism. Educated at Oxford, principally in medicine and science, he later became physician and adviser to the future 3rd earl of Shaftesbury (1667–72). He moved to France, but after Shaftesbury's fall in 1683 he fled to the Netherlands, where he supported the future William III. Locke returned to England after the Glorious Revolution (1688–89) to become commissioner of appeals, a post he held until his death. In his major philosophical work, *Essay Concerning Human Understanding* (1690), he argued that knowledge begins in sensation or introspection rather than in innate ideas, as the philosophers of rationalism held. In *Two Treatises of Government* (1690), he defended a doctrine of natural rights and a conception of political authority as limited and conditional on the ruler's fulfillment of his obligation to serve the public good. A classic formulation of the principles of political liberalism, this work influenced the American and French revolutions and the Constitution of the United States.

thought that revolution is justified when the sovereign fails to fulfill these obligations. Indeed, it appears that he began writing his major work of political theory, *Two Treatises of Government* (1690), precisely in order to justify the revolution of two years before.

By the time Locke had published his *Treatises*, politics in England had become a contest between two loosely related parties, the Whigs and the Tories. These parties were the ancestors of Britain's modern Liberal Party and Conservative Party, respectively. Locke was a notable Whig,

WHIG AND TORY

The Whigs and the Tories were two opposing political parties or factions in England, particularly during the 18th century. Originally "Whig" and "Tory" were terms of abuse introduced in 1679 during the heated struggle over the bill to exclude James, duke of York (afterward James II), from the succession. Whig—whatever its origin in Scottish Gaelic—was a term applied to horse thieves and, later, to Scottish Presbyterians; it connoted nonconformity and rebellion and was applied to those who claimed the power of excluding the heir from the throne. Tory was an Irish term suggesting a papist outlaw and was applied to those who supported the hereditary right of James despite his Roman Catholic faith.

The Glorious Revolution (1688–89) greatly modified the division in principle between the two parties, for it had been a joint achievement. Thereafter most Tories accepted something of the Whig doctrines of limited constitutional monarchy rather than divine-right absolutism. In the early to mid-18th century aristocratic groups and connections regarded themselves as Whigs by sentiment and tradition. The die-hard Tories were discredited as Jacobites, supporters of the exiled Stuart king James II and his descendants after the Glorious Revolution, who sought the restoration of the Stuart heirs to the throne.

The reign of George III (1760–1820) brought a shift of meanings to the two words. No Whig Party as such existed at the time, only a series of aristocratic groups and family connections operating in Parliament through patronage and influence. Nor was there a Tory Party, only Tory sentiment, tradition, and temperament surviving among certain families and social groups. Real party alignments began to take shape only after 1784, when profound political issues that deeply stirred public opinion were arising, such as the

The devil watches gleefully as representatives of two opposing parties, the Whigs and the Tories, fight for political power in England. Hulton Archive/Getty Images

controversy over the American Revolution. After 1784 William Pitt the Younger emerged as the leader of a new Tory Party, which broadly represented the interests of the country gentry, the merchant classes, and official administerial groups. In opposition, a revived Whig Party, led by Charles James Fox, came to represent the interests of religious dissenters, industrialists, and others who sought electoral, parliamentary, and philanthropic reforms.

The French Revolution and the wars against France soon further complicated the division between parties. A large section of the more moderate Whigs deserted Fox and supported Pitt. After 1815 and a period of party confusion, there eventually emerged the conservatism of Sir Robert Peel and Benjamin Disraeli, earl of Beaconsfield, and the liberalism of Lord John Russell and William Ewart Gladstone, with the party labels of Conservative and Liberal assumed by each faction, respectively. Although the label Tory has continued to be used to designate the Conservative Party, Whig has ceased to have much political meaning.

and it is conventional to view liberalism as derived from the attitudes of Whig aristocrats, who were often linked with commercial interests and who had an entrenched suspicion of the power of the monarchy. The Whigs dominated English politics from the death of Queen Anne in 1714 to the accession of King George III in 1760.

In addition to Hobbes and Locke, the 18th-century philosopher Jean-Jacques Rousseau also examined the idea of the social contract. Rousseau held that in the state of nature people are unwarlike but also undeveloped in reasoning and morality; in surrendering their individual freedom, they acquire political liberty and civil rights within a system of laws based on the "general will" of the governed. The various notions of the social contract influenced the shapers of the American Revolution and the French Revolution and the constitutions that followed them.

JEAN-JACQUES ROUSSEAU

(b. June 28, 1712, Geneva, Switz. — d. July 2, 1778,
Ermenonville, France)

Jean-Jacques Rousseau was a Swiss-French philosopher whose ideas contributed to the development of liberalism. At age 16 he fled Geneva for Savoy, where he became the steward and later the lover of the baronne de Warens, a benevolent aristocrat. At age 30, having furthered his education and social position under her influence, Rousseau moved to Paris, where he joined Denis Diderot at the centre of the philosophes (French intellectuals of the period known as the Enlightenment); he wrote on music and economics for Diderot's *Encyclopédie*. His first major work, the *Discourse on the Arts and Sciences* (1750), argued that man is good by nature but has been corrupted by society and civilization; Rousseau's belief in the natural goodness of man set him apart from Roman Catholic writers who, like him, were hostile to the idea of progress. In the *Discourse on the Origin and Foundations of Inequality Among Men* (1754), he argued against Thomas Hobbes that human life before the formation of societies was healthy, happy, and free and that vice arose as the result of social organization and especially the introduction of private property. Civil society, he held, comes into being only to ensure peace and to protect property, which not everyone has; it thus represents a fraudulent social contract that reinforces inequality. In *The Social Contract* (1762), which begins with the memorable line, "Man was born free, but he is everywhere in chains," Rousseau argues that a civil society based on a genuine social contract rather than a fraudulent one would provide people with a better kind of freedom in exchange for their natural independence, namely, political liberty, which he understands as obedience to a self-imposed law created by the "general will." In 1762 the publication of *Émile*, a treatise on education, produced outrage, and Rousseau was forced to flee to Switzerland. He began showing signs of mental instability c. 1767, and he died insane. His *Confessions* (1781–88), which he modeled on the work of the same title by St. Augustine, is among the most famous autobiographies.

LIBERALISM AND DEMOCRACY

The early liberals worked to free individuals from two forms of social constraint—religious conformity and aristocratic privilege—that had been maintained and enforced through the powers of government. The aim of the early liberals was thus to limit the power of government over the individual while holding it accountable to the governed. As Locke and others argued, this required a system of government based on majority rule—that is, one in which government executes the expressed will of a majority of the electorate. The chief institutional device for attaining this goal was the periodic election of legislators by popular vote and of a chief executive by popular vote or the vote of a legislative assembly.

But in answering the crucial question of who is to be the electorate, classical liberalism fell victim to ambivalence, torn between the great emancipating tendencies generated by the revolutions with which it was associated and middle-class fears that a wide or universal franchise would undermine private property. Benjamin Franklin spoke for the Whig liberalism of the Founding Fathers of the United States when he stated: "As to those who have no landed property in a county, the allowing them to vote for legislators is an impropriety. They are transient inhabitants, and not so connected with the welfare of the state, which they may quit when they please, as to qualify them properly for such privilege."

John Adams, in his *Defense of the Constitutions of Government of the United States of America* (1787), was more explicit. If the majority were to control all branches of government, he declared, "debts would be abolished first; taxes laid heavy on the rich, and not at all on others; and at last a downright equal division of everything be demanded and voted." French statesmen such as François Guizot and Adophe Thiers expressed similar sentiments well into the 19th century.

Most 18th- and 19th-century liberal politicians thus feared popular sovereignty; for a long time, consequently, they limited suffrage to property owners. In Britain even the important Reform Bill of 1867 did not completely abolish property qualifications for the right to vote. In France, despite the ideal of universal male suffrage proclaimed in 1789 and reaffirmed in the Revolutions of 1830, there were no more than 200,000 qualified voters in a population of about 30,000,000 during the reign of Louis-Philippe, the "citizen king" who had been installed by the ascendant bourgeoisie in 1830. In the United States, the brave language of the Declaration of Independence notwithstanding, it was not until 1860 that universal male suffrage prevailed—for whites. In most of Europe, universal male suffrage remained a remote ideal until late in the 19th century. Racial and sexual prejudice also served to limit the franchise—and, in the case of slavery in the United States, to deprive large numbers of people of virtually any hope of freedom. Efforts to extend the vote to women met with little success until the early years of the 20th century. Indeed, Switzerland, which is sometimes called the world's oldest continuous democracy, did not grant full voting rights to women until 1971.

Despite the misgivings of men of the propertied classes, a slow but steady expansion of the franchise prevailed throughout Europe in the 19th century—an expansion driven in large part by the liberal insistence that "all men are created equal." But liberals also had to reconcile the principle of majority rule with the requirement that the power of the majority be limited. The problem was to accomplish this in a manner consistent with democratic principles. If hereditary elites were discredited, how could the power of the majority be checked without giving disproportionate power to property owners or to some other "natural" elite?

SEPARATION OF POWERS

The liberal solution to the problem of limiting the powers
of a democratic majority employed various devices. The
first was the separation of powers—i.e., the distribution
of power between such functionally differentiated agen-
cies of government as the legislature, the executive, and
the judiciary. This arrangement, and the system of checks
and balances by which it was accomplished, received its
classic embodiment in the Constitution of the United
States and its political justification in the Federalist papers
(1787–88), by Alexander Hamilton, James Madison, and
John Jay. Of course, such a separation of powers also could
have been achieved through a "mixed constitution"—that
is, one in which power is shared by, and governing functions appropriately differentiated between, a monarch, a
hereditary chamber, and an elected assembly; this was in
fact the system of government in Great Britain at the
time of the American Revolution. The U.S. Constitution
also contains elements of a mixed constitution, such as
the division of the legislature into the popularly elected
House of Representatives and the "aristocratic" Senate,
the members of which originally were chosen by the state
governments. But it was despotic kings and functionless
aristocrats—more functionless in France than in Britain—
who thwarted the interests and ambitions of the middle
class, which turned, therefore, to the principle of
majoritarianism.

PERIODIC ELECTIONS

The second part of the solution lay in using staggered
periodic elections to make the decisions of any given
majority subject to the concurrence of other majorities

distributed over time. In the United States, for example, presidents are elected every four years and members of the House of Representatives every two years, and one-third of the Senate is elected every two years to terms of six years. Therefore, the majority that elects a president every four years or a House of Representatives every two years is different from the majority that elects one-third of the Senate two years earlier and the majority that elects another one-third of the Senate two years later. These bodies, in turn, are "checked" by the Constitution, which was approved and amended by earlier majorities. In Britain an act of Parliament immediately becomes part of the uncodified constitution; however, before acting on a highly controversial issue, Parliament must seek a popular mandate, which represents a majority other than the one that elected it. Thus, in a constitutional democracy, the power of a current majority is checked by the verdicts of majorities that precede and follow it.

RIGHTS

The third part of the solution followed from liberalism's basic commitment to the freedom and integrity of the individual, which the limitation of power is, after all, meant to preserve. From the liberal perspective, the individual is not only a citizen who shares a social contract with his fellows but also a person with rights upon which the state may not encroach if majoritarianism is to be meaningful. A majority verdict can come about only if individuals are free to some extent to exchange their views. This involves, beyond the right to speak and write freely, the freedom to associate and organize and, above all, freedom from fear of reprisal. But the individual also has rights apart from his role as citizen. These rights

secure his personal safety and hence his protection from
arbitrary arrest and punishment. Beyond these rights are
those that preserve large areas of privacy. In a liberal
democracy there are affairs that do not concern the state.
Such affairs may range from the practice of religion to
the creation of art and the raising of children by their
parents. For liberals of the 18th and 19th centuries they
also included most of the activities through which
individuals engage in production and trade. Eloquent
declarations affirming such rights were embodied in the
British Bill of Rights (1689), the U.S. Declaration of
Independence (1776) and Constitution (ratified 1788), the
French Declaration of the Rights of Man and of the
Citizen (1789), and the basic documents of countries
throughout the world that later used these declarations
as their models. These documents and declarations
asserted that freedom is more than the right to cast a
vote in an occasional election; it is the fundamental right
of people to live their own lives.

CLASSICAL LIBERALISM IN ACTION

Until the 17th century, democratic theorists and political
leaders largely ignored the possibility that a legislature
might consist neither of the entire body of citizens, as in
Greece and Rome, nor of representatives chosen by and
from a tiny oligarchy or hereditary aristocracy, as in the
Italian republics. An important break in the prevailing
orthodoxy occurred during and after the English Civil
Wars, when the Levelers and other radical followers
of Puritanism demanded broader representation in
Parliament, expanded powers for Parliament's lower
house, the House of Commons, and universal manhood
suffrage. Further revolutionary developments in England,

its North American colonies, and France exemplified the successful implementation of political systems espousing the precepts of classical liberalism—particularly representative democracy and natural rights.

IN ENGLAND

Among the assemblies created in Europe during the Middle Ages, the one that most profoundly influenced the development of representative government was the English Parliament. Less a product of design than an unintended consequence of opportunistic innovations, Parliament grew out of councils that were called by kings for the purpose of redressing grievances and for exercising judicial functions. In time, Parliament began to deal with important matters of state, notably the raising of revenues needed to support the policies and decisions of the monarch. As its judicial functions were increasingly delegated to courts, it gradually evolved into a legislative body. By the end of the 15th century, the English system displayed some of the basic features of modern parliamentary government: for example, the enactment of laws now required the passage of bills by both houses of Parliament and the formal approval of the monarch.

Other important features had yet to be established, however. England's political life was dominated by the monarchy for centuries after the Middle Ages. During the English Civil Wars, led on one side by radical Puritans, the monarchy was abolished and a republic— the Commonwealth—was established (1649), though the monarchy was restored in 1660. By about 1800, significant powers, notably including powers related to the appointment and tenure of the prime minister, had shifted to Parliament. This development was strongly influenced by the emergence of political factions in Parliament during the early years of the 18th century. These factions, known as Whigs and Tories, later became the full-fledged Liberal and Conservative parties, respectively. To king and Parliament alike it became increasingly apparent that laws could not be passed nor taxes raised without the support of a Whig or Tory leader who could muster a majority of votes in the House of Commons. To gain that support, the monarch was forced to select as prime minister the leader of the majority party in the Commons and to accept the leader's suggestions for the composition of the cabinet. That the monarch should have to yield to Parliament in this area became manifest during a constitutional crisis in 1782, when King George III (reigned 1760–1820) was compelled, much against his will, to accept a Whig prime minister and cabinet—a situation he regarded, according to one scholar, as "a violation of the Constitution, a defeat for his policy, and a personal humiliation." By 1830 the constitutional principle that the choice of prime minister, and thus the cabinet, reposed with the House of Commons had become firmly entrenched in the (uncodified) British Constitution.

Parliamentary government in Britain was not yet a democratic system, however. Mainly because of property requirements, the franchise was held by only about 5 percent of the British population over 20 years of age. The Reform Act of 1832, which is generally viewed as a historic threshold in the development of parliamentary democracy in Britain, extended the suffrage to about 7 percent of the adult population. It would require further acts of Parliament in 1867, 1884, and 1918 to achieve universal male suffrage and one more law, enacted in 1928, to secure the right to vote for all adult women.

The English Civil Wars

The English Civil Wars pitted the Royalists—supporters of the monarchy of Charles I (and his son and successor, Charles II)—against opposing groups in each of Charles's kingdoms, including Parliamentarians in England, Covenanters in Scotland, and Confederates in Ireland. The civil wars are traditionally considered to have begun in England in August 1642, when Charles I raised an army against the wishes of Parliament, ostensibly to deal with a rebellion in Ireland. But the period of conflict actually began earlier in Scotland, with the Bishops' Wars of 1639–40, and in Ireland, with the Ulster Rebellion of 1641. Throughout the 1640s, war between king and Parliament ravaged England, but it also struck all of the kingdoms held by the House of Stuart—and, in addition to war between the various British and Irish dominions, there was civil war within each of the Stuart states. For this reason the English Civil Wars might more properly be called the British Civil Wars or the Wars of the Three Kingdoms. The wars finally ended in 1651 with the flight of Charles II to France and, with him, the hopes of the British monarchy.

The first major battle fought on English soil—the Battle of Edgehill (October 1642)—quickly demonstrated that a clear advantage was enjoyed by neither the Royalists (also known as the Cavaliers) nor the Parliamentarians (also known as the Roundheads for their short-cropped hair, in contrast to the long hair and wigs associated with the Cavaliers).

The result was an effective military stalemate until the triumph of the Roundheads at the Battle of Marston Moor (July 2, 1644). This decisive victory deprived the king of two field armies and, equally important, paved the way for

Battle of Naseby, *by an unknown artist. The victory of the Parliamentarian
New Model Army, under Sir Thomas Fairfax and Oliver Cromwell, over
the Royalist army, commanded by Prince Rupert, at the Battle of Naseby
(June 14, 1645) marked a decisive turning point in the English Civil Wars.*
© Photos.com/Jupiterimages

the reform of the parliamentary armies with the creation
of the New Model Army, completed in April 1645. This
centralized standing army, with central funding and direction, now moved against the Royalist forces. The New
Model Army's closely fought victory at the Battle of
Naseby proved the turning point in parliamentary fortunes and marked the beginning of a string of stunning
successes that eventually forced the king to surrender to
the Scots at Newark on May 5, 1646.

While the Scottish Covenanters had made a significant
contribution to Parliament's victory in the first English

THE LEVELER MOVEMENT

The Levelers were a republican and democratic faction in England during the period of the Civil Wars and Commonwealth. The name Levelers was given by enemies of the movement to suggest that its supporters wished to "level men's estates."

The Leveler movement originated in 1645–46 among radical supporters of Parliament in and around London. The Civil War had been waged in the name of Parliament and people: the Levelers demanded that real sovereignty should be transferred to the House of Commons (to the exclusion of king and lords); that manhood suffrage, a redistribution of seats, and annual or biennial sessions of Parliament should make that legislative body truly representative; and that government should be decentralized to local communities. They put forward a program of economic reform in the interests of small property holders—complete equality before the law, the abolition of trading monopolies, the reopening of enclosed land, security of land tenure for copyholders, no conscription (impressment) or billeting, drastic law reform, the abolition of tithes (and so of a state church), and complete freedom of religious worship and organization. Disappointed by Parliament's attitude, the Levelers turned directly to the people—and to the New Model Army.

In April 1647 the army rank and file elected agitators who were largely influenced by Leveler ideas. The generals had to accept an army council that included these ordinary soldiers, as well as officers. At Putney, in October 1647, this representative body discussed the Agreement of the People, a document presented by the Levelers as a new social contract to reestablish the state that had been dissolved by Parliament's victory in the Civil War. The

Putney debates on this document ended in deadlock, however, and the generals restored discipline in the army by force.

The Levelers never won national support. Their sea-green colours held London's streets, and the troops listened to them eagerly, but propaganda was difficult among a population used to taking its ideas from the church and the landed aristocracy. Yet their appeal to reason against arguments drawn from precedent or biblical authority marks a milestone in political thought.

Civil War, during the second (1648) and third English Civil Wars (1650–51) they supported the king. The execution of Charles I in January 1649 merely served to galvanize Scottish (and Irish) support for the king's son, Charles II, who was crowned king of the Scots on Jan. 1, 1651. However, the resounding victory of Parliamentarian leader Oliver Cromwell at Worcester (Sept. 3, 1651) and Charles II's subsequent flight to France not only gave Cromwell control over England but also effectively ended the wars of—and the wars in—the three kingdoms.

The Glorious Revolution

The Glorious Revolution (1688–89), sometimes referred to as the Bloodless Revolution, describes the events in English history that resulted in the deposition of James II and the accession of his daughter Mary II and her husband, William III, prince of Orange and stadtholder of the Netherlands.

After the accession of James II in 1685, his overt Roman Catholicism alienated the majority of the population. In 1687 he issued a Declaration of Indulgence, suspending the penal laws against dissenters and recusants, and in April 1688 ordered that a second Declaration of Indulgence be read from every pulpit on two successive Sundays. William Sancroft, the archbishop of Canterbury, and six other bishops petitioned him against this and were prosecuted for seditious libel. Their acquittal almost coincided with the birth of a son to James's Roman Catholic queen, Mary of Modena (June 1688). This event promised an indefinite continuance of his policy and brought discontent to a head. Seven eminent Englishmen, including one bishop and six prominent politicians of both Whig and Tory persuasions, wrote to William of Orange, inviting him to come over with an army to redress the nation's grievances.

William was both James's nephew and his son-in-law, and, until the birth of James's son, his wife, Mary, was heir apparent. William's chief concern was to check the over-growth of French power in Europe, and he welcomed England's aid. Thus, having been in close touch with the leading English malcontents for more than a year, he accepted their invitation. Landing at Brixham on Tor Bay (November 5), he advanced slowly on London, as support fell away from James II. James's daughter Anne and his best general, John Churchill, were among the deserters to William's camp; thereupon James fled to France.

William was now asked to carry on the government and summon a Parliament. When this Convention Parliament met (Jan. 22, 1689), it agreed, after some debate, to treat James's flight as an abdication and to offer the Crown, with an accompanying Declaration of Right, to William and Mary jointly. Both gift and conditions were accepted. Thereupon the convention turned itself into a proper Parliament and large parts of the Declaration into a Bill of Rights. This bill gave the succession to Mary's sister, Anne, in default of issue to Mary; barred Roman

Catholics from the throne; abolished the Crown's power to suspend laws; condemned the power of dispensing with laws "as it hath been exercised and used of late"; and declared a standing army illegal in time of peace.

The settlement marked a considerable triumph for Whig views. If no Roman Catholic could be king, then no kingship could be unconditional. The adoption of the

BILL OF RIGHTS (1689)

The British Bill of Rights (1689), formally known as An Act Declaring the Rights and Liberties of the Subject and Settling the Succession of the Crown, is one of the basic instruments of the British constitution, the result of the long 17th-century struggle between the Stuart kings and the English people and Parliament. With the Toleration Act (1689), granting religious toleration to all Protestants, the Triennial Act (1694), ordering general elections to be held every three years, and the Act of Settlement (1701), providing for the Hanoverian succession, the Bill of Rights provided the foundation on which the government rested after the Glorious Revolution (1688–89).

The main purpose of the act was unequivocally to declare illegal various practices of James II. Among such practices proscribed were the royal prerogative of dispensing with the law in certain cases, the complete suspension of laws without the consent of Parliament, and the levying of taxes and the maintenance of a standing army in peacetime without specific parliamentary authorization. A number of clauses sought to eliminate royal interference in parliamentary matters, stressing that elections must be free and that members must have complete freedom of speech. Certain forms of interference in the course of justice were also proscribed.

exclusionist solution lent support to John Locke's contention that government was in the nature of a social contract between the king and his people represented in Parliament. The revolution permanently established Parliament as the ruling power of England.

IN THE UNITED STATES

Classical liberalism in America may be said to begin with the Founding Fathers, the most prominent statesmen of America's Revolutionary generation. They were responsible for the successful war for colonial independence from Great Britain, the liberal ideas celebrated in the Declaration of Independence, and the republican form of government defined in the United States Constitution. While there are no agreed-upon criteria for inclusion, membership in this select group customarily requires conspicuous contributions at one or both of the foundings of the United States: during the American Revolution, when independence was won, or during the Constitutional Convention, when nationhood was achieved. The following 10 Founding Fathers, presented alphabetically, represent the "gallery of greats" that has stood the test of time: John Adams, Samuel Adams, Benjamin Franklin, Alexander Hamilton, Patrick Henry, Thomas Jefferson, James Madison, John Marshall, George Mason, and George Washington.

At the most general level, these men created the first modern nation-state based on liberal principles. These include the democratic principle that political sovereignty in any government resides in the citizenry rather than in a divinely sanctioned monarchy; the capitalistic principle that economic productivity depends upon the release of individual energies in the marketplace rather than on state-sponsored policies; the moral principle that the individual, not the society or the state, is the sovereign unit in the political equation; and the judicial principle that all citizens are equal before the law. Moreover, this liberal formula has become the preferred political recipe for success in the modern world, vanquishing the European monarchies in the 19th century and the totalitarian regimes of Germany, Japan, and the Soviet Union in the 20th century.

More specifically, the Founding Fathers managed to defy conventional wisdom in four unprecedented achievements: first, they won a war for colonial independence against the most powerful military and economic power in the world; second, they established the first large-scale republic in the modern world; third, they invented political parties that institutionalized the concept of a legitimate opposition; and fourth, they established the principle of the legal separation of church and state, though it took several decades for that principle to be implemented in all the states. Finally, all these achievements were won without recourse to the guillotine or the firing squad, which is to say without the violent purges that accompanied subsequent revolutions in France, Russia, and China.

The American Revolution

The American Revolution won political independence for 13 of Britain's North American colonies, which formed the United States of America. After the end of the costly French and Indian War (1763), Britain imposed new taxes, through such acts as the Stamp Act and the Sugar Act, and trade restrictions on the colonies, fueling growing resentment and strengthening the colonists' objection to their lack of representation in the British Parliament. An early expression of this resentment was the formation of organizations known as the Sons of Liberty in the summer of 1765. These groups rallied support for colonial resistance through the use of petitions, assemblies, and propaganda, and they sometimes resorted to violence against officials of the mother country. Instrumental in preventing the enforcement of the Stamp Act, they remained an active pre-Revolutionary force against the crown.

Eventually, determined to achieve independence, the colonies formed the Continental Army, composed chiefly of minutemen, to challenge Britain's large organized militia. The war began when Britain sent a force to destroy rebel military stores at Concord, Mass. After fighting broke out on April 19, 1775 (in the Battles of Lexington and Concord), rebel forces began a siege of Boston that ended when American forces, under Henry Knox, forced out the British troops, under William Howe, on March 17, 1776, in the Battle of Bunker Hill.

Britain offered the Americans a pardon in exchange for surrender; however, the Americans refused. Instead, they drafted the Declaration of Independence and declared themselves independent of British rule on July 4, 1776. British forces retaliated by driving George Washington's army from New York to New Jersey. On December 25, Washington crossed the Delaware River and won the battles of Trenton and Princeton. The British army split to cover more territory, which proved a fatal error. In engaging the Americans in Pennsylvania, notably in the Battle of the Brandywine, they left the troops in the north vulnerable. Despite a victory in the Battle of Ticonderoga, British troops, under John Burgoyne, were defeated by Horatio Gates and Benedict Arnold in the Battle of Saratoga (Oct. 17, 1777). Washington quartered his 11,000 troops through a bleak winter at Valley Forge, where they received training from Frederick Steuben. This additional military knowledge gave them victory in Monmouth, N.J., on June 28, 1778.

France, which had been secretly furnishing aid to the Americans since 1776, finally declared war on Britain in

June 1778. French troops assisted American troops in the south, culminating in the successful Siege of Yorktown, where Charles Cornwallis surrendered his forces on Oct. 19, 1781, bringing an end to the war on land. War continued at sea, fought chiefly between Britain and the United States' European allies. The last battle of the war was won by the American navy under John Barry in March 1783 in the Straits of Florida. With the Treaty of Paris (Sept. 3, 1783), Britain recognized the independence of the United States east of the Mississippi River and ceded Florida to Spain.

The Declaration of Independence

The landmark Declaration of Independence was approved by the Continental Congress on July 4, 1776, and announced the independence of 13 of Britain's North American colonies. The day on which final separation was officially voted was July 2, although the 4th, the day on which the Declaration of Independence was adopted, has always been celebrated in the United States as the great national holiday—the Fourth of July, or Independence Day.

The Declaration of Independence was written largely by Thomas Jefferson, who had displayed talent as a political philosopher and polemicist in his work *A Summary View of the Rights of British America*, published in 1774. At the request of his fellow committee members he wrote the first draft. It can be said, as John Adams did, that the declaration contained nothing really novel in its political philosophy, which was derived from John Locke, Algernon Sidney, and other English theorists. It may also be asserted that the argument offered was not without flaws in history and logic. Substantially abandoning contention on the basis of the rights of Englishmen, the declaration put forth the more fundamental doctrines of natural rights and of government under social contract. Claiming that Parliament never truly possessed sovereignty over the

Image of the Declaration of Independence (1776) taken from an engraving made by printer William J. Stone in 1823. National Archives, Washington, D.C.

colonies and that the crown of right exercised it only under contract, the declaration contended that George III, with the support of a "pretended" legislature, had persistently violated the agreement between himself as governor and the Americans as the governed. A long list of accusations was offered toward proving this contention. The right and duty of revolution were then invoked.

THOMAS JEFFERSON

(b. April 13, 1743, Shadwell, Va. — d. July 4, 1826,
Monticello, Va., U.S.)

Thomas Jefferson was the Founding Father who drafted the
Declaration of Independence and went on to become the
third president of the United States (1801–09). A planter
and lawyer, he became a member of Virginia's House of
Burgesses. In 1773 he initiated the Virginia Committee of
Correspondence with Richard Henry Lee and Patrick
Henry, and the following year he wrote the influential *A
Summary View of the Rights of British America*, stating that
the British Parliament had no authority to legislate for the
colonies. A delegate to the Second Continental Congress,
he was appointed to the committee to draft the Declaration
of Independence and became its primary author. He was
elected governor of Virginia (1779–81) but was unable to
organize effective opposition when British forces invaded
the colony (1780–81). Criticized for his conduct, he retired,
vowing to remain a private citizen. Again a member of the
Continental Congress (1783–85), he drafted the first of
the Northwest Ordinances for dividing and settling the
Northwest Territory. In 1785 he succeeded Benjamin
Franklin as U.S. minister to France. In 1790 he was appointed
by George Washington to become the country's first secretary of state. He quickly became embroiled in a bitter
conflict with Alexander Hamilton over the country's foreign policy and their opposing interpretations of the
Constitution. Their divisions gave rise to political factions
and eventually to political parties. Jefferson served as vice
president (1797–1801) under John Adams.

In 1801 Jefferson was sworn in as the country's third
president. As president, Jefferson attempted to implement
his liberal ideas of reducing the powers of the embryonic

federal government; he also dispensed with a great deal of the ceremony and formality that had attended the office of president to that time. In 1803 he oversaw the Louisiana Purchase, which doubled the land area of the country.

In 1809 he retired to his plantation, Monticello, where he pursued his interests in science, philosophy, and architecture. Though a lifelong slaveholder, Jefferson was an anomaly among the Virginia planter class for his support of gradual emancipation.

One of the country's Founding Fathers and author of the Declaration of Independence, Thomas Jefferson personified liberal ideals as the third president of the United States. MPI/ Hulton Archive/Getty Images

The Declaration of Independence has been a source of inspiration outside the United States. It encouraged colonists in South America to strive toward overthrowing the Spanish empire there, and it was quoted with enthusiasm by the Marquis de Mirabeau during the French Revolution. It remains a great historical landmark in that it contained the first formal assertion by a whole people of their right to a government of their own choice. What Locke had contended for as an individual, the Americans proclaimed as a body politic; moreover, they made good the argument by force of arms.

IN FRANCE

Soon after France assisted the United States of America in the Revolutionary War against Great Britain, it experienced its own revolution, similarly inspired by the precepts of classical liberalism. The French Revolution culminated in the overthrow of the French monarchy and the establishment of a republic.

The French Revolution

The French Revolution shook France between 1787 and 1799 and reached its first climax there in 1789, ending the ancien régime ("old order"). Although historians disagree on the causes of the Revolution, classical liberalism was undoubtedly one of the forces behind it. The liberal philosophers known as the philosophes, who advocated liberal political and social reform, and who belonged to the intellectual movement known as the Enlightenment, had been read more widely in France than anywhere else.

The Revolution took shape in France when the controller general of finances arranged the summoning of an assembly of "notables" (prelates, great noblemen, and a few representatives of the bourgeoisie) in February 1787 to propose reforms designed to eliminate the budget deficit by increasing the taxation of the privileged classes. The assembly refused to take responsibility for the reforms and suggested the calling of the Estates-General, which represented the clergy, the nobility, and the Third Estate (the commoners) and which had not met since 1614. The king, Louis XVI, promised to convene the Estates-General in 1789.

The Estates-General met at Versailles on May 5, 1789. They were immediately divided over a fundamental issue: should they vote by head, giving the advantage to the Third Estate, or by estate, in which case the two privileged orders of the realm might outvote the third? On June 17 the bitter struggle over this legal issue finally drove the deputies of the Third Estate to declare themselves the National Assembly; they threatened to proceed, if necessary, without the other two orders. They were supported by many of the parish priests, who outnumbered the aristocratic upper clergy among the church's deputies. When royal officials locked the deputies out of their regular meeting hall on June 20, they occupied the king's indoor tennis court (*jeu de paume*) and swore an oath not to disperse until they had given France a new constitution. The king grudgingly gave in and urged the nobles and the remaining clergy to join the assembly, which took the official title of National Constituent Assembly on July 9; at the same time, however, he began gathering troops to dissolve it.

These two months of prevarication at a time when the problem of maintaining food supplies had reached its

The storming of the Bastille on July 14, 1789, undated coloured engraving.
© Photos.com/Jupiterimages

climax infuriated the towns and the provinces. Rumours of an "aristocratic conspiracy" by the king and the privileged to overthrow the Third Estate led to the Great Fear of July 1789, when the peasants were nearly panic-stricken. The gathering of troops around Paris provoked insurrection in the capital. On July 14, 1789, the Parisian crowd seized the Bastille prison, a symbol of royal tyranny. Again the king had to yield; visiting Paris, he showed his recognition of the sovereignty of the people by wearing the tricolour cockade, a hat decoration of blue, white, and red ribbons representing the new order.

On Aug. 26, 1789, the National Constituent Assembly introduced the Declaration of the Rights of Man and of the Citizen, proclaiming liberty, equality, the inviolability of property, and the right to resist oppression. The king refused to sanction it. The Parisians rose again and on October 5 marched to the palace of Versailles. The next day they brought the royal family back to Paris. The National Constituent Assembly followed the court, and in Paris it continued to work on the new constitution. The French population participated actively in the new political culture created by the Revolution. Dozens of uncensored newspapers kept citizens abreast of events, and political clubs allowed them to voice their opinions.

The National Constituent Assembly completed the abolition of feudalism, suppressed the old "orders," established civil equality among men (at least in metropolitan France, since slavery was retained in the colonies), and made more than half the adult male population eligible to vote, although only a small minority met the requirement for becoming a deputy. The decision to nationalize the lands of the Roman Catholic Church in France to pay off the public debt led to a widespread redistribution of property. The National Constituent Assembly tried to create a monarchical regime in which the legislative and executive powers were shared between the king and an assembly. This regime might have worked if the king had really wanted to govern with the new authorities, but Louis XVI was weak and vacillating and was the prisoner of his aristocratic advisers. On June 20–21, 1791, he tried to flee the country, but he was stopped at Varennes and brought back to Paris.

By early 1792 both radicals, eager to spread the principles of the Revolution, and the king, hopeful that war would either strengthen his authority or allow foreign armies to rescue him, supported an aggressive policy. France declared war against Austria on April 20, 1792. In the first phase of the war (April–September 1792), France suffered defeats; Prussia joined the war in July, and an Austro-Prussian army crossed the frontier and advanced rapidly toward Paris. The French forces checked the Prussians on Sept. 20, 1792, at Valmy. On the same day, a new assembly, the National Convention, met. The next day it proclaimed the abolition of the monarchy and the establishment of the republic.

In the second phase of the war (September 1792–April 1793), the revolutionaries got the better of the enemy. Meanwhile, the National Convention was divided between the Girondins, who wanted to organize a bourgeois republic in France and to spread the Revolution over the whole of Europe, and the Montagnards ("Mountain Men"), who, with the radical leader Maximilien de Robespierre, wanted to give the lower classes a greater share in political and economic power. Despite efforts made by the Girondins, Louis XVI was judged by the Convention, condemned to death for treason, and executed on Jan. 21, 1793; the queen, Marie-Antoinette, was guillotined nine months later.

In the spring of 1793, the war entered a third phase, marked by new French defeats. Austria, Prussia, and Great Britain formed a coalition, to which most of the rulers of Europe adhered. These reverses strengthened the

The last prisoners awaiting execution during the Reign of Terror in 1794, undated engraving. © Photos.com/Jupiterimages

extremists. The Girondin leaders were driven from the National Convention, and the Montagnards, who had the support of the Paris sansculottes (workers, craftsmen, and shopkeepers), seized power and kept it until 9 Thermidor, year II, of the new French republican calendar (July 27, 1794). The Montagnards were bourgeois liberals like the Girondins but under pressure from the sansculottes, and, in order to meet the requirements of defense, they adopted a radical economic and social policy. They introduced the Maximum (government control of prices), taxed the rich, brought national assistance to the poor and to the disabled, declared that education should be free and compulsory, and ordered the confiscation and sale of the property of émigrés. Opposition was broken by the Reign of Terror (19 Fructidor, year I–9 Thermidor, year II

[Sept. 5, 1793–July 27, 1794]), which entailed the arrest of at least 300,000 suspects, 17,000 of whom were sentenced to death and executed while more died in prisons or were killed without any form of trial.

The war entered its fourth phase in the spring of 1794. A brilliant victory over the Austrians at Fleurus on 8 Messidor, year II (June 26, 1794) made the Terror and the economic and social restrictions seem pointless. Robespierre, "the Incorruptible," who had sponsored the restrictions, was overthrown in the National Convention on 9 Thermidor, year II (July 27, 1794), and executed the

SANSCULOTTE

The sansculottes (French: "without knee breeches") were the more militant supporters of the French Revolution, especially in the years 1792 to 1795. Sansculottes presented themselves as members of the poorer classes or leaders of the common people, but during the Reign of Terror public functionaries and educated men also adopted the label to demonstrate their patriotism.

The distinctive costume of the typical sansculotte was the pantalon (long trousers) in place of the culotte (silk breeches) worn by the upper classes, as well as the carmagnole (short jacket) and the red cap of liberty. Jacques-René Hébert's popular newspaper, *Le Père Duchesne*, did much to spread the image of the sansculotte: a woodcut on the front page of each issue showed a man in Revolutionary costume, holding a musket and smoking a pipe.

The influence of the sansculottes declined sharply after Hébert's execution in March 1794. The defeat of the desperate popular uprisings in the spring of 1795 marked the end of their public role.

following day. Soon after his fall the Maximum was abolished, the social laws were no longer applied, and efforts toward economic equality were abandoned. Reaction set in; the National Convention began to debate a new constitution, and royalists tried to seize power in Paris but were crushed by the young general Napoleon Bonaparte on 13 Vendémiaire, year IV (Oct. 5, 1795). A few days later the National Convention dispersed.

The constitution of the year III, which the National Convention had approved, placed executive power in a Directory of five members and legislative power in two chambers, the Council of Ancients and the Council of the Five Hundred (together called the Corps Législatif). This regime, a bourgeois republic, might have achieved stability had not war perpetuated the struggle between revolutionaries and counterrevolutionaries throughout Europe. The war, moreover, embittered existing antagonisms between the Directory and the legislative councils in France and often gave rise to new ones. These disputes were settled by coups d'état, chiefly those of 18 Fructidor, year V (Sept. 4, 1797), which removed the royalists from the Directory and from the councils, and of 18 Brumaire, year VIII (Nov. 9, 1799), in which Bonaparte abolished the Directory and became the leader of France as its "first consul."

After the victory of Fleurus, the progress of the French armies in Europe had continued. The majority of the directors had inherited the Girondin desire to spread the Revolution over Europe and listened to the appeals of Jacobins (radical revolutionaries) abroad. Thus French troops in 1798 and 1799 entered Switzerland, the Papal States, and Naples and set up the Helvetic, Roman, and Parthenopean republics. However, a new coalition of Austria, Russia, Turkey, and Great Britain won great successes during the spring and summer of 1799 and drove

JACOBIN CLUB

The Society of the Friends of the Constitution, or the Society of the Jacobins, Friends of Liberty and Equality, was the most famous political group of the French Revolution. It was commonly called the Jacobin Club because its sessions were held in a former convent of the Dominicans, who were known in Paris as Jacobins. The group, which became identified with extreme egalitarianism and violence, led the Revolutionary government from mid-1793 to mid-1794.

The Jacobins originated in 1789; their purpose was to protect the gains of the Revolution against a possible aristocratic reaction. By July 1790 there were about 1,200 members in the Parisian club and 152 affiliate clubs. In July 1791 the Jacobin Club split over a petition calling for the removal of Louis XVI after his unsuccessful attempt to flee France; many of the moderate deputies left to join the rival club of the Feuillants. Maximilien de Robespierre was one of the few deputies who remained, and he assumed a position of prominence in the club.

After the overthrow of the monarchy, in August 1792, the club entered a new phase as one of the major groups directing the Revolution. It acquired a democratic character with the admission of the leftist Montagnard deputies in the National Convention (the new legislature) and also a more popular one as it responded to the demands of the Parisian working and artisan class. It agitated for the execution of the king (January 1793) and for the overthrow of the moderate Girondins (June 1793).

With the establishment of the Revolutionary dictatorship, beginning in the summer of 1793, the local Jacobin clubs became instruments of the Reign of Terror. (In 1793 there were probably 5,000 to 8,000 clubs throughout France, with a nominal membership of 500,000.) The

Parisian club supported Robespierre in his attacks on the enemies of the Revolution. After the fall of Robespierre in 1794, the Parisian club, now a symbol of dictatorship and terror, was temporarily closed. It reopened briefly as a centre of opposition but was permanently closed in November 1794. Some local clubs lasted until 1799–1800 despite their having been officially banned.

back the French armies to the frontiers. Bonaparte thereupon returned to France. His coup d'état of 18–19 Brumaire (Nov. 9–10, 1799) overthrew the Directory and substituted yet another government, the Consulate. Bonaparte declared the Revolution over, and indeed it was; under the Consulate, the principles of representation and legislative supremacy were discarded. The Consulate lasted until Bonaparte declared himself emperor in 1804.

Declaration of the Rights of Man and of the Citizen

The French Declaration of the Rights of Man and of the Citizen is one of the basic charters of human liberties, containing the principles that inspired the French Revolution. Its 17 articles, adopted between Aug. 20 and Aug. 26, 1789, by France's National Assembly, served as the preamble to the Constitution of 1791.

The basic principle of the Declaration was that all "men are born and remain free and equal in rights" (Article 1), which were specified as the rights of liberty, private property, the inviolability of the person, and resistance to oppression (Article 2). All citizens were equal before the law and were to have the right to participate in legislation directly or indirectly (Article 6); no one was to be arrested without a judicial order (Article 7). Freedom of religion (Article 10) and freedom of speech (Article 11) were safeguarded within the bounds of public "order" and "law." The document reflects the interests of the elites who wrote it: property was given the status of an inviolable right, which could be taken by the state only if an indemnity were given (Article 17); offices and position were opened to all citizens (Article 6).

The sources of the Declaration included the major thinkers of the French Enlightenment, such as Charles-Louis de Secondat, baron de La Brède et de Montesquieu, who had urged the separation of powers, and Jean-Jacques Rousseau, who wrote of general will—the concept that the

CHARLES-LOUIS DE SECONDAT, BARON DE LA BRÈDE ET DE MONTESQUIEU

(b. Jan. 18, 1689, Château La Brède, near Bordeaux, France—d. Feb. 10, 1755, Paris)

Montesquieu, a French philosophe (intellectual) and satirist, was a key figure in the history of liberal politics. Born into a noble family, he held public office in Bordeaux from 1714. His satirical *Persian Letters* (1721) was hugely successful. From 1726 he traveled widely to study social and political institutions. His magnum opus, the enormous *The Spirit of the Laws* (1750), contained an original classification of governments by their manner of conducting policy, an argument for the separation of the legislative, judicial, and executive powers, and a celebrated but less influential theory of the political influence of climate. The work profoundly influenced European and American political thought and was relied on by the framers of the U.S. Constitution. His other works include *Causes of the Greatness and Decadence of the Romans* (1734).

state represents the general will of the citizens. The idea that the individual must be safeguarded against arbitrary police or judicial action was anticipated by writers such as Voltaire. French jurists and economists such as the physiocrats had insisted on the inviolability of private property. Other influences on the authors of the Declaration were foreign documents such as the Virginia Declaration of Rights (1776) in North America and the manifestos of the Dutch Patriot movement of the 1780s. The French Declaration went beyond these models, however, in its scope and in its claim to be based on principles that are fundamental to man and therefore universally applicable.

LIBERALISM IN THE 19TH CENTURY

In the 19th century liberalism met with a series of successes and failures as people in various countries struggled to establish representative government. Some in Europe staged revolutions that failed to overthrow monarchies, while others, particularly in Latin America, succeeded in freeing themselves from colonial rule.

EUROPE

Following the liberal revolutions of the late 18th century, liberalism, as an ideology and in practice, became the preeminent reform movement in Europe during the 19th century. Its fortunes, however, varied with the historical conditions in each country—the strength of the crown, the élan of the aristocracy, the pace of industrialization, and the circumstances of national unification. The national character of a liberal movement could even be affected by religion. Liberalism in Roman Catholic countries such as France, Italy, and Spain, for example, tended to acquire anticlerical overtones, and liberals in those countries tended to favour legislation restricting the civil authority and political power of the Catholic clergy.

In Great Britain the Whigs had evolved by the mid-19th century into the Liberal Party, whose reformist programs became the model for liberal political parties throughout Europe. Liberals propelled the long campaign that abolished Britain's slave trade in 1807 and slavery itself throughout the British dominions in 1833. The liberal project of broadening the franchise in Britain bore fruit in the Reform Bills of 1832, 1867, and 1884–85. The sweeping reforms achieved by Liberal Party governments led by William Gladstone for 14 years between 1868 and 1894 marked the apex of British liberalism.

Liberalism in continental Europe often lacked the fortuitous combination of broad popular support and a powerful liberal party that it had in Britain. In France the Revolutionary and Napoleonic governments pursued liberal goals in their abolition of feudal privileges and their modernization of the decrepit institutions inherited from the ancien régime. After the Bourbon Restoration in 1815, however, French liberals were faced with the decades-long task of securing constitutional liberties and enlarging popular participation in government under a reestablished monarchy, goals not substantially achieved until the formation of the Third Republic in 1871.

Elsewhere in Europe liberalism inspired nationalistic aspirations to the creation of unified, independent, constitutional states with their own parliaments and the rule of law; among the most prominent exponents were the leaders of the Risorgimento movement for Italian unification and the nationalist reformer Lajos Kossuth in Hungary. But the failure of the Revolutions of 1848 highlighted liberals' weaknesses. Liberals' inability to unify the German states in the mid-19th century was attributable in large part to the dominant role of a militarized Prussia and the reactionary influence of Austria. The liberal-inspired unification of Italy was delayed until the 1860s by the armies of Austria and of Napoleon III of France and by the opposition of the Vatican.

Nevertheless, liberalism was a transforming force in Europe throughout the 19th century. Industrialization and modernization, for which classical liberalism provided ideological justification, wrought great changes. The feudal system fell, a functionless aristocracy lost its privileges, and monarchs were challenged and curbed. Capitalism

REVOLUTIONS OF 1848

The Revolutions of 1848 were a series of republican revolts against European monarchies, beginning in Sicily, and spreading to France, Germany, Italy, and the Austrian Empire. They all ended in failure and repression, and were followed by widespread disillusionment among liberals.

The revolutionary movement began in Italy with a local revolution in Sicily in January 1848; and, after the revolution of February 24 in France, the movement extended throughout the whole of Europe with the exception of Russia, Spain, and the Scandinavian countries. In Great Britain it amounted to little more than a Chartist demonstration (Chartism was a working-class movement for parliamentary reform) and a republican agitation in Ireland. In Belgium, The Netherlands, and Denmark it manifested itself in peaceful reforms of existing institutions; but democratic insurrections broke out in the capitals of the three great monarchies, Paris, Vienna, and Berlin, where the governments, rendered powerless by their fear of "the revolution," did little to defend themselves. The revolution was successful in France alone, where the Second Republic and universal manhood suffrage were established.

In Austria the new ministers promised to grant constitutions, and in Prussia King Frederick William IV, who led the movement for the unification of Germany, hoisted the black, red, and gold flag that had become the symbol of German unity. The German governments agreed to the convocation of three constituent assemblies at Berlin, Vienna, and Frankfurt by which democratic constitutions were to be drafted for Prussia, Austria, and Germany. In Italy, at first, the revolution only took the form of a nationalist rising against Austria led by the king of Sardinia under the Italian tricolour, the "white, red and green." The republic was proclaimed in 1849, and then only in Rome and Tuscany. Within the Austrian empire the nationalities subjected to the German Government of Vienna agitated for a national government, and Hungary succeeded in organizing itself on an autonomous basis.

However, the restoration had commenced even before the revolution was over, and it was accomplished by the armies that had remained faithful to their respective governments. The immediate result of the reaction became manifest in the withdrawal of liberal democratic or nationalist concessions which had been made during the revolution: universal manhood suffrage, liberty of the press and of assembly. Absolute monarchy was reestablished in Germany, Austria, and Italy; and the governments strengthened the police forces and organized a persecution of the popular press and associations that paralyzed political life. Yet the restoration of the old order was not entirely complete: universal manhood suffrage was not abolished in France; and in Prussia the Constitution of January 1850, which established an elective assembly, was retained.

replaced the static economies of the Middle Ages, and the middle class was left free to employ its energies by expanding the means of production and vastly increasing the wealth of society. As liberals set about limiting the power of the monarchy, they converted the ideal of constitutional government, accountable to the people through the election of representatives, into a reality.

LATIN AMERICA

In the Western Hemisphere in the 19th century, the Latin American wars for independence were the most dramatic example of the liberal assault against authoritarian rule. Between 1808 and 1826 all of Latin America except the Spanish colonies of Cuba and Puerto Rico slipped out of the hands of the Iberian powers who had ruled the region for three centuries. The rapidity and timing of that dramatic change were the result of a combination of long-building tensions in colonial rule and a series of external events.

Reforms imposed by the Spanish Bourbon monarchs in the 18th century provoked great instability in the relations between the rulers and their colonial subjects in the Americas. Many Creoles (those of Spanish parentage but who were born in America) felt Bourbon policy to be an unfair attack on their wealth, political power, and social status. More generally, Creoles reacted angrily against the crown's preference for peninsulars (colonial residents who had been born in the Iberian Peninsula— i.e., Spain and Portugal) in administrative positions and its declining support of the caste system and the Creoles' privileged status within it. After hundreds of years of proven service to Spain, the American-born elites felt that the Bourbons were now treating them like a recently conquered nation.

In cities throughout the region, Creole frustrations increasingly found expression in ideas derived from the Enlightenment. Imperial prohibitions proved unable to stop the flow of potentially subversive English, French, and North American works into the colonies of Latin America. Creole participants in conspiracies against Portugal and Spain at the end of the 18th and the beginning of the 19th century showed familiarity with such European Enlightenment thinkers as Thomas Hobbes, John Locke, Montesquieu, and Jean-Jacques Rousseau. The Enlightenment clearly informed the aims of dissident Creoles and inspired some of the later, great leaders of the independence movements across Latin America. Although these ideas were not, strictly speaking, causes of independence, they did help foster a more questioning attitude toward traditional institutions and authority.

In 1810 a Cortes (Parliament) emerged in Cádiz, Spain, to represent both Spain and Spanish America. Two years later it produced a new, liberal constitution that proclaimed Spain's American possessions to be full members of the kingdom and not mere colonies. Yet the Creoles who participated in the new Cortes were denied equal representation. Moreover, the Cortes would not concede permanent free trade to the Americans and obstinately refused to grant any degree of meaningful autonomy to the overseas dominions. Having had a taste of freedom during their political and economic isolation from the mother country, Spanish Americans did not easily consent to a reduction of their power and autonomy.

By this time a trend was clear. Without denouncing Spanish King Ferdinand VII, Creoles throughout most of Spanish America were moving toward the establishment of their own autonomous governments. Transforming these early initiatives into a break with Spanish control required tremendous sacrifice. Over the next decade and a half,

Spanish Americans had to defend with arms their movement toward independence. (By contrast, the Portuguese colony of Brazil gained its independence with little of the violence that marked similar transitions in Spanish America. Dom Pedro, the Portuguese prince regent residing in Brazil, proclaimed Brazil's independence on Sept. 7, 1822, and subsequently became its first emperor.)

South America

The movements that liberated Spanish South America arose from opposite ends of the continent. From the north came the movement led most famously by Simón Bolívar, the scion of an old aristocratic Creole family in Caracas and a dynamic figure known as the Liberator. From the south proceeded another powerful force, this one directed by the more circumspect José de San Martín. After difficult conquests of their home regions, the two movements spread the cause of independence through other territories, finally meeting on the central Pacific coast. From there, troops under northern generals finally stamped out the last vestiges of loyalist resistance in Peru and Bolivia by 1826.

In May 1810 prominent Creoles in Buenos Aires, capital of the Viceroyalty of the Río de la Plata (which included the territory now comprising Argentina, Uruguay, Paraguay, and Bolivia), forced the last Spanish viceroy there to consent to a *cabildo abierto*, an extraordinary open meeting of the municipal council and local notables. Although shielding itself with a pretense of loyalty to Ferdinand, the junta produced by that session marked the end of Spanish rule in Buenos Aires and its hinterland. After its revolution of May 1810, the region was the only one to resist reconquest by loyalist troops throughout the period of the independence wars.

Simón Bolívar—"the Liberator"—was one of two men (the other was José de San Martín) who brought independence to South America in the early 19th century. Hulton Archive/Getty Images

Distinct interests and long-standing resentment of the viceregal capital led different regions in the south to pursue separate destinies. Montevideo and its surroundings became the separate Estado Oriental ("Eastern State," later Uruguay). Paraguay resisted Buenos Aires' military and set out on a path of relative isolation from the outside world. By the time Bolívar's armies finally completed the liberation of Upper Peru (then renamed Bolivia in the Liberator's honour), the region had long since separated itself from Buenos Aires.

The main thrust of the southern independence forces met much greater success on the Pacific coast. In 1817 San Martín, a Latin American–born former officer in the Spanish military, directed 5,000 men in a dramatic crossing of the Andes and struck at a point in Chile where loyalist forces had not expected an invasion. In alliance with Chilean patriots under the command of Bernardo O'Higgins, San Martín's army restored independence to a region whose highly factionalized junta had been defeated by royalists in 1814. With Chile as his base, San Martín then faced the task of freeing the Spanish stronghold of Peru. Final destruction of loyalist resistance in the highlands required the entrance of northern armies.

Meanwhile, Creoles in the Viceroyalty of New Granada (which included present-day Colombia, Panama, Ecuador, and Venezuela) organized revolutionary governments that proclaimed some social and economic reforms in 1810, and in Venezuela they openly declared a break with Spain the following year. Forces loyal to Spain fought the Venezuelan patriots from the start, leading to a pattern in which patriot rebels held the capital city and its surroundings but could not dominate large areas of the countryside. In 1812 loyalist forces crushed the rebels' military, driving Bolívar and others to seek refuge in New Granada proper (the heart of the viceroyalty). Bolívar returned to Venezuela with a new army in 1813 but achieved only short-lived victories. The army led by loyalist José Tomás Boves demonstrated the key military role that the *llaneros* (cowboys) came to play in the region's struggle. Turning the tide against independence, these highly mobile, ferocious fighters made up a formidable military force that pushed Bolívar out of his home country once more.

By 1815 the independence movements in Venezuela and almost all across Spanish South America seemed moribund. A large military expedition sent by Ferdinand VII in that year reconquered Venezuela and most of New Granada. Yet another invasion led by Bolívar in 1816 failed miserably.

The following year a larger and revitalized independence movement emerged, winning the struggle in the north and taking it into the Andean highlands. The mercurial Bolívar galvanized this initiative. A hero and symbol of South American independence, Bolívar did not produce victory by himself, of course; still, he was of fundamental importance to the movement as an ideologue, military leader, and political catalyst. In his most famous writing, the "Jamaica Letter" (composed during one of his periods of exile, in 1815), Bolívar affirmed his undying faith in the cause of independence, even in the face of the patriots' repeated defeats. While laying out sharp criticisms of Spanish colonialism, the document also looked toward the future. For Bolívar, the only path for the former colonies was the establishment of an autonomous, centralized republican government.

A group of *llaneros* of mixed ethnicity led by José Antonio Páez proved crucial to the patriots' military victories in 1818–19. A major step in that success came in the subduing of the loyalist defenders of Bogotá in 1819. After leading his army up the face of the eastern Andes, Bolívar dealt a crushing defeat to his enemies in the Battle of

Boyacá. But consolidating victory in the north proved difficult. A congress that Bolívar had convened in Angostura in 1819 named him president of Gran Colombia, a union of what are today Venezuela, Colombia, Panama, and Ecuador. In reality, sharp divisions permeated the region and ultimately dashed Bolívar's hopes of uniting the former Spanish colonies into a single new nation. Still, the tide had turned in favour of independence, and further energetic military campaigns liberated New Granada and Venezuela by 1821. A constituent congress held that year in Cúcuta chose Bolívar president of a now much more centralized Gran Colombia.

Leaving his trusted right-hand man, Francisco de Paula Santander, in Bogotá to rule the new government, Bolívar then pushed on into Ecuador and the central Andes. There the southern and northern armies came together in a pincer movement to quash the remaining loyalist strength. In 1822 San Martín and Bolívar came face-to-face in a celebrated but somewhat mysterious encounter in Guayaquil, Ecuador. Accounts of their meeting vary widely, but apparently San Martín made the realistic evaluation that only Bolívar and his supporters could complete the liberation of the Andes. From that point on, the northerners took charge of the struggle in Peru and Bolivia. After standing by while Spanish forces threatened to recapture the lands that San Martín's armies had emancipated, Bolívar responded to the calls of Peruvian Creoles and guided his soldiers to victory in Lima. While he organized the government there, his lieutenants set out to win the highlands of Peru and Upper Peru. One of them, the Venezuelan Antonio José de Sucre, directed the patriots' triumph at Ayacucho in 1824, which turned out to be the last major battle of the war. Within two years independence fighters mopped up the last of loyalist resistance, and South America was free of Spanish control.

Mexico and Central America

The independence of Mexico, like that of Peru, came late. As was the case in Lima, Mexican cities had a powerful segment of Creoles and peninsular Spaniards whom the old imperial system had served well. Mexican Creoles, like those in Peru, had the spectre of a major social uprising to persuade them to cling to Spain and stability for a while longer. For many of the powerful in Mexican society, a break with Spain promised mainly a loss of traditional status and power and possibly social revolution.

In 1810 the Bajío region produced a unique movement led by a radical priest, Miguel Hidalgo y Costilla. When officials discovered the conspiracy that Hidalgo and other Creoles had been planning in Querétaro, the priest appealed directly to the indigenous and mestizo populace. A rich agricultural and mining zone, the Bajío had recently undergone difficult economic times that hit those rural and urban workers particularly hard. Thus many of them responded eagerly to Hidalgo's famous Grito de Dolores ("Cry of Dolores"). Although framed as an appeal for resistance to the peninsulars, the Grito was in effect a call for independence.

Under the banner of the Virgin of Guadalupe, the movement's ranks swelled rapidly. Hidalgo's untrained army grew to have some 80,000 members as it conquered towns and larger cities and ultimately threatened Mexico City itself. Perhaps fearing the atrocities his troops might commit there, Hidalgo prevented the movement from entering Mexico City. Shortly afterward troops of the Spanish viceregal government caught up with the rebels. After a dramatic military defeat, Hidalgo was captured in early 1811 and executed.

The death of its first leader did not mean the end of Mexico's first independence campaign. Soon another priest, the mestizo José María Morelos y Pavón, took over the reins of the movement. With the defeat and death of Morelos in 1815, however, the potential national scope of the movement came to an effective end. Although smaller forces continued to harass the powerful through guerrilla warfare in several regions, the popular movement for independence in Mexico was no longer a grave threat to elite power.

Final independence came instead as a conservative initiative led by military officers, merchants, and the Roman Catholic Church. In Spain in 1820 liberals carried out a revolt intended to eliminate the special privileges of the church and the military. Anxious over that threat to the strength of ththose two pillars of Mexican government, and newly confident in their ability to keep popular forces in check, Creoles turned against Spanish rule in 1820–21. Two figures from the early rebellion played central roles in liberating Mexico. One, Vicente Guerrero, had been an insurgent chief; the other, Agustín de Iturbide, had been an officer in the campaign against the popular independence movement. The two came together behind an agreement known as the Iguala Plan. Centred on provisions of independence, respect for the church, and equality between Mexicans and peninsulars, the plan gained the support of many Creoles, Spaniards, and former rebels. As royal troops defected to Iturbide's cause, the new Spanish administrator was soon forced to accept the inevitability of Mexican independence. A year later, in 1822, Iturbide engineered his own coronation as Agustín I, emperor of Mexico.

The following year, a revolt that included the former insurgent Guadalupe Victoria (who, like Guerrero, had abandoned the cause of a popular independence) cut short Iturbide's tenure as monarch. The consequences of that overthrow extended from Mexico through Central America. In Mexico the rebellion ushered in a republic and introduced Antonio López de Santa Anna, who occupied a central place in the nation's politics for several decades. The provinces of the Kingdom of Guatemala—which included what are today the Mexican state of Chiapas and the nations of Guatemala, El Salvador, Honduras, Nicaragua, and Costa Rica—had adhered to Iturbide's Mexico by 1822. With the exception of Chiapas, these Central American provinces split off from Mexico in the wake of Iturbide's fall. They formed a federation, the United Provinces of Central America, which held together only until 1838, when regionalism led to the creation of separate countries in the region.

MODERN LIBERALISM

By the end of the 19th century, there was increasing disenchantment with classical liberalism's ideal of a market economy. A small number of businessmen held vast amounts of wealth and power, while great masses of people lived in poverty or worked in deplorable conditions. Thus, modern liberals came to believe that the government should correct this inequality, notably through programs that aided the needy and laws that regulated working conditions. Modern liberalism took shape in the Progressive movement, was furthered by trade unionism, and gained increased strength after the Great Depression and World War II.

THE PROGRESSIVE MOVEMENT IN THE UNITED STATES

During the 19th century the United States presented a quite different situation than that in Europe or Latin America—there was not a monarchy, an aristocracy, nor an established church against which liberalism could react. Indeed, liberalism was so well established in the United

States' constitutional structure, its political culture, and its jurisprudence that there was no distinct role for a liberal party to play, at least until the late 19th and early 20th centuries.

At that time, the Progressive movement, one of the country's most remarkable expressions of modern liberalism, became apparent. Generally speaking, progressivism was the response of various groups to problems raised by the rapid industrialization and urbanization that followed the Civil War. These problems included the spread of slums and poverty; the exploitation of labour; the breakdown of democratic government in the cities and states caused by the emergence of political organizations, or machines, allied with business interests; and a rapid movement toward financial and industrial concentration. Many Americans feared that these gigantic combinations of economic and political power might destroy the country's historic traditions of responsible democratic government and free economic opportunity for all.

Actually there was not, either in the 1890s or later, any single Progressive movement. The numerous movements for reform on the local, state, and national levels were too diverse, and sometimes too mutually antagonistic, ever to coalesce into a national crusade. But they were generally motivated by common assumptions and goals—e.g., the repudiation of individualism and laissez-faire, concern for the underprivileged and downtrodden, the control of government by the rank and file, and the enlargement of governmental power in order to bring industry and finance under a measure of popular control.

The origins of progressivism were as complex and are as difficult to describe as the movement itself. In the vanguard were various agrarian crusaders, such as the Grangers and the Populists and Democrats under William Jennings

Bryan, with their demands for stringent railroad regulation and national control of banks and the money supply. At the same time a new generation of economists, sociologists, and political scientists was undermining the philosophical foundations of the laissez-faire state and constructing a new ideology to justify democratic collectivism; and a new school of social workers was establishing

POPULIST MOVEMENT

The Populist Movement in the United States was a politically oriented coalition of agrarian reformers in the Midwest and South that advocated a wide range of economic and political legislation in the late 19th century. Throughout the 1880s local political action groups known as Farmers' Alliances sprang up among Midwesterners and Southerners, who were discontented because of crop failures, falling prices, and poor marketing and credit facilities. Although it won some significant regional victories, the alliances generally proved politically ineffective on a national scale. Thus in 1892 their leaders organized the Populist Party, sometimes called the People's Party, and the Farmers' Alliances melted away. While trying to broaden their base to include labour and other groups, the Populists remained almost entirely agrarian-oriented. They demanded an increase in the circulating currency (to be achieved by the unlimited coinage of silver), a graduated income tax, government ownership of the railroads, a tariff for revenue only, the direct election of U.S. senators, and other measures designed to strengthen political democracy and give farmers economic parity with business and industry.

In 1892 the Populist presidential candidate, James B. Weaver, polled 22 electoral votes and more than 1,000,000

popular votes. By fusing with the Democrats in certain
states, the party elected several members to Congress, three
governors, and hundreds of minor officials and legislators,
nearly all in the northern Midwest. In the South, however,
most farmers refused to endanger white supremacy by voting against the Democratic Party. Additional victories were
won in the 1894 midterm election, but in 1896 the Populists
allowed themselves to be swept into the Democratic cause
by their mutual preoccupation with the Free Silver
Movement. The subsequent defeat of Democratic presidential candidate William Jennings Bryan signalled the
collapse of one of the most challenging protest movements
in the United States since the Civil War. The Progressive
Party later embraced some of the Populist causes.

*Soon after aligning itself with the Democrats and failed presidential
candidate William Jennings Bryan, who advocated unlimited coinage of silver, the fledgling Populist Party lost its power and eventually
faded away.* MPI/Hulton Archive/Getty Images

settlement houses and going into the slums to discover the extent of human degradation. Allied with them was a growing body of ministers, priests, and rabbis—proponents of what was called the social Gospel—who struggled to arouse the social concerns and consciences of their parishioners. Finally, journalists called "muckrakers" probed into all the dark corners of American life and carried their message of reform through mass-circulation newspapers and magazines.

By 1901 the reform upheaval was too strong to be contained within urban centres or even state boundaries. Moreover, certain problems with which only the federal government was apparently competent to deal cried out for solution. Pres. William McKinley's assassination in September 1901 brought to the presidency an entirely different kind of man—Theodore Roosevelt. Roosevelt had broad democratic sympathies; moreover, thanks to his experience as police commissioner of New York City and governor of New York State, he was the first president to have an intimate knowledge of modern urban problems. By 1906 he was the undisputed spokesman of national progressivism and by far its best publicity agent.

In 1901, Americans were perhaps most alarmed about the spread of so-called trusts, or industrial combinations, which they thought were responsible for the steady price increases that had occurred each year since 1897. Ever alert to the winds of public opinion, Roosevelt responded by activating the Sherman Anti-Trust Act of 1890, which had lain dormant because of Grover Cleveland's and McKinley's refusal to enforce it and also because of the Supreme Court's ruling of 1895 that the measure did not apply to combinations in manufacturing. Beginning in 1902 with a suit to dissolve a northwestern railroad monopoly, Roosevelt moved next against the so-called Beef Trust,

*Trust-buster Teddy Roosevelt appealed to American citizens, who were
wary of industrial monopolies, which they deemed responsible for sky-
rocketing prices.* Hulton Archive/Getty Images

then against the oil, tobacco, and other monopolies. In every case the Supreme Court supported the administration, going so far in the oil and tobacco decisions of 1911 as to reverse its 1895 decision.

Roosevelt was so much the idol of the masses of 1908 that he could have easily gained the Republican nomination in that year. After his election in 1904, however, he had announced that he would not be a candidate four years later; adhering stubbornly to his pledge, he arranged the nomination of his secretary of war, William Howard Taft of Ohio, who easily defeated William Jennings Bryan. Taft might have made an ideal president during a time of domestic tranquility, but his tenure in the White House was far from peaceful. National progressivism was nearly at high tide; and a large group of Republican progressives, called "insurgents," sat in both houses of Congress. These Republicans, like a majority of Americans, demanded such reforms as tariff reductions, an income tax, the direct election of senators, and even stricter railroad and corporation regulations.

Republican insurgents were determined to prevent Taft's renomination in 1912. They found their leader in Roosevelt, who had become increasingly alienated from Taft and who made a whirlwind campaign for the presidential nomination in the winter and spring of 1912. Roosevelt swept the presidential primaries, even in Taft's own state of Ohio; but Taft and conservative Republicans controlled the powerful state organizations and the Republican National Committee and were able to nominate Taft by a narrow margin. Convinced that the bosses had stolen the nomination from him, Roosevelt led his followers out of the Republican convention. In August they organized the Progressive ("Bull Moose") Party and named Roosevelt to lead the third-party cause.

Taft's single objective in the 1912 campaign was to defeat Roosevelt. The real contest was between Roosevelt and Democrat Woodrow Wilson for control of the Progressive majority. Campaigning strenuously on a platform that he called the New Nationalism, Roosevelt demanded effective control of big business through a strong federal commission, radical tax reform, and a whole series of measures to put the federal government squarely into the business of social and economic reform. By contrast Wilson seemed conservative with a program he called the New Freedom; it envisaged a concerted effort to destroy monopoly and to open the doors of economic opportunity to small businessmen through drastic tariff reduction, banking reform, and severe tightening of the antitrust laws.

Roosevelt outpolled Taft in the election, but he failed to win many Democratic Progressives away from Wilson, who won by a huge majority of electoral votes, though receiving only about 42 percent of the popular vote. Wilson oversaw the enactment of a number of progressive policies during his two terms, but the era came to an end after World War I (1914–18) and was succeeded by a period of conservatism.

Interwar Liberalism

The further development of liberalism in Europe was brutally interrupted in 1914–18 by the prolonged slaughter of World War I. The war overturned four of Europe's great imperial dynasties—Germany, Austria-Hungary, Russia, and Ottoman Turkey—and thus at first appeared to give added impetus to liberal democracy. Europe was reshaped by the Treaty of Versailles on the principle of national self-determination, which in practice meant the breakup of the German, Austro-Hungarian, and Ottoman empires into nationally homogeneous states. The League of Nations, an organization for international cooperation, was created in the hope that negotiation would replace war as a means of settling international disputes.

But the trauma of the war had created widespread disillusionment about the entire liberal view of progress toward a more humane world. The harsh peace terms imposed by the victorious Allies, together with the misery created by the Great Depression, beginning in 1929, enfeebled Germany's newly established Weimar Republic and set the stage for the Nazi seizure of power in 1933. In Italy, meanwhile, dissatisfaction with the peace settlement led directly to the takeover by the Fascist Party in 1922. Liberalism was also threatened by Soviet communism, which seemed to many to have inherited the hopes for progress earlier associated with liberalism itself.

While liberalism came under political attack in the interwar period, the Great Depression threatened the very survival of the market economy. The boom-and-bust character of the business cycle had long been a major defect of market economies, but the Great Depression, with its seemingly endless downturn in business activity and its soaring levels of unemployment, confounded classical economists and produced real pessimism about the viability of capitalism.

The wrenching hardships inflicted by the Great Depression eventually convinced Western governments that complex modern societies needed some measure of rational economic planning. The New Deal (1933–39), the domestic program undertaken by Pres. Franklin D. Roosevelt to lift the United States out of the Great Depression, typified modern liberalism in its vast expansion of the scope of governmental activities and its increased regulation of business. Among the measures that New Deal legislation provided were emergency assistance and temporary jobs to the unemployed, restrictions on banking and financial industries, more power for trade unions to organize and bargain with employers, and establishment of the Social Security program of retirement benefits and unemployment, and disability insurance.

THE TRADE UNION MOVEMENT

Trade unionism originated in the 19th century in Great Britain, continental Europe, and the United States. In many countries it is synonymous with the term "labour movement." Trade unions consist of labourers in a particular trade, industry, or company, created for the purpose of securing improvements in pay, benefits, working conditions, or social and political status through collective bargaining.

Though the movement started in the 19th century, smaller associations of workers started appearing in Britain in the 18th century. These remained sporadic and short-lived through most of the 19th century, in part because of the hostility they encountered from employers and government groups that resented this new form of political and economic activism. At that time unions and unionists were regularly prosecuted under various restraint-of-trade and conspiracy statutes in both Britain and the United States. British unionism received its legal foundation in the Trade-Union Act of 1871. In the United States the same effect was achieved, albeit more slowly and uncertainly, by a series of court decisions that whittled away at the use of injunctions, conspiracy laws, and other devices against unions.

While union organizers in both countries faced similar obstacles, their approaches evolved quite differently: the British movement favoured political activism, which led to the formation of the Labour Party in 1906, while American unions pursued collective bargaining as a means of winning economic gains for their workers. The founding of the American Federation of Labor (AFL) by several unions of skilled workers in 1886 marked the beginning of a continuous, large-scale labour movement in the United States. Its member groups comprised national trade or craft unions that organized local unions and negotiated wages, hours, and working conditions.

During the 20th century, craft unions lost ground to industrial unions. This shift was both historic and controversial because the earliest unions had developed in order to represent skilled workers. These groups believed that unskilled workers were unsuitable for union organization. In 1935, for example, the AFL opposed attempts to organize the unskilled and ultimately expelled a small group of member unions that were attempting to do so. The expelled unions formed the Congress of Industrial Organizations (CIO), which by 1941 had assured the success of industrial unionism by organizing the steel and automobile industries. When the AFL and the CIO merged in 1955, they represented between them some 15 million workers. At the same time, mass unions began appearing in Britain and several European countries, and before the end of the century the industrial unions—embracing large numbers of unskilled or semiskilled workers—were recognized as powerful negotiating forces.

By the end of the 20th century the globalization of the workforce had brought new challenges to the labour movement, effectively weakening collective bargaining in industries whose workers could be replaced by a cheaper labour force in a different part of the world. Labour unions have nonetheless had a lasting influence. The principles and practices of trade unionism are embedded in the economic systems of most industrial countries.

Labour unions in America were at the apex of their bargaining power when the formidable AFL joined forces with the CIO in 1955. Michael Rougier/Time & Life Pictures/Getty Images

Postwar Liberalism Through the 1960s

Liberalism, in strategic alliance with Soviet communism, ultimately triumphed over fascism in World War II (1939–45), and liberal democracy was reestablished in West Germany, Italy, and Japan. As Western Europe, North America, and Japan entered a period of steady economic growth and unprecedented prosperity after the war, attention shifted to the institutional factors that prevented such economies from fully realizing their productive potential, especially during periods of mass unemployment and depression. Great Britain, the United States, and other Western industrialized nations committed their national governments to promoting full employment, the maximum use of their industrial capacity, and the maximum purchasing power of their citizenry. The old rhetoric about "sharing the wealth" gave way to a concentration on growth rates, as liberals—inspired by the English economist John Maynard Keynes—used the government's power to borrow, tax, and spend not merely to counter contractions of the business cycle but to encourage expansion of the economy. Here, clearly, was a program less disruptive of class harmony and the basic consensus essential to a democracy than the old Robin Hood method of taking from the rich and giving to the poor.

A further and final expansion of social welfare programs occurred in the liberal democracies during the postwar decades. Notable measures were undertaken in Britain by the Labour government of Prime Minister Clement Attlee and in the United States by the Democratic administration of Pres. Lyndon B. Johnson as part of his Great Society program of national reforms. These measures created the modern welfare state, which provided not only the usual forms of social insurance but also pensions, unemployment benefits, subsidized medical care, family allowances, and government-funded higher education. By the 1960s social welfare was thus provided "from the cradle to the grave" throughout much of Western Europe—particularly in the Scandinavian countries—in Japan and Canada, and to a lesser extent in the United States.

The liberal democratic model was adopted in Asia and Africa by most of the new nations that emerged from the dissolution of the British and French colonial empires in the 1950s and early '60s. The new nations almost invariably adopted constitutions and established parliamentary governments, believing that these institutions would lead to the same freedom and prosperity that had been achieved in Europe. The results, however, were mixed, with genuine parliamentary democracy taking root in some countries but succumbing in many others to military or socialist dictatorships.

CONTEMPORARY LIBERALISM

The three decades of unprecedented general prosperity that the Western world experienced after World War II marked the high tide of modern liberalism. But the slowing of economic growth that gripped most Western countries beginning in the mid-1970s presented a serious challenge to modern liberalism. By the end of that decade economic stagnation, combined with the cost of maintaining the social benefits of the welfare state, pushed governments increasingly toward politically untenable levels of taxation and mounting debt.

As modern liberals struggled to meet the challenge of stagnating living standards in mature industrial economies, others saw an opportunity for a revival of classical liberalism. The intellectual foundations of this revival were primarily the work of the Austrian-born British economist

Friedrich von Hayek and the American economist Milton Friedman. One of Hayek's greatest achievements was to demonstrate, on purely logical grounds, that a centrally planned economy is impossible. Friedman, as one of the founders of the modern monetarist school of economics, held that the business cycle is determined mainly by the supply of money and by interest rates, rather than by government fiscal policy—contrary to the long-prevailing view of Keynes and his followers. These arguments were enthusiastically embraced by the major conservative political parties in Britain and the United States, which had never abandoned the classical liberal conviction that the market, for all its faults, guides economic policy better than governments do. Revitalized conservatives achieved power with the lengthy administrations of Prime Minister Margaret Thatcher (1979–90) in Britain and Pres. Ronald Reagan (1981–89) in the United States. The clearest sign of the importance of this "neoclassical" version of liberalism was the emergence of libertarianism as a political force.

In the two decades following the elections of Thatcher and Reagan, modern liberalism appeared to be in dispirited decline. Most sectors of the British and American economies were deregulated or privatized, and regulations governing the banking, insurance, and financial industries— many in place since the New Deal—were watered down or eliminated in the 1980s and '90s. The resulting lack of oversight was a major factor in a worldwide financial crisis that began in 2007–08 and threatened to turn into a global depression. In 2009 newly elected U.S. Pres. Barack Obama undertook, with widespread popular support, a "new New Deal" in which banks were re-regulated and the automobile industry radically restructured. Modern liberalism appeared to gain a new lease on life.

Contemporary liberalism remains deeply concerned with reducing economic inequalities and helping the poor,

Nobel Prize–winning economist Milton Friedman is credited with reviving classical liberalism in contemporary America. Many conservatives embraced the economic tenets of this "neoclassical" liberalism.. Keystone/Hulton Archive/Getty Images

but it also has extended the concept of individual rights to various struggles for social justice. The prototypical mass movement in this regard was the American civil rights movement of the 1950s and '60s, which resulted in legislation forbidding most forms of discrimination against a large African American minority. In the 1970s there arose similar movements struggling for equal rights for women, gays and lesbians, people with disabilities, and other minorities or disadvantaged social groups. Moreover, the relaxation in most developed countries of long-standing restrictions on contraception, divorce, abortion, and homosexuality was inspired in part by the traditional liberal insistence on individual choice.

DEMOCRATIC PARTY

The U.S. Democratic Party is one of the country's two leading parties and has historically been the party of labour, minorities, and progressive reformers. In the 1790s a group of Thomas Jefferson's supporters called themselves "Democratic Republicans" or "Jeffersonian Republicans" to demonstrate their belief in the principle of popular government and their opposition to monarchism. The party adopted its present name in the 1830s, during the presidency of Andrew Jackson. Democrats won nearly every presidential election in the years 1836–60, but the issue of slavery split the party. The Southern Democrats called for the protection of slavery in the new territories, whereas the Northern Democrats, led by Stephen A. Douglas, advocated allowing each territory to decide by popular sovereignty whether to accept slavery within its borders. As a result, in 1860 the new antislavery Republican Party won its first national victory under

Abraham Lincoln. From 1861 to 1913 the only Democratic president was Grover Cleveland; in these years the party was basically conservative and agrarian-oriented, and its members were opposed to protective tariffs. It returned to power under Woodrow Wilson, instituting greater federal regulation of banking and industry, but the Republicans' frank embrace of big business drew voters amid the prosperity of the 1920s. Democrats became dominant again in 1932, electing Franklin D. Roosevelt. A coalition of urban workers, small farmers, liberals, and others sustained Democrats in office until 1953, and the party regained the presidency with the election of John F. Kennedy in 1960. In the 1970s and '80s the Democrats held the presidency only during the single term of Jimmy Carter (1976–81) but retained majority control of the House of Representatives. They regained the presidency in 1992 with the election of Bill Clinton but lost control of both the House and the Senate in 1994. In the presidential election of 2000, Clinton's vice president, Al Gore, was defeated by a Republican, George W. Bush. In 2004, the party's presidential nominee, John Kerry, was defeated by Bush, and the Democrats lost seats in both houses of Congress. Aided by growing opposition to the Iraq War, Democrats regained control of both the House and the Senate following the 2006 midterm elections. In the 2008 presidential election Democratic nominee Barack Obama defeated Republican John McCain, and the Democrats increased their majorities in both the House and the Senate. The modern Democratic Party generally supports a strong federal government with powers to regulate business and industry in the public interest; federally financed social services and benefits for the poor, the unemployed, the aged, and other groups; and the protection of civil rights.

LIBERTARIANISM

Libertarianism is a variant of liberalism that puts individual liberty at the centre of its political philosophy. Liberalism seeks to define and justify the legitimate powers of government in terms of certain natural or God-given individual rights—such as the rights to life, liberty, private property, freedom of speech and association, freedom of worship, government by consent, equality under the law, and moral autonomy (the pursuit of one's own conception of happiness, or the "good life"). The purpose of government, according to liberals, is to protect these and other individual rights, and in general liberals have contended that government power should be limited to that which is necessary to accomplish this task. Libertarians are classical liberals who strongly emphasize the individual right to liberty. They contend that the scope and powers of government should be constrained so as to allow each individual as much freedom of action as is consistent with a like freedom for everyone else. Thus, they believe that individuals should be free to behave and to dispose of their property as they see fit, provided that their actions do not infringe on the equal freedom of others.

In the late 19th and early 20th centuries, many liberals began to worry that persistent inequalities of wealth and the tremendous pace of social change were undermining democracy and threatening other classical liberal values, such as the right to moral autonomy. Fearful of what they considered a new despotism of the wealthy, modern liberals advocated government regulation of markets and major industries, heavier taxation of the rich, the legalization of trade unions, and the introduction of various government-funded social services, such as mandatory accident insurance. In the 20th century, so-called welfare state

INDIVIDUALISM

Modern individualism emerged in Britain with the ideas of Scottish economist Adam Smith and English philosopher Jeremy Bentham. The concept was described by French political scientist Alexis de Tocqueville as fundamental to the American temper. Individualism places great value on self-reliance, on privacy, and on mutual respect. Negatively, it embraces opposition to authority and to all manner of controls over the individual, especially when exercised by the state. All individualists believe that government should keep its interference in the lives of individuals at a minimum, confining itself largely to maintaining law and order, preventing individuals from interfering with others, and enforcing agreements (contracts) voluntarily arrived at. Individualism also implies a property system according to which each person or family enjoys the maximum of opportunity to acquire property and to manage and dispose of it as he or they see fit. Although economic individualism and political individualism in the form of democracy advanced together for a while, in the course of the 19th century they eventually proved incompatible, as newly enfranchised voters came to demand governmental intervention in the economic process. Individualistic ideas lost ground in the later 19th and early 20th century with the rise of large-scale social organization and the emergence of political theories opposed to individualism, particularly communism and fascism. Individualism, often emphasized in the tenets of classical liberalism and libertarianism, reemerged in the latter half of the 20th century with the defeat of fascism and the fall of communist regimes in the Soviet Union and Eastern Europe.

liberalism, or social democracy, emerged as the dominant form of liberalism, and the term *liberalism* itself underwent a significant change in definition in English-speaking countries. Particularly after World War II, most self-described liberals no longer supported completely free markets and minimal government, though they continued to champion other individual rights, such as the right to freedom of speech. As liberalism became increasingly associated with government intervention in the economy and social-welfare programs, some classical liberals abandoned the old term and began to call themselves "libertarians."

Nevertheless, despite the historical growth in the scope and powers of government, in the early 21st century the political and economic systems of most Western countries—especially the United Kingdom and the United States—continued to be based largely on classical liberal principles. Accordingly, libertarians in those countries tended to focus on smaller deviations from liberal principles, creating the perception among many that their views were radical or extreme. Explicitly libertarian political parties (such as the Libertarian Party in the United States and the Libertarianz Party in New Zealand), where they did exist, garnered little support, even among self-professed libertarians. Most politically active libertarians supported classical liberal parties (such as the Free Democratic Party in Germany or the Flemish Liberals and Democrats in Belgium) or conservative parties (such as the Republican Party in the United States or the Conservative Party in Great Britain); they also backed pressure groups advocating policies such as tax reduction, the privatization of education, and the decriminalization of drugs and other so-called victimless crimes. There were also small but vocal groups of libertarians in Scandinavia, Latin America, India, and China.

Chapter 2: Conservatism

The political doctrine of conservatism emphasizes the value of traditional institutions and practices. In other words, conservatism is a preference for the historically inherited rather than the abstract and ideal. This preference has traditionally rested on an organic conception of society—that is, on the belief that society is not merely a loose collection of individuals but a living organism comprising closely connected, interdependent members. Conservatives thus favour institutions and practices that have evolved gradually and are manifestations of continuity and stability. Government's responsibility is to be the servant, not the master, of existing ways of life, and politicians must therefore resist the temptation to transform society and politics. This suspicion of government activism distinguishes conservatism not only from radical forms of political thought but also from liberalism, which is a modernizing, antitraditionalist movement dedicated to correcting the evils and abuses resulting from the misuse of social and political power. In *The Devil's Dictionary* (1906), the American writer Ambrose Bierce cynically (but not inappropriately) defined the conservative as "a statesman who is enamored of existing evils, as distinguished from the Liberal, who wishes to replace them with others." Conservatism must also be distinguished from the reactionary outlook, which favours the restoration of a previous, and usually outmoded, political or social order.

It was not until the late 18th century, in reaction to the upheavals of the French Revolution (1789), that conservatism began to develop as a distinct political attitude and movement. The term *conservative* was introduced after 1815 by supporters of the newly restored Bourbon monarchy in France, including the author and diplomat François-Auguste-René, vicomte de Chateaubriand. In 1830 the British politician and writer John Wilson Croker used the term to describe the British Tory Party, and John C. Calhoun, an ardent defender of states' rights in the United States, adopted it soon afterward. The originator of modern, articulated conservatism (though he never used the term himself) is generally acknowledged to be the British parliamentarian and political writer Edmund Burke, whose *Reflections on the Revolution in France* (1790) was a forceful expression of conservatives' rejection of the French Revolution and a major inspiration for counter-revolutionary theorists in the 19th century. For Burke and other pro-parliamentarian conservatives, the violent, untraditional, and uprooting methods of the revolution outweighed and corrupted its liberating ideals. The general revulsion against the violent course of the revolution provided conservatives with an opportunity to restore pre-Revolutionary traditions, and several brands of conservative philosophy soon developed.

A common way of distinguishing conservatism from both liberalism and radicalism is to say that conservatives reject the optimistic view that human beings can be morally improved through political and social change. Conservatives who are Christians sometimes express this point by saying that human beings are guilty of original sin. Skeptical conservatives merely observe that human history, under almost all imaginable political and social circumstances, has been filled with a great deal of evil. Far from believing that human nature is essentially good or that human beings are fundamentally rational, conservatives tend to assume that human beings are driven by their passions and desires — and are therefore naturally prone to selfishness, anarchy, irrationality, and violence. Accordingly, conservatives look to traditional political and cultural institutions to curb humans' base and destructive instincts. In Burke's words, people need "a sufficient restraint upon their passions," which it is the office of government "to bridle and subdue." Families, churches, and schools must teach the value of self-discipline, and those who fail to learn this lesson must have discipline imposed upon them by government and law. Without the restraining power of such institutions, conservatives believe, there can be no ethical behaviour and no responsible use of liberty.

Conservatism is as much a matter of temperament as of doctrine. It may sometimes even accompany left-wing politics or economics—as it did, for example, in the late 1980s, when hard-line communists in the Soviet Union were often referred to as "conservatives." Typically, however, the conservative temperament displays two characteristics that are scarcely compatible with communism. The first is a distrust of human nature, rootlessness (social disconnectedness), and untested innovations, together with a corresponding trust in unbroken historical continuity and in the traditional frameworks for conducting human affairs. Such frameworks may be political, cultural, or religious, or they may have no abstract or institutional expression at all.

The second characteristic of the conservative temperament, which is closely related to the first, is an aversion to abstract argument and theorizing. Attempts by philosophers and revolutionaries to plan society in advance, using political principles purportedly derived from reason alone, are misguided and likely to end in disaster, conservatives say. In this respect the conservative temperament contrasts markedly with that of the liberal. Whereas the liberal consciously articulates abstract theories, the conservative instinctively embraces concrete traditions. For just this reason, many authorities on conservatism have been led to deny that it is a genuine ideology, regarding it instead as a relatively inarticulate state of mind. Whatever the merits of this view, it remains true that the best insights of conservatism seldom have been developed into sustained theoretical works comparable to those of liberalism and radicalism.

In opposition to the "rationalist blueprints" of liberals and radicals, conservatives often insist that societies are so complex that there is no reliable and predictable connection between what governments try to do and what actually happens. It is therefore futile and dangerous, they believe, for governments to interfere with social or economic realities—as happens, for example, in government attempts to control wages, prices, or rents.

The claim that society is too complex to be improved through social engineering naturally raises the question, "What kind of understanding of society is possible?" The most common conservative answer emphasizes the idea of tradition. People are what they are because they have inherited the skills, manners, morality, and other cultural resources of their ancestors. An understanding of tradition—specifically, a knowledge of the history of one's own society or country—is therefore the most valuable cognitive resource available to a political leader, not because it is a source of abstract lessons but because it puts him directly in touch with the society whose rules he may be modifying.

Conservative influences operate indirectly—i.e., other than via the programs of political parties—largely by virtue of the fact that there is much in the general human temperament that is naturally or instinctively conservative, such as the fear of sudden change and the tendency to act habitually. These traits may find collective expression in, for example, a resistance to imposed political change and in the entire range of convictions and preferences that contribute to the stability of a particular culture. In all societies, the existence of such cultural restraints on political innovation constitutes a fundamental conservative bias, the implications of which were aphoristically expressed by the 17th-century English statesman Viscount Falkland: "If it is not necessary to change, it is necessary not to change." Mere inertia, however, has rarely sufficed to protect conservative values in an age dominated by rationalist dogma and by social change related to continuous technological progress.

Conservatism has often been associated with traditional and established forms of religion. After 1789 the appeal of religion redoubled, in part because of a craving for security in an age of chaos. The Roman Catholic Church, because of its roots in the Middle Ages, has appealed to more conservatives than has any other religion. Although he was not a Catholic, Burke praised Catholicism as "the most effectual barrier" against radicalism. But conservatism has had no dearth of Protestant, Jewish, Islamic, and strongly anticlerical adherents.

THE BURKEAN FOUNDATIONS

Although conservatives sometimes claim philosophers as ancient as Aristotle and Cicero as their forebears, the first explicitly conservative political theorist is generally considered to be Edmund Burke. In 1790, when the French Revolution still seemed to promise a bloodless utopia, Burke predicted in his *Reflections on the Revolution in France*—and not by any lucky blind guess but by an analysis of its rejection of tradition and inherited values—that the revolution would descend into terror and dictatorship. In their rationalist contempt for the past, he charged, the revolutionaries were destroying time-tested institutions

Edmund Burke analyzed the political climate of his time (late 18th century) before formulating his politcal theory of conservatism, which had its roots in the Whig support for limited governmental interference. Hulton Archive/ Getty Images

without any assurance that they could replace them with anything better. Political power is not a license to rebuild society according to some abstract, untested scheme; it is a trust to be held by those who are mindful of both the value of what they have inherited and of their duties to their inheritors. (It should be noted that although Burke's prediction about the Revolution proved true, French revolutionaries varied in their approach to the overthrow of the old order; the Club of the Feuillants, for example, supported a constitutional monarchy.)

For Burke, the idea of inheritance extended far beyond property to include language, manners and morals, and appropriate responses to the human condition. To be human is to inherit a culture, and politics cannot be understood outside that culture. In contrast to the Enlightenment philosophers Thomas Hobbes, John Locke, and Jean-Jacques Rousseau, each of whom conceived of political society as based on a hypothetical social contract among the living, Burke argued that

> Society is indeed a contract . . . [But, a]s the ends of such a partnership cannot be obtained in many generations, it becomes a partnership not only between those who are living, but between those who are living, those who are dead, and those who are to be born . . . Changing the state as often as there are floating fancies, . . . no one generation could link with the other. Men would be little better than the flies of a summer.

Because the social contract as Burke understood it involves future generations as well as those of the present and the past, he was able to urge improvement through political change, but only as long as the change is evolutionary: "A disposition to preserve and an ability to improve, taken together, would be my standard of a statesman."

Burke's conservatism was not an abstract doctrine; it represented the particular conservatism of the unwritten British constitution. In the politics of his time Burke was a Whig, and he bequeathed to later conservative thinkers the Whig belief in limited government. This belief was partly why Burke defended the American Revolution (1775–83), which he believed was a justified defense of traditional liberties against the untraditional tyranny of King George III.

Burke shocked his contemporaries by insisting with brutal frankness that "illusions" and "prejudices" are socially necessary. He believed that most human beings are innately depraved, steeped in original sin, and unable to better themselves with their feeble reason. Better, he said, to rely on the "latent wisdom" of prejudice, which accumulates slowly through the years, than to "put men to live and trade each on his own private stock of reason." Among such prejudices are those that favour an established church and a landed aristocracy; members of the latter, according to Burke, are the "great oaks" and "proper chieftains" of society, provided that they temper their rule with a spirit of timely reform and remain within the constitutional framework.

In Burke's writings the entire political wisdom of Europe is formulated in a new idiom, designed to bring out the folly of French revolutionaries intoxicated by sudden power and abstract ideas of a perfect society. For Burke, modern states are so complex that any attempt to reform them on the basis of metaphysical doctrines alone is bound to end in despotism. The passion and eloquence with which he developed this argument contributed significantly to the powerful conservative reactions against the French Revolution throughout Europe in the late 18th and early 19th centuries.

CLUB OF THE FEUILLANTS

The Club of the Feuillants was a conservative political club of the French Revolution that met in a former monastery of the Feuillants (Reformed Cistercians) in Paris. It was founded after Louis XVI's flight to Varennes (June 20, 1791), when a number of deputies, led by Antoine Barnave, Adrien Duport, and Alexandre de Lameth, left the Jacobin Club in opposition to a petition calling for the replacement of the king. These deputies, unlike those who remained with the radical Jacobins, feared the radicalization of the Revolution, thinking it would result in the destruction of the monarchy and of private property.

The Feuillants made up a substantial group in the Legislative Assembly, elected in September 1791 to implement the newly written constitution. They sat on the right of the Assembly (indicating their conservative attitude), opposed the democratic movement, and upheld the constitutional monarchy. But the Jacobins gradually overshadowed the Feuillants, and the club disappeared when the insurrection of Aug. 10, 1792, overthrew the monarchy.

MAISTRE AND LATIN CONSERVATISM

Among the thinkers influenced by Burke was the French diplomat and polemicist Joseph de Maistre, who developed his own more extreme brand of conservatism, known as Latin conservatism, early in the 19th century. Whereas Burkean conservatism was evolutionary, the conservatism of Maistre was counterrevolutionary. Both men favoured tradition over the radical innovations of the French Revolution, but the traditions they favoured were very different: Burke rejected the revolution for the sake of traditional liberties, Maistre for the sake of traditional authority—especially the authority of monarch and church. Burke was not authoritarian but constitutionalist—and always parliamentary—whereas Maistre, in stressing the authority of the traditional elite, is often justifiably called not conservative but reactionary.

Indeed, Maistre rejected the entire heritage of the Enlightenment, attributing the revolutionary disorders of Europe to pernicious Enlightenment ideas. He presented a picture of human beings as essentially emotional and prone to disorder and evil unless controlled within a tight political structure dominated by rulers, priests, and the threat of the public executioner. Against the French Revolutionary slogan "Liberty, equality, fraternity," Maistre proclaimed the value of "Throne and altar." His program called for a restoration of hereditary and absolute monarchy in France, though it would be a more religious and less frivolous monarchy than before. The Bourbon Restoration in France after 1815 did in fact attempt to create a modified version of the ancien régime somewhat resembling that suggested by Maistre, but the Bourbons were overthrown in 1830.

Maistre's writings were an important source of conservative thought in Spain, Italy, and France in the first half of the 19th century. But no work by Maistre or any other enemy of the Jacobins (the radical leaders of the French Revolution from 1793 to 1794) has approached the influence of Burke's classic essay, which became the basis of all subsequent conservative arguments against the French Revolution. Whereas Maistre's rigid, hierarchical conservatism has died out, Burke's more flexible brand is stronger than ever, permeating all political parties of the West that stress gradual, as opposed to radical or revolutionary, change.

CONSERVATISM IN THE 19TH CENTURY

The 19th century was in many ways antithetical to conservatism, both as a political philosophy and as a program of particular parties identified with conservative interests. The Enlightenment had engendered widespread belief in the possibility of improving the human condition—a belief, that is, in the idea of progress—and a rationalist disposition to tamper with or discard existing institutions or practices in pursuit of that goal. The French Revolution gave powerful expression to this belief, and the early Industrial Revolution and advances in science reinforced it. The resulting rationalist politics embraced a broad segment of the political spectrum, including liberal reformism, trade-union socialism (or social democracy), and ultimately Marxism. In the face of this constant rationalist innovation, conservatives often found themselves forced to adopt a merely defensive role, so that the political initiative lay always in the other camp.

METTERNICH AND THE CONCERT OF EUROPE

The massive social upheavals of the Revolutionary and Napoleonic periods provoked a reaction of more immediate and far-reaching consequence than the writings of conservative theorists. During the period 1815–48, the Austrian statesman Klemens, prince von Metternich, a major influence in Austria and in Europe generally, devoted his energies to erecting an antirevolutionary chain of international alliances throughout Europe.

Metternich was a dominating figure at the Congress of Vienna, the international peace conference convened in 1814 near the close of the Napoleonic wars. The peace

Austrian foreign affairs minister Klemens, prince von Metternich, played a major role at the Congress of Vienna, which resulted in a peace settlement based on conservative principles. Hulton Archive/ Getty Images

settlement, reached at Vienna in 1815, was based on conservative principles shared by the Austrian delegate, Metternich; the British delegate, Robert Stewart, Viscount Castlereagh; the French delegate, Charles-Maurice de Talleyrand, prince de Bénévent; and the formerly liberal Russian tsar Alexander I. These principles were traditionalism, in reaction to 25 years of rapid change; legitimism (hereditary monarchy as the only lawful rule); and restoration of monarchs ousted after 1789.

The European great powers also attempted to enforce peace through periodic conferences between governments that gave rise to a period of international cooperation known as the Concert of Europe. The Concert system, which amounted to a rudimentary form of international governance, was used to arbitrate peacefully several international disputes and to suppress liberal uprisings within the borders of the member states.

According to Metternich, the liberal revolutions of the 1820s and '30s in Spain and parts of Italy and Germany were "unhistorical" and unrealistic. Liberals were engaged in a futile attempt to impose the English institutions of parliamentary government and constitutional monarchy in places where they had no historical roots. Using arguments borrowed from Burke, he insisted on the need for continuity with the past and orderly, organic development. Hence his sarcastic comments on the liberal revolutions in Naples and elsewhere, "A people who can neither read nor write, whose last word is the dagger—fine material for constitutional principles! . . . The English constitution is the work of centuries . . . There is no universal recipe for constitutions."

The Retreat of Old-Style Conservatism

The settlement engineered by Metternich at the Congress of Vienna was reactionary in that it aimed at reinstating the political and social order that existed before the French Revolution. Nevertheless, the restored monarchies in France, Austria, and Spain thought it prudent to sanction the formation of parliamentary institutions as a sop to liberal sentiment. Political parties were hardly necessary in these states, given the limited powers accorded to the new parliaments and the narrowness of the franchise. As a result, the monarchies' most reliable supporters, the aristocratic landowners and the clergy, were able to secure the allegiance of the general population. They were especially influential in rural areas, where an inherently conservative peasantry was still relatively unaffected by industrialization and other modern innovations.

This political settlement proved untenable within a few decades of the Restoration, chiefly because of the increasing discontent of urban liberals. City dwellers tended to be more active politically than rural people, and as urban populations grew in both absolute and relative size owing to the Industrial Revolution, their festering discontent began to threaten the Restoration establishment. In the face of their agitations and revolts, conservatives gradually lost ground, and after the Revolutions of 1848 — which resulted in the exile of Metternich and of King Louis-Philippe of France—conservative factions either lost power to liberals and nationalists or clung to influence only in coalitions with other groups.

French conservatives remained loyal to the restored monarchy, but the revolutions of 1830 and 1848 dealt successive blows to that institution, and before the end of the 19th century royalists in France faced the disconcerting fact that there were no less than three families claiming a nonexistent French throne. Supporters of French conservatism among the Roman Catholic clergy, the military officer class, and the landed aristocracy remained haunted

by nostalgia for the ancien régime and thus collided with
the aspirations of the growing and powerful middle class.

Conservatism and Nationalism

Industrialization hastened the decline of old-style
conservatism because it tended to strengthen the
commerce-minded middle class and to create a new industrial working class with a diminished allegiance to old
institutions. Between 1830 and 1880 liberalism won
repeated victories over the conservative establishment in
Western Europe. Conservatives, like other political groups,
had to establish majorities in parliament if they wanted to
hold power, and the progressive expansion of the franchise
meant that they had to cultivate support from a broad
electorate. But their chief source of strength, the rural
peasantry, was declining in numbers relative to other social
groups and was in any case too small to support an effective national party.

Conservative parties eventually solved this problem by
identifying themselves with nationalist sentiments. This
strategy was pursued most vigorously in Germany, where
the unification of the German states into a single nation
became a central preoccupation of both liberals and conservatives by the middle of the 19th century. The Prussian
chancellor Otto von Bismarck used nationalist sentiments
stirred up by Prussia's successful wars against Denmark
(1864), Austria (1866), and France (1870–71) to create a
united Germany under the Prussian monarchy in 1871. The
conservative governments he headed as Germany's chancellor for the next 20 years undertook various social welfare
measures—such as pensions and unemployment benefits—to draw working-class support away from the leftist
Social Democratic Party. Although Bismarck protected the

dominant position of the Prussian landowning (Junker) and officer classes, his social welfare measures mitigated class conflict and facilitated a social cohesion in Germany that lasted to the end of World War I.

By the end of the 19th century, conservative parties throughout Europe had adopted the nationalist strategy. This gave them increased popular appeal in an era of intensifying patriotic feeling, but it also contributed to the climate of international rivalry that culminated in the outbreak of World War I in 1914. Conservative parties were almost invariably the staunchest and most intractable supporters of this war.

Great Britain

In the 17th and 18th centuries conservative political causes in Great Britain were defended by the Tories, a Parliamentary faction representing landed gentry, established merchant classes, and the clergy. This faction became the Tory Party in 1784 and finally adopted the label "Conservative" after 1831. As the Conservative Party it retained great power throughout the 19th century, consistently receiving the support of about half the electorate.

Although the party was shaken by the Whig Reform Bill of 1832 and by other measures of the Whig and Liberal parties that undermined the power of the landed gentry, it was rescued by the fertile imagination and astute management of Benjamin Disraeli, who was prime minister in 1868 and again from 1874 to 1880. Disraeli nurtured the party's support among the working class by extending the franchise to industrial workers in the Reform Bill of 1867. His policy of "Tory democracy," as it came to be known, combined a desire to mitigate the harsh conditions that

As Queen Victoria's prime minister, Benjamin Disraeli held great sway over 19th-century British politics, ushering in a new era of conservative policy. Hulton Archive/Getty Images

unrestrained capitalism imposed on ordinary workers with a belief in the value of the class system and established institutions such as the monarchy and the church. Under Disraeli the party was able to broaden its electoral support and thereby outflank the Liberal Party and the new commercial class it represented.

Disraeli's successor as party leader, Lord Salisbury, was prime minister in 1885 and again from 1886 to 1892 and from 1895 to 1902; Arthur Balfour led another Conservative government from 1902 to 1905. This era of Conservative rule was marked by imperialism, high tariffs, and the gradual erosion of the party's working-class vote.

UNITED STATES

Politics in the United States never quite conformed to the doctrinal patterns exhibited in continental Europe or even Britain, mainly because there was never a monarchy, an aristocracy, or an established church for conservatives to defend or for liberals to attack. John Adams, Alexander Hamilton, and the Federalists of the late 18th and early 19th centuries were conservative in their emphasis on order and security, but in other respects they were closer to classical liberalism. Although they may have shared Burke's respect for a "natural aristocracy," they had no use for a hereditary one. The nearest thing to an American aristocracy was the wealthy plantation-owning class in the South before the American Civil War (1861–65). Members of this class generally favoured the rights of states against the power of the federal government, and prominent defenders of this position, such as John C. Calhoun, have properly been seen as conservative thinkers.

But if there was relatively little explicit conservatism in the United States in the 19th century, the political history of the country was also remarkably resistant to revolutionary radicalism. The American working class generally shared the hopeful individualism of the middle class. As a result, the common view of the United States until well into the 20th century was that it was a country of one basic political tradition: liberalism. For a long time it seemed that conservatism could not take root in a country founded on the liberal doctrines of the Founding Fathers.

CHRISTIAN DEMOCRACY IN EUROPE

By the end of the 19th century, industrialization had created a large and turbulent working class whose increasing involvement in politics gave it a powerful voice. All Christian churches, but especially the Roman Catholic Church, faced anticlerical attacks from liberal reformers on the one hand and working-class socialists on the other. The Catholic church responded, notably under Pope Leo XIII (reigned 1878–1903), by developing social doctrines and political movements that combined protection of the church's institutional interests with policies of social justice intended to draw industrial workers back to the faith. This movement, which eventually came to be called Christian Democracy, achieved varying degrees of success in France, Germany, and Italy in the late 19th and 20th centuries. Christian Democrats were conservative in their affirmation of the right to private property as basic to a Christian society, but they also insisted that the rich look after the needs of the poor. Christian Democracy, in other words, recognized both a legal structure that protected private property and a moral imperative to use property in a compassionate way. In practical politics, Christian Democrats tended to be opportunists who aligned themselves with the ideological centre.

SOCIAL DARWINISM

Social Darwinism contends that persons, groups, and races are subject to the same laws of natural selection as Charles Darwin had perceived in plants and animals in nature. The theory was used to support laissez-faire capitalism and political conservatism in the late 19th and early 20th centuries. According to social Darwinists the weak were diminished and their cultures delimited, while the strong grew in power and in cultural influence over the weak. Social Darwinists held that the life of humans in society was a struggle for existence ruled by "survival of the fittest," a phrase proposed by the British philosopher and scientist Herbert Spencer.

The social Darwinists—notably Spencer and Walter Bagehot in England and William Graham Sumner in the United States—believed that the process of natural selection acting on variations in the population would result in the survival of the best competitors and in continuing improvement in the population. Societies, like individuals, were viewed as organisms that evolve in this manner.

Class stratification thus was justified on the basis of "natural" inequalities among individuals, for the control of property was said to be a correlate of superior and inherent moral attributes such as industriousness, temperance, and frugality. Attempts to reform society through state intervention or other means would, therefore, interfere with natural processes; unrestricted competition and defense of the status quo were in accord with biological selection. The poor were the "unfit" and should not be aided; in the struggle for existence, wealth was a sign of success.

At the societal level, social Darwinism was used as a philosophical rationalization for imperialist, colonialist,

and racist policies, sustaining belief in Anglo-Saxon or
Aryan cultural and biological superiority. Social Darwinism
declined during the 20th century as an expanded knowledge
of biological, social, and cultural phenomena undermined,
rather than supported, its basic tenets.

CONSERVATISM SINCE THE TURN OF THE 20TH CENTURY

The Allied victory in World War I (1914–18) resulted in the
downfall of four great imperial dynasties—those in Russia,
Austria-Hungary, Germany, and Ottoman Turkey—that
were the last major bastions of conservatism based on
monarchy, landed aristocracy, and an established church.
After the war, conservative parties became the standard-
bearers of frustrated nationalism in Germany as well as in
Italy and other former Allied countries. In a process that
began in the 1930s and intensified during World War II
(1939–45), conservative parties across central and Eastern
Europe were destroyed or co-opted by the totalitarian
regime of Nazi Germany.

European conservative parties began to recover their
strength only after 1946, and then only in Western Europe,
since Soviet power had extirpated all conservative political organizations in Eastern Europe. To the chagrin of
Western European socialists, conservative parties—or,
more commonly, Christian Democratic parties in which
various moderate and conservative elements had coalesced—began to win elections in West Germany and
other countries. After the defeat of the fascist regimes,
and given socialism's apparent inability to speedily rebuild
shattered postwar economies, many Europeans turned

once more to conservative policies, which seemed to promise both economic growth and democratic freedoms. This revived conservatism was by now completely shorn of its old aristocratic associations. Instead, it emphasized the raising of living standards through a market economy and the provision of a wide array of social services by the state. For the rest of the century conservative parties were characterized by liberal individualism tinged with a strong sense of social conscience—as well as by an implacable opposition to communism.

GREAT BRITAIN

At the start of the 20th century, the Conservative Party in Great Britain seemed to stand at the summit of its popularity. This ascendancy was temporarily halted by the Liberal victory in the general election of 1906. By this time, however, the Liberals had begun to lose trade-union and working-class supporters to the Labour Party, and the Labour victory of 1924 spelled the end of the Liberal Party as an effective political force. During the next four decades the Conservatives formed the government most of the time. Their success was partly the result of their having absorbed large numbers of formerly Liberal middle-class voters. The Conservative Party thus became a union of old Tory and Liberal interests combined against Labour.

In the interwar period, conservatism in Britain became closely identified with the defense of middle- and upper-class privileges, an unconstructive opposition to socialism, and, during the 1930s, appeasement (a deal-making and commercialist approach to the rising Nazi menace). However, following the introduction of a mixed economy and the vast extension of state welfare services under the Labour government of Clement Attlee after 1945, the Conservatives reversed very few of their predecessors' innovations when they returned to power in 1951. Instead they claimed to be better able to administer the welfare state efficiently. Indeed, to some extent they even tried to outbid their opponents with their own programs of social spending, including measures to encourage the construction of new homes. Three decades later this era of liberal-conservative accommodation came to a dramatic close under the government of Margaret Thatcher, whose energetic brand of conservatism stressed individual initiative, strident anticommunism, and laissez-faire economics. Thatcher's commitment to individual initiative was so strong, in fact, that she virtually repudiated the organic view of traditional conservatives when she declared, "there is no such thing as society." By this she meant that what is conventionally called "society" is nothing more than a collection of self-interested individuals. This view had much more in common with modern libertarianism than with the older conservatism of Burke. Thatcher's Tory successors had a rather less extreme individualistic orientation and reincorporated some of the communitarian elements of traditional conservatism into their ideology.

Continental Europe

Conservatism elsewhere in Western Europe was generally represented by two or more parties, ranging from the liberal centre to the moderate and extreme right. The three types of conservative party were the agrarian (particularly in Scandinavia), the Christian Democratic, and those parties allied closely with big business. These categories are very general and are not mutually exclusive.

The Christian Democratic parties had the longest history, their predecessors having emerged in the 19th century to support the church and the monarchy against liberal and radical elements. After World War I, supporters of business became the predominant element in these parties. In Italy clerical interests remained strongly represented in the Christian Democratic Party (from 1993 the Italian Popular Party), which dominated governments in that country for four decades from 1945. This party never possessed a coherent policy, however, because it was little more than a disparate alliance of moderate and conservative interest groups. The Christian Democrats anchored a long series of governing coalitions with smaller centrist parties and the Italian Socialist Party. These coalitions, while often politically ineffective and increasingly corrupt, served to exclude the large Italian Communist Party (which, after various name changes is now subsumed within the Democratic Party) from power through the end of the Cold War. When the Soviet Union collapsed in 1991 and communism was no longer perceived as a threat to Europe, the Christian Democrats lost much of their support. Their eclipse coincided with the growth of other conservative and nationalist groups formerly outside the mainstream of Italian politics—such as the Northern League, which called for the creation of a federated Italian republic, and the National Alliance (until 1994 the Italian Social Movement), which many regarded as neofascist—and with the founding in 1994 of a new conservative party, Forza Italia ("Go, Italy!"), by the media tycoon Silvio Berlusconi.

In Germany, a country divided between Roman Catholics and Protestants, the church played a far less significant role in the main conservative party, the Christian Democratic Union. After 1950, following an internal debate over economic and social questions, the party adopted a program that included support for a market economy and a strong commitment to maintaining and improving social insurance and other social welfare programs. Illustrating the conservative temper of Germany's

political climate since the end of World War II, the opposition Social Democratic Party of Germany progressively
eliminated the socialist content of its program, to the
point of embracing the profit motive in a party congress at
Bad Godesberg in 1959. In power continuously from 1982
to 1998, the Christian Democrats presided over the unification of East Germany with West Germany following the
collapse of Soviet-supported communist regimes across
Eastern Europe in 1989–90. From the 1990s German conservatives, with some exceptions, adhered to an ideology
of minimal government, deregulation, privatization, and
the reining-in of the welfare state. Putting these ideas into
political practice, however, proved difficult if not impossible, since many Germans continued to support an
extensive safety net of unemployment insurance and other
social welfare programs.

In contrast to Italy and Germany, no Christian
Democratic party emerged in France to represent moderate conservative opinion. Instead, a large proportion of
French conservatives supported parties such as Rally for
the Republic (now the Union for a Popular Movement)—
which espoused a highly nationalistic conservatism based
on the legacy of Charles de Gaulle, president of France
from 1958 to 1969—or anti-immigration groups such as the
National Front, led by Jean-Marie Le Pen; the latter party,
some argued, was not so much conservative as reactionary
or neofascist. Gaullist conservatism emphasized tradition
and order and aimed at a politically united Europe under
French leadership. Gaullists espoused divergent views on
social issues, however. The large number of Gaullist and
non-Gaullist conservative parties, their lack of stability,
and their tendency to identify themselves with local issues
made it difficult to categorize these groups in simple terms.
In the early 21st century, French conservatives of several
stripes were united by a number of developments. One was

the theme of "law and order," sounded strongly by interior minister (and later president) Nicolas Sarkozy. Unemployed youths in suburban Paris and elsewhere—many of whom were immigrants or the children of immigrants—engaged in periodic rioting to protest their plight and were met with stiff (and popular) police resistance. Another thread uniting French conservatives was the perceived threat to French values from immigrants, especially Muslims. One of the values allegedly in danger was the strict secular character of public education. When young Muslim women insisted on wearing veils to school, the French state reacted strongly—a reaction that seems, in retrospect, to have succeeded less in reaffirming French values than in further alienating Muslims from French society.

In general, conservatism in Europe has exerted a pervasive political influence since the start of the 20th century, finding expression in parties of very different character. These parties have espoused traditional middle-class values and opposed unnecessary state involvement in economic affairs and radical attempts at income redistribution. They also have been characterized by an absence of ideology and often by the lack of any well-articulated political philosophy.

JAPAN

The Meiji Restoration (1868) in Japan brought about the fall of the Tokugawa shogunate (a hereditary military dictatorship) and returned control of the country to direct imperial rule under the emperor Meiji. The political and social changes that took place after the restoration were significant and extensive, involving not only the abolition of feudal institutions but also the introduction of Western political ideas. In the 1880s a growing popular rights movement called for the creation of a constitutional government and wider participation through deliberative assemblies. Responding to these pressures, the government in 1885 formed a Cabinet system, and in 1886 work on a constitution began. Finally in 1889 the constitution, presented as a gift from the emperor to the people, was officially promulgated. It established a bicameral parliament, called the Diet (*gikai*), to be elected through a limited voting franchise. The first Diet was convened the following year, 1890.

Yet despite these dramatic developments, Japanese politics continued to be shaped primarily by traditional loyalties and attitudes. Except for the period of military government during the 1930s and '40s, conservative rule in Japan has been nearly uninterrupted since the beginning of party politics in the 1880s. Conservative parties—the two most important of which merged to form the Liberal-Democratic Party in 1955—were dominated by personalities rather than by ideology and dogma; and personal loyalties to leaders of factions within the party, rather than commitment to policy, determined the allegiance of conservative members of the Diet.

The Liberal-Democratic Party has been intimately linked with big business, and its policies have been guided primarily by the objective of fostering a stable environment for the development of Japan's market economy. To this end, the party has functioned primarily as a broker between conflicting business interests.

In the early 21st century there was a resurgence of Japanese nationalism, much of it centring on how the history of Japan in the 20th century—particularly the period before and during World War II—was to be taught. Conservative nationalists insisted that the Japanese military had done nothing wrong and had indeed acted honourably and that stories of widespread war crimes were fabricated by Japan's enemies, both foreign and domestic.

Just how pervasive and influential this resurgent national-ism might be remains to be seen.

UNITED STATES

The perception of the United States as an inherently lib-eral country began to change in the wake of the New Deal, the economic relief program undertaken by the Democratic administration of Pres. Franklin D. Roosevelt in 1933 to help raise the country out of the Great Depression. This program greatly expanded the federal government's involvement in the economy through the regulation of private enterprise, the levying of higher taxes on corpora-tions and the wealthy, and the expansion of social welfare programs. The Republican Party, drawing on the support of big business, the wealthy, and prosperous farmers, stub-bornly opposed the New Deal.

As Democratic liberals moved to the left in endorsing a larger role for government, Republicans generally clung to a 19th-century version of liberalism that called for the government to avoid interfering in the market. This pol-icy produced little success for Republicans at the polls. In matters of foreign policy, however, the Old Right, as these staunch conservatives were known, was powerful and popular enough to prevent the United States from entering World War II until the Japanese attack on the U.S. naval base at Pearl Harbor, Hawaii, in 1941. By the time the Republicans regained the presidency in 1953, they had accepted most of the New Deal reforms and were preoccupied with the battle against communists at home and abroad.

In the first decades after the war, the United States, like Britain, gradually expanded social services and increased government regulation of the economy. In the 1970s, however, the postwar economic growth that the

United States and other Western countries had relied on
to finance social welfare programs began to slacken, just as
Japan and other East Asian nations were finally attaining
Western levels of prosperity. Whatever the causes of the
West's economic stagnation, it became clear that liberal
policies of governmental activism were incapable of solv-
ing the problem.

At this point a new group of mainly American conservatives, the so-called neoconservatives, arose to argue that
high levels of taxation and the government's intrusive regulation of private enterprise were hampering economic
growth. No less troubling, in their view, was the way in
which social welfare policies were leading those who
received welfare benefits to become increasingly depend-
ent upon government. The neoconservatives generally
accepted a modest welfare state—indeed, they were sometimes described as disenchanted welfare liberals—but they
insisted that social welfare programs should help people
help themselves, not make them permanent wards of the
state. In this and other respects neoconservatives saw
themselves as defenders of middle-class virtues such as
thrift, hard work, and self-restraint, all of which they took
to be under attack in the cultural upheaval of the reputedly
hedonistic 1960s. They also took a keen interest in foreign
affairs, adopting an interventionist stance that set them
apart from the isolationist tendencies of earlier conservatives. Many of them argued that the United States had both
a right and a duty to intervene in the affairs of other nations
in order to combat the influence of Soviet communism and
to advance American interests; some even claimed that the
United States had a duty to remake the non-Western
world on the model of American democratic capitalism.
Among American political leaders, the chief representatives of neoconservatism were the Republican presidents
Ronald Reagan (1981–89) and George W. Bush (2001–09).

Ronald Reagan, 1983. U.S. Department of Defense

Its most articulate advocates, however, were academics who entered politics, such as New York Sen. Daniel Patrick Moynihan and Jeane Kirkpatrick, who served as ambassador to the United Nations (UN) during the Reagan administration.

REPUBLICAN PARTY

The Republican Party, or the Grand Old Party (GOP), was formed in 1854 by former members of the Whig, Democratic, and Free Soil parties who chose the party's name to recall the Jeffersonian Republicans' concern with the national interest above sectional interests and states' rights. The new party opposed slavery and its extension into the territories, as provided by the Kansas-Nebraska Act. Its first presidential candidate, John C. Frémont, won 11 states in 1856; its second, Abraham Lincoln, won the 1860 election by carrying 18 states. Its association with the Union victory in the American Civil War allowed it a long period of dominance nationally, though it was uncompetitive in the South for more than a century after the war. Republican candidates won 14 of 18 presidential elections between 1860 and 1932, through support from an alliance of Northern and Midwestern farmers and big-business interests.

In 1912 the party split between a progressive wing led by Theodore Roosevelt and a conservative wing led by Pres. William Howard Taft; the rift enabled the Democratic candidate, Woodrow Wilson, to win that year's election. The Republican Party's inability to counter the impact of the Great Depression led to its ouster from power in 1933; in 1953 the presidency of Dwight D. Eisenhower brought a moderate wing of the party to prominence. The party's platform remained conservative, emphasizing anticommunism, reduced government regulation of the economy, and lower taxes; many members also opposed civil rights legislation. In the 1950s the GOP gained new support from middle-class suburbanites and white Southerners disturbed by the integrationist policies of the national Democratic Party. Richard Nixon, who narrowly lost the 1960 presidential race, won narrowly in 1968 and by a landslide in 1972, but he was forced to resign in 1974 as a result of the Watergate scandal, which centred on illegal activities on the part of Nixon and his administration.

Ronald Reagan, who had assumed the leadership of the conservative wing of the Republican Party after Barry Goldwater's defeat in the presidential election of 1964, won the presidency in 1980 and 1984. Reagan introduced deep tax cuts and launched a massive buildup of U.S. military forces. His vice president, George H.W. Bush, was elected in 1988 and enjoyed enormous popularity after success in the Persian Gulf War, but an anemic economy led to his defeat in 1992 by Democrat Bill Clinton. The defeat was offset in 1994, when the Republicans regained control of the House of Representatives for the first time in 40 years.

In 2000 George W. Bush narrowly won the presidency in one of the closest and most controversial elections in U.S. history. In 2004 he won reelection. In part because of growing opposition to the Iraq War, Republicans lost control of both the House and the Senate following the 2006 midterm elections. In the 2008 presidential election, the Republican nominee, Sen. John McCain, was defeated by Democrat Barack Obama. The Democrats also increased their majorities in both the House and the Senate during that election.

Today, the Republican Party continues to emphasize tax cuts, traditional social values, and a strong national defense.

CONSERVATISM'S PROSPECTS

Division, not unity, marked conservatism around the world during the first decade of the 21st century—this despite the defeat of conservatism's chief nemesis of the previous 50 years, Soviet communism. But perhaps this fissure is not surprising. Anticommunism was the glue that held the conservative movement together, and without this common enemy the many differences between conservatives of different kinds became all too painfully clear. In Europe, for example, conservatives split over issues such as the desirability of a united Europe, the advantages of a single European currency (the euro, introduced in the countries of the European Union in 2002), and the region's proper role in policing troubled areas such as the Balkans and the Middle East.

Conservatism was even more divided in the United States. Abortion, immigration, national sovereignty, "family values," and the "war on terror," both at home and abroad, were among the issues that rallied supporters but divided adherents into various camps, from neoconservatives and "paleoconservatives" (descendants of the Old Right, who regarded neoconservatives as socially liberal and imperialistic in foreign affairs) to cultural traditionalists among "religious right" groups such as the Christian Coalition and the Moral Majority. The camps battled one another as well as their perceived enemies in the so-called "culture wars" from the 1990s through the first decade of the 21st century.

By the time of the Congressional elections of 2006 and the presidential election of 2008, however, it was clear that such infighting had taken its toll. Two military invasions and occupations abroad, in Afghanistan and Iraq, had proved enormously expensive in American lives and treasure and cast doubt on the wisdom of the neoconservatives' call for a more interventionist U.S. foreign policy backed by military might. While American conservatives had long called for smaller government, balanced budgets, and leaving education to the states, the policies of the George W. Bush administration contradicted those allegedly key tenets of conservatism. And the global economic crisis that began in 2007–08, during the final year of the Bush administration, turned Americans' attention away from cultural issues such as same-sex marriage and toward more material concerns. The "new New Deal" introduced by Democratic Pres. Barack Obama's administration in 2009 angered and upset many conservatives, whose ranks nevertheless remained divided.

Chapter 3: Socialism

In stark contrast to liberalism, socialism calls for public rather than private ownership or control of property and natural resources. According to socialists, individuals do not live or work in isolation but live in cooperation with one another. Furthermore, everything that people produce is in some sense a social product, and everyone who contributes to the production of a good is entitled to a share in it. Society as a whole, therefore, should own or at least control property for the benefit of all its members.

This conviction puts socialism in opposition to capitalism, which is based on private ownership of the means of production and allows individual choices in a free market to determine how goods and services are distributed. Socialists complain that capitalism necessarily leads to unfair and exploitative concentrations of wealth and power in the hands of the relative few who emerge victorious from free-market competition—people who then use their wealth and power to reinforce their dominance in society. Because such people are rich, they may choose where and how to live, and their choices in turn limit the options of the poor. As a result, terms such as *individual freedom* and *equality of opportunity* may be meaningful for capitalists but can only ring hollow for working people, who must do the capitalists' bidding if they are to survive. As socialists see it, true freedom and true equality require social control of the resources that provide the basis for prosperity in any society. Karl Marx and Friedrich Engels made this point in *Manifesto of the Communist Party* (1848) when they proclaimed that in a socialist society "the condition for the free development of each is the free development of all." (Writers of the 19th century tended to use the terms communism and socialism interchangeably; today communism is widely understood to be the revolutionary form of socialism described by Marx.)

This fundamental conviction nevertheless leaves room for socialists to disagree among themselves with regard to two key points. The first concerns the extent and the kind of property that society should own or control. Some socialists have thought that almost everything except personal items such as clothing should be public property. This is true, for example, of the society envisioned by the English humanist Sir Thomas More in his *Utopia* (1516), which describes a pagan and communist city-state in which institutions and policies are entirely governed by reason. Other socialists, however, have been willing to accept or even welcome private ownership of farms, shops, and other small or medium-sized businesses.

The second disagreement concerns the way in which society is to exercise its control of property and other resources. In this case the main camps consist of loosely defined groups of centralists and decentralists. On the centralist side are socialists who want to invest public control of property in some central authority, such as the state—or the state under the guidance of a political party, as was the case in the Soviet Union. Those in the decentralist camp believe that decisions about the use of public property and resources should be made at the local, or lowest-possible, level by the people who will be most directly affected by those decisions. This conflict has persisted throughout the history of socialism as a political movement.

ORIGINS

The origins of socialism as a political movement lie in the Industrial Revolution. Its intellectual roots, however, reach back almost as far as recorded thought—even as far as Moses, according to one history of the subject. Socialist or communist ideas certainly play an important part in the ideas of the ancient Greek philosopher Plato, whose *Republic* depicts an austere society in which men and women of the "guardian" class share with each other not only their few material goods but also their spouses and children. Early Christian communities also practiced the sharing of goods and labour, a simple form of socialism subsequently followed in certain forms of monasticism. Several monastic orders continue these practices today.

Christianity and Platonism were combined in More's *Utopia*, which apparently recommends communal ownership as a way of controlling the sins of pride, envy, and greed. Land and houses are common property on More's imaginary island of Utopia, where everyone works for at least two years on the communal farms and people change houses every 10 years so that no one develops pride of possession. Money has been abolished, and people are free to take what they need from common storehouses. All the Utopians live simply, moreover, so that they are able to meet their needs with only a few hours of work a day, leaving the rest for leisure.

More's *Utopia* is not so much a blueprint for a socialist society as it is a commentary on the failings he perceived in the supposedly Christian societies of his day. Religious and political turmoil, however, soon inspired others to try to put utopian ideas into practice. Common ownership was one of the aims of the brief Anabaptist regime in the Westphalian city of Münster during the Protestant Reformation, and several communist or socialist sects sprang up in England in the wake of the Civil Wars (1642–51). Chief among them was the Diggers, whose members claimed that God had created the world for people to share, not to divide and exploit for private profit. When they acted on this belief by digging and planting on land that was not legally theirs, they ran afoul of Oliver Cromwell's Protectorate, which forcibly disbanded them.

Whether utopian or practical, these early visions of socialism were largely agrarian. This remained true as late as the French Revolution, when the journalist François-Noël Babeuf and other radicals complained that the Revolution had failed to fulfill the ideals of liberty, equality, and fraternity. Adherence to "the precious principle of equality," Babeuf argued, requires the abolition of private property and common enjoyment of the land and its fruits.

DIGGERS

Diggers were agrarian communists who flourished in England in 1649–50 and were led by Gerrard Winstanley and William Everard. In April 1649 about 20 poor men assembled at St. George's Hill, Surrey, and began to cultivate the common land. These Diggers held that the English Civil Wars had been fought against the king and the great landowners; now that Charles I had been executed, land should be made available for the very poor to cultivate. (Food prices had reached record heights in the late 1640s.) The numbers of the Diggers more than doubled during 1649. Their activities alarmed England's government and roused the hostility of local landowners, who were rival claimants to the common lands. The Diggers were harassed by legal actions and mob violence, and by the end of March 1650 their colony was dispersed. The Diggers themselves abjured the use of force. The Diggers also called themselves True Levelers, but their communism was denounced by the leaders of the Levelers.

Such beliefs led to his execution for conspiring to overthrow the government. The publicity that followed his
trial and death, however, made him a hero to many in the
19th century who reacted against the emergence of industrial capitalism.

UTOPIAN SOCIALISM

Conservatives who saw the settled life of agricultural society disrupted by the insistent demands of industrialism
were as likely as their radical counterparts to be outraged
by the self-interested competition of capitalists and the
squalor of industrial cities. The radicals distinguished
themselves, however, by their commitment to equality
and their willingness to envision a future in which industrial power and capitalism were divorced. To their moral
outrage at the conditions that were reducing many workers to pauperism, the radical critics of industrial capitalism
added a faith in the power of people to put science and an
understanding of history to work in the creation of a new
and glorious society. The term *socialist* came into use about
1830 to describe these radicals, some of the most important of whom subsequently acquired the title of "utopian"
socialists.

One of the first utopian socialists was the French aristocrat Claude-Henri de Saint-Simon. Saint-Simon did not
call for public ownership of productive property, but he
did advocate public control of property through central
planning, in which scientists, industrialists, and engineers
would anticipate social needs and direct the energies of
society to meet them. Such a system would be more efficient than capitalism, according to Saint-Simon, and it
even has the endorsement of history itself. Saint-Simon
believed that history moves through a series of stages,
each of which is marked by a particular arrangement of

social classes and a set of dominant beliefs. Thus, feudalism, with its landed nobility and monotheistic religion, was giving way to industrialism, a complex form of society characterized by its reliance on science, reason, and the division of labour. In such circumstances, Saint-Simon argued, it makes sense to put the economic arrangements of society in the hands of its most knowledgeable and productive members, so that they may direct economic production for the benefit of all.

Another early socialist, Robert Owen, was himself an industrialist. Owen first attracted attention by operating textile mills in New Lanark, Scotland, that were both highly profitable and, by the standards of the day, remarkably humane: no children under age 10 were employed. Owen's fundamental belief was that human nature is not fixed but formed. If people are selfish, depraved, or vicious, it is because social conditions have made them so. Change the conditions, he argued, and people will change; teach them to live and work together in harmony, and they will do so. Thus, Owen set out in 1825 to establish a model of social organization, which he called New Harmony, on land he had purchased in the U.S. state of Indiana. This was to be a self-sufficient, cooperative community in which property was commonly owned. New Harmony failed within a few years, taking most of Owen's fortune with it, but he soon turned his attention to other efforts to promote social cooperation—trade unions and cooperative businesses, in particular.

Similar themes mark the writings of François-Marie-Charles Fourier, a French clerk whose imagination, if not his fortune, was as extravagant as Owen's. Modern society breeds selfishness, deception, and other evils, Fourier charged, because institutions such as marriage, the male-dominated family, and the competitive market confine people to repetitive labour or a limited role in life and thus

A wealthy industrialist by trade, Welshman Robert Owen was a socialist at heart. He established a short-lived cooperative community—what he believed to be a utopian society—in the United States in the 1820s. Hulton Archive/Getty Images

frustrate the need for variety. By setting people at odds with each other in the competition for profits, moreover, the market in particular frustrates the desire for harmony. Accordingly, Fourier envisioned a form of society that would be more in keeping with human needs and desires. Such a "phalanstery," as he called it, would be a largely self-sufficient community of about 1,600 people organized according to the principle of "attractive labour," which holds that people will work voluntarily and happily if their work engages their talents and interests. All tasks become tiresome at some point, however, so each member of the phalanstery would have several occupations, moving from one to another as his interest waned and waxed. Fourier left room for private investment in his utopian community, but every member was to share in ownership, and inequality of wealth, though permitted, was to be limited.

The ideas of common ownership, equality, and a simple life were taken up in the visionary novel *Voyage en Icarie* (1840; *Travels in Icaria*), by the French socialist Étienne Cabet. Icaria was to be a self-sufficient community, combining industry with farming, of about one million people. In practice, however, the Icaria that Cabet founded in Illinois in the 1850s was about the size of a Fourierist phalanstery, and dissension among the Icarians prompted Cabet to depart in 1856.

OTHER EARLY SOCIALISTS

Other socialists in France began to agitate and organize in the 1830s and '40s; they included Louis Blanc, Louis-Auguste Blanqui, and Pierre-Joseph Proudhon. Blanc, the author of *L'Organisation du travail* (1839; *The Organization of Labour*), promoted a scheme of state-financed but worker-controlled "social workshops" that would guarantee work for everyone and lead gradually to a socialist society.

Blanqui, by contrast, was a revolutionary who spent more than 33 years in prison for his insurrectionary activities. Socialism cannot be achieved without the conquest of state power, he argued, and this conquest must be the work of a small group of conspirators. Once in power, the revolutionaries would form a temporary dictatorship that would confiscate the property of the wealthy and establish state control of major industries.

In *Qu'est-ce que la propriété?* (1840; *What Is Property?*), Proudhon memorably declared, "Property is theft!" This assertion was not quite as bold as it appears, however, since Proudhon had in mind not property in general but property that is worked by anyone other than its owner. In contrast to a society dominated by capitalists and absentee landlords, Proudhon's ideal was a society in which everyone had an equal claim, either alone or as part of a small cooperative, to possess and use land and other resources as needed to make a living. Such a society would operate on the principle of mutualism, according to which individuals and groups would exchange products with one another on the basis of mutually satisfactory contracts. All this would be accomplished, ideally, without the interference of the state, for Proudhon was an anarchist who regarded the state as an essentially coercive institution. Yet his anarchism did not prevent him from urging Napoleon III to make free bank credit available to workers for the establishment of mutualist cooperatives—a proposal the emperor declined to adopt.

MARXIAN SOCIALISM

Despite their imagination and dedication to the cause of the workers, none of the early socialists met with the full approval of Karl Marx, who is unquestionably the most important theorist of socialism. In fact, Marx and his longtime friend and collaborator Friedrich Engels were largely responsible for attaching the label "utopian," which they intended to be derogatory, to Saint-Simon, Fourier, and Owen, whose "fantastic pictures of future society" they contrasted to their own "scientific" approach to socialism. The path to socialism proceeds not through the establishment of model communities that set examples of harmonious cooperation to the world, according to Marx and Engels, but through the clash of social classes. "The history of all hitherto existing society is the history of class struggles," they proclaimed in the *Manifesto of the Communist Party*. A scientific understanding of history, they believed, shows that these struggles will culminate in the triumph of the working class and the establishment of socialism.

SOCIALISM AFTER MARX

By the time of Marx's death in 1883, many socialists had begun to call themselves "Marxists." His influence was particularly strong within the Social Democratic Party of Germany (SPD), which was formed in 1875 by the merger of a Marxist party and a party created by Marx's German rival, Ferdinand Lassalle. According to Marx's *Critique of the Gotha Programme* (1891), Lassalle had "conceived the workers' movement from the narrowest national standpoint"; that is, Lassalle had concentrated on converting Germany to socialism, whereas Marx thought that socialism had to be an international movement. Even worse, Lassalle and his followers had sought to gain control of the state through elections in hopes of using "state aid" to establish producers' cooperatives. Marx's belief in the revolutionary transformation of society soon prevailed in the SPD, but his controversy with Lassalle and the Lassalleans testifies to the existence of other important currents in socialist thought in the late 19th century.

CHRISTIAN SOCIALISM

Caught up in these currents were men and women who seemed to agree on little but their condemnation of capitalism. Many prominent socialists were militant atheists, for example, but others expressly connected socialism to religion. Even the rationalist Saint-Simon had called for a "new Christianity" that would join Christian social teachings with modern science and industry to create a society that would satisfy basic human needs. His followers attempted to put this idea into practice, giving rise to a Saint-Simonian sect sometimes called "the religion of the engineers." This combination of an appeal to universal brotherhood and a faith in enlightened management also animated the best-selling utopian novel *Looking Backward* (1888), by the American journalist Edward Bellamy. In England the Anglican clergymen Frederick Denison Maurice and Charles Kingsley initiated a Christian socialist movement at the end of the 1840s on the grounds that the competitive individualism of laissez-faire capitalism was incompatible with the spirit of Christianity. Similar concerns inspired socialists in other countries, including the Russian novelist, anarchist, and pacifist Leo Tolstoy.

Although neither Christianity nor any other religion was a dominant force within socialist theory or politics, the connection between Christianity and socialism persisted through the 20th century. One manifestation of this connection was liberation theology—sometimes characterized as an attempt to marry Marx and Jesus—which emerged among Roman Catholic theologians in Latin America in the 1960s. Another, perhaps more modest, manifestation is the Christian Socialist Movement in Britain, which affiliates itself with the British Labour Party. Several members of Parliament have belonged to the Christian Socialist Movement, including Prime Minister Gordon Brown, the son of a Methodist minister, and his predecessor, Tony Blair, an Anglican who converted to Catholicism not long after he left office.

FABIAN SOCIALISM

As anarcho-communists (communists espousing anarchism, the belief that government is harmful and unnecessary) argued for a form of socialism so decentralized that it required the abolition of the state, a milder and markedly centralist version of socialism, Fabianism, emerged in Britain. Fabian Socialism was so called because the members of the Fabian Society admired the tactics of the Roman general Fabius Cunctator (Fabius the Delayer), who avoided pitched battles and gradually wore down Hannibal's forces. Instead of revolution, the Fabians favoured "gradualism" as the way to bring about socialism. Their notion of socialism, like Saint-Simon's, entailed social control of property through an effectively and impartially administered state—a government of enlightened experts. The Fabians themselves were mostly middle-class intellectuals—including George Bernard Shaw, Sidney and Beatrice Webb, Graham Wallas, and H.G. Wells—who thought that persuasion and education were more likely to lead to socialism, however gradually, than violent class warfare. Rather than form their own political party or work through trade unions, moreover, the Fabians aimed at gaining influence within existing parties. They eventually exercised considerable influence within Britain's Labour Party, though they had little to do with its formation in the early 1900s.

SYNDICALISM

Near the anarcho-communists on the decentralist side of
socialism were the syndicalists. Inspired in part by
Proudhon's ideas, syndicalism developed at the end of the
19th century out of the French trade-union movement—
syndicat being the French word for trade union. It was a
significant force in Italy and Spain in the early 20th century until it was crushed by the fascist regimes in those
countries. In the United States, syndicalism appeared in
the guise of the Industrial Workers of the World, or
"Wobblies," founded in 1905.

The hallmarks of syndicalism were workers' control and
"direct action." Syndicalists such as Fernand Pelloutier dis-
trusted both the state, which they regarded as an agent of
capitalism, and political parties, which they thought were
incapable of achieving radical change. Their aim was to
replace capitalism and the state with a loose federation of
local workers' groups, which they meant to bring about
through direct action—especially a general strike of workers that would bring down the government as it brought the
economy to a halt. Georges Sorel elaborated on this idea in
his *Réflexions sur la violence* (1908; *Reflections on Violence*), in
which he treated the general strike not as the inevitable
result of social developments but as a "myth" that could lead
to the overthrow of capitalism if only enough people could
be inspired to act on it.

INDUSTRIAL WORKERS OF THE WORLD

Forty-three groups who opposed the American Federation
of Labor's acceptance of capitalism and its refusal to

include unskilled workers in craft unions founded the Industrial Workers of the World (IWW) in Chicago in 1905. Among the founders of the IWW were William D. ("Big Bill") Haywood of the Western Federation of Miners (WFM), Daniel De Leon of the Socialist Labor Party, and Eugene V. Debs of the Socialist Party. Debs eventually withdrew his support as the group grew more radical.

Prior to the founding of the IWW, members of the WFM had called a series of strikes in Cripple Creek, Colorado (1894); Leadville, Colorado (1896); Coeur d'Alene, Idaho (1899); and Telluride, Colorado (1903). State militia halted the Cripple Creek strike in 1904, which prompted the WFM to form the first incarnation of the IWW.

Under Haywood's leadership, the IWW gained greater prominence as a revolutionary organization dedicated to controlling the means of production by the workers. Its tactics often led to arrests and sensational publicity; when IWW organizer Joe Hill was executed in 1915 on a disputed murder charge, he became a martyr and folk hero for the labour movement. The organization won its greatest victories in the mining and lumbering industries of the Pacific Northwest.

The IWW was the only labour organization to oppose U.S. participation in World War I, which IWW leaders protested by attempting to limit copper production in western states. The federal government responded by prosecuting and convicting some of those leaders under the newly enacted Sabotage and Espionage Acts. In the postwar years, the IWW underwent further scrutiny and prosecution by local officials responding to widespread antiradical sentiments. By 1925 membership in the IWW had dwindled to insignificance.

Guild Socialism

Related to syndicalism but nearer to Fabianism in its reformist tactics, Guild Socialism was an English movement that attracted a modest following in the first two decades of the 20th century. Inspired by the medieval guild, an association of craftsmen who determined their own working conditions and activities, theorists such as Samuel G. Hobson and G.D.H. Cole advocated the public ownership of industries and their organization into guilds, each of which would be under the democratic control of its trade union. The role of the state was less clear: some Guild Socialists envisioned it as a coordinator of the guilds' activities, while others held that its functions should be limited to protection or policing. In general, however, the Guild Socialists were less inclined to invest power in the state than were their Fabian compatriots.

Social Democracy

By the time of the Russian Revolution of 1917 and the subsequent establishment of the communist Soviet Union, a fissure had clearly developed between communists and socialists. Socialists who repudiated the use of revolution to establish a socialist society, and who eschewed communism's militancy and totalitarianism, came to be known as social democrats. Their political ideology, social democracy, advocated a peaceful, evolutionary transition of society from capitalism to socialism using established political processes. Because it represented a change in basic Marxist doctrine, social democracy was originally known as revisionism.

The social-democratic movement grew out of the efforts of August Bebel, who with Wilhelm Liebknecht cofounded the German Social Democratic Workers' Party in 1869 and then effected the merger of their party with the General German Workers' Union in 1875 to form what came to be called the Social Democratic Party of Germany (Sozialdemokratische Partei Deutschlands). Bebel imbued social democracy with the belief that socialism must be installed through lawful means rather than by force. After the election of two Social Democrats to the Reichstag (legislature) in 1871, the party grew in political strength until in 1912 it became the largest single party in voting strength, with 110 out of 397 seats in the Reichstag. The success of the Social Democratic Party in Germany encouraged the spread of social democracy to other countries in Europe.

The growth of German social democracy owed much to the influence of the German political theorist Eduard Bernstein. In his *Die Voraussetzungen des Sozialismus und die Aufgaben der Sozialdemokratie* (1899; "The Preconditions of Socialism and the Tasks of Social Democracy"; Eng. trans. *Evolutionary Socialism*), Bernstein challenged the Marxist orthodoxy that capitalism was doomed, pointing out that capitalism was overcoming many of its weaknesses, such as unemployment, overproduction, and the inequitable distribution of wealth. Ownership of industry was becoming more widely diffused, rather than more concentrated in the hands of a few. Whereas Marx had declared that the subjugation of the working class would inevitably culminate in socialist revolution, Bernstein argued that success for socialism depended not on the continued and intensifying misery of the working class but rather on eliminating that misery. He further noted that social conditions were improving and that with universal suffrage the working class could establish socialism by electing socialist representatives.

After World War II, social-democratic parties came to power in several nations of Western Europe—e.g., West Germany, Sweden, and Great Britain (in the Labour Party)—and laid the foundations for modern European social-welfare programs. With its ascendancy, social

LABOUR PARTY

The British Labour Party was founded from the labour movement and has historically had strong links with trade unions, leading it to promote an active role for the state in the creation of economic prosperity and the provision of social services. In opposition to the Conservative Party, it has been Britain's major democratic socialist party since the early 20th century. In 1900 the Trades Union Congress and the Independent Labour Party (founded 1893) established the Labour Representation Committee, which took the name Labour Party in 1906. In 1918 it became a socialist party with a democratic constitution, and by 1922 it had supplanted the Liberal Party as the official opposition party. In 1924 James Ramsay MacDonald formed the first Labour government, with Liberal support. The party was out of power from 1935 until a spectacular recovery in 1945 brought in Clement R. Attlee's government (until 1951), which introduced a system of social welfare, including a national health service, and extensive nationalization of industry. Labour regained power under Harold Wilson (1964–70) and later James Callaghan (1974–79), but it foundered because of economic problems and worsening relations with its trade-union allies. In 1983 Michael Foot's radical program resulted in a massive Labour defeat. Neil Kinnock moved the party toward the centre, but only in 1997 did Tony Blair and his "New Labour" agenda succeed in returning Labour to power.

democracy changed gradually, most notably in West Germany. These changes generally reflected a moderation of the 19th-century socialist doctrine of wholesale nationalization of business and industry. Although the principles of the various social-democratic parties began to diverge somewhat, certain common fundamental principles emerged. In addition to abandoning violence and revolution as tools of social change, social democracy took a stand in opposition to totalitarianism. The Marxist view of democracy as a "bourgeois" facade for class rule was abandoned, and democracy was proclaimed essential for socialist ideals. Increasingly, social democracy adopted the goal of state regulation, but not state ownership, of business and industry as sufficient to further economic growth and equitable income.

Chapter 4: Communism

While socialism calls for public ownership of much of society's resources—usually defined as state control—communism aims to replace private property and a profit-based economy with public ownership and communal control of at least the major means of production (e.g., mines, mills, and factories) and the natural resources of a society. Communism is thus a form of socialism—a higher and more advanced form, according to its advocates. Exactly how communism differs from socialism has long been a matter of debate, but the distinction rests largely on the communists' adherence to the revolutionary socialism of Karl Marx.

In his *Critique of the Gotha Programme* (1875), Marx identified two phases of communism that would follow the predicted overthrow of capitalism: the first would be a transitional system in which the working class would control the government and economy yet still find it necessary to pay people according to how long, hard, or well they worked; the second would be fully realized communism—a society without class divisions or government, in which the production and distribution of goods would be based upon the principle "From each according to his ability, to each according to his needs." Marx's followers, especially the Russian revolutionary Vladimir Ilich Lenin, took up this distinction.

In *State and Revolution* (1917), Lenin asserted that socialism corresponds to Marx's first phase of communist society and communism proper to the second. Lenin and the Bolshevik wing of the Russian Social-Democratic Workers' Party reinforced this distinction in 1918, the year after they seized power in Russia, by taking the name

All-Russian Communist Party. Since then, communism has been largely, if not exclusively, identified with the form of political and economic organization developed in the Soviet Union and adopted subsequently in the People's Republic of China and other countries ruled by communist parties.

For much of the 20th century, in fact, about one-third of the world's population lived under communist regimes. These regimes were characterized by the rule of a single party that tolerated no opposition and little dissent. In place of a capitalist economy, in which individuals compete for profits, moreover, party leaders established a command economy in which the state controlled property and its bureaucrats determined wages, prices, and production goals. The inefficiency of these economies played a large part in the collapse of the Soviet Union in 1991, and the remaining communist countries (excepting North Korea) are now allowing greater economic competition while holding fast to one-party rule. Whether they will succeed in this endeavour remains to be seen. Succeed or fail, however, communism is clearly not the world-shaking force it was in the 20th century.

MARXISM

It was neither a religious upheaval nor a civil war but a technological and economic revolution—the Industrial Revolution of the late 18th and early 19th centuries—that provided the impetus and inspiration for modern communism. This revolution, which achieved great gains in economic productivity at the expense of an increasingly miserable working class, encouraged Karl Marx to think that the class struggles that dominated history were leading inevitably to a society in which prosperity would be

KARL MARX

(b. May 5, 1818, Trier, Rhine province, Prussia [Ger.]—d.
March 14, 1883, London, Eng.)

Karl Marx was a German political philosopher, economic
theorist, and revolutionary who, with Friedrich Engels,
developed the fundamental ideology of communism. He
studied humanities at the University of Bonn (1835) and law
and philosophy at the University of Berlin (1836–41), where
he was exposed to the works of G.W.F. Hegel, a German ide-
alist philosopher. Working as a writer in Cologne and Paris
(1842–45), he became active in leftist politics. In Paris he met
Engels, a German socialist philosopher, who would become
his lifelong collaborator. Expelled from France in 1845, Marx
moved to Brussels, where his political orientation matured
and he and Engels made names for themselves through their
writings. Marx was invited to join a secret left-wing group in
London, for which he and Engels wrote the *Manifesto of the
Communist Party* (1848). In that same year, Marx organized
the first Rhineland Democratic Congress in Germany and
opposed the king of Prussia when he dissolved the Prussian
Assembly. Exiled, he moved to London in 1849, where he
spent the rest of his life. He worked part-time as a European
correspondent for the *New York Tribune* (1851–62) while writing his major critique of capitalism, *Das Kapital* (3 vol.,
1867–94). He was a leading figure in the First International,
a federation of workers' groups, from 1864 until the defec-
tion of Mikhail Aleksandrovich Bakunin in 1872.

shared by all through common ownership of the means of
production.

Marx and his friend and coauthor, Friedrich Engels,
maintained that the poverty, disease, and early death that
afflicted the proletariat (the industrial working class)

The belief that society's ills could be traced historically to a disparity between the haves and the have-nots led Karl Marx to write the Manifesto of the Communist Party. Henry Guttmann/Hulton Archive/Getty Images

were endemic to capitalism: they were systemic and structural problems that could be resolved only by replacing
capitalism with communism. Under this alternative system, the major means of industrial production—such as
mines, mills, factories, and railroads—would be publicly
owned and operated for the benefit of all. Marx and
Engels presented this critique of capitalism and a brief
sketch of a possible future communist society in *Manifesto
of the Communist Party* (1848), which they wrote at the
commission of a small group of radicals called the
Communist League.

Marx, meanwhile, had begun to lay the theoretical and
(he believed) scientific foundations of communism, first
in *The German Ideology* (written 1845–46, published 1932)
and later in *Das Kapital* (1867; *Capital*). His theory has
three main aspects: first, a materialist conception of history; second, a critique of capitalism and its inner workings;
and third, an account of the revolutionary overthrow of
capitalism and its eventual replacement by communism.

According to Marx's materialist theory, history is a
series of class struggles and revolutionary upheavals,
leading ultimately to freedom for all. Marx derived his
views in part from the philosophy of G. W. F. Hegel, who
conceived of history as the dialectical self-development
of "spirit." In contrast to Hegel's philosophical idealism,
however, Marx held that history is driven by the material
or economic conditions that prevail in a given age.
"Before men can do anything else," Marx wrote, "they
must first produce the means of their subsistence."
Without material production there would be no life and
thus no human activity.

According to Marx, material production requires two
things: "material forces of production"—roughly, raw
materials and the tools required to extract and process

THE COMMUNIST MANIFESTO

The *Manifesto of the Communist Party* (German: *Manifest Der Kommunistischen Partei*; 1848) was a pamphlet written by Marx and Engels to serve as the platform of the Communist League. It became one of the principal programmatic statements of the European socialist and communist parties in the 19th and early 20th centuries.

The *Manifesto* embodied the authors' materialistic conception of history ("The history of all hitherto existing society is the history of class struggles"), and it surveyed that history from the age of feudalism down to 19th-century capitalism, which was destined, they declared, to be overthrown and replaced by a workers' society. The communists, the vanguard of the working class, constituted the section of society that would accomplish the "abolition of private property" and "raise the proletariat to the position of ruling class."

The *Manifesto* opens with the dramatic words "A spectre is haunting Europe—the spectre of communism" and ends by stating, "The proletarians have nothing to lose but their chains. They have a world to win. Workingmen of all countries, unite!"

them—and "social relations of production"—the division of labour through which raw materials are extracted and processed. Human history is the story of both elements' changing and becoming ever more complex. In primitive societies the material forces were few and simple—for example, grains and the stone tools used to grind them into flour. With the growth of knowledge and technology came successive upheavals, or "revolutions," in the forces and relations of production and in the complexity of both.

For example, iron miners once worked with pickaxes and shovels, which they owned, but the invention of the steam shovel changed the way they extracted iron ore. Since no miner could afford to buy a steam shovel, he had to work for someone who could. Industrial capitalism, in Marx's view, is an economic system in which one class—the ruling bourgeoisie—owns the means of production while the working class or proletariat effectively loses its independence, the worker becoming part of the means of production, a mere "appendage of the machine."

The second aspect of Marx's theory is his critique of capitalism. Marx held that human history had progressed through a series of stages, from ancient slave society through feudalism to capitalism. In each stage a dominant class uses its control of the means of production to exploit the labour of a larger class of workers. But internal tensions or "contradictions" in each stage eventually lead to the overthrow and replacement of the ruling class by its successor. Thus, the bourgeoisie overthrew the aristocracy and replaced feudalism with capitalism; so too, Marx predicted, will the proletariat overthrow the bourgeoisie and replace capitalism with communism.

Marx acknowledged that capitalism was a historically necessary stage of development that had brought about remarkable scientific and technological changes—changes that greatly increased aggregate wealth by extending humankind's power over nature. The problem, Marx believed, was that this wealth—and the political power and economic opportunities that went with it—was unfairly distributed. The capitalists reap the profits while paying the workers a pittance for long hours of hard labour. Yet it is the workers who create economic value, according to Marx's labour theory of value, which holds that the worth of a commodity is determined by the amount of labour required to produce it. Under capitalism, Marx claimed, workers are not paid fully or fairly for their labour because the capitalists siphon off surplus value, which they call profit. Thus, the bourgeois owners of the means of production amass enormous wealth, while the proletariat falls further into poverty. This wealth also enables the bourgeoisie to control the government or state, which does the bidding of the wealthy and the powerful to the detriment of the poor and the powerless.

The exploitation of one class by another remains hidden, however, by a set of ideas that Marx called ideology. "The ruling ideas of every epoch," he wrote in *The German Ideology*, "are the ideas of the ruling class." By this, Marx meant that the conventional or mainstream ideas taught in classrooms, preached from pulpits, and communicated through the mass media are ideas that serve the interests of the dominant class. In slave societies, for example, slavery was depicted as normal, natural, and just. In capitalist societies the free market is portrayed as operating efficiently, fairly, and for the benefit of all, while alternative economic arrangements such as socialism are derided or dismissed as false or fanciful. These ideas serve to justify or legitimize the unequal distribution of economic and political power. Even exploited workers may fail to understand their true interests and accept the dominant ideology—a condition that later Marxists called "false consciousness." One particularly pernicious source of ideological obfuscation is religion, which Marx called "the opium of the people" because it purportedly dulls the critical faculties and leads workers to accept their wretched condition as part of God's plan.

Besides inequality, poverty, and false consciousness, capitalism also produces "alienation." By this, Marx meant that the worker is separated or estranged from (1) the product of his labour, which he does not own; (2) the process of production, which under factory conditions makes him "an appendage of the machine"; (3) the sense of satisfaction that he would derive from using his human capacities in unique and creative ways; and (4) other human beings, whom he sees as rivals competing for jobs and wages.

Marx believed that capitalism is a volatile economic system that will suffer a series of ever-worsening crises—recessions and depressions—that will produce greater unemployment, lower wages, and increasing misery among the industrial proletariat. These crises will convince the proletariat that its interests as a class are implacably opposed to those of the ruling bourgeoisie. Armed with revolutionary class consciousness, the proletariat will seize the major means of production along with the institutions of state power—police, courts, prisons, and so on—and establish a socialist state that Marx called "the revolutionary dictatorship of the proletariat." The proletariat will thus rule in its own class interest, as the bourgeoisie did before, in order to prevent a counterrevolution by the displaced bourgeoisie. Once this threat disappears, however, the need for the state will also disappear. Thus, the interim state will be replaced by a classless communist society.

Marx's vision of communist society is remarkably (and perhaps intentionally) vague. Unlike earlier "utopian socialists," whom Marx and Engels derided as unscientific and impractical—including Claude-Henri de Saint-Simon, Charles Fourier, and Robert Owen—Marx did not produce detailed blueprints for a future society. Some features that he did describe, such as free education for all and a graduated income tax, are now commonplace. Other features, such as public ownership of the major means of production and distribution of goods and services according to

DICTATORSHIP OF THE PROLETARIAT

In Marxism, the dictatorship of the proletariat refers to rule by the proletariat—the economic and social class consisting of industrial workers who derive income solely from their labour—during the transitional phase between the abolition of capitalism and the establishment of communism. During this transition, the proletariat is to suppress resistance to the socialist revolution by the bourgeoisie, destroy the social relations of production underlying the class system, and create a new, classless society. With the disappearance of classes, then, the state will "wither away."

The dictatorship of the proletariat originally was conceived by Karl Marx as a dictatorship by the majority class. Because Marx regarded all governments as class dictatorships, he viewed proletarian dictatorship as no worse than any other form of government. However, the Bolshevik Revolution in Russia in 1917 resulted in a dictatorship not of the majority class of proletarians but of a political party that claimed to represent proletarian interests. Contrary to Marx's vision and as George Orwell (1903–50), Mikhail Aleksandrovich Bakunin (1814–76), and others had foreseen, the proposed dictatorship of the proletariat eventually became a dictatorship of former proletarians.

the principle "From each according to his ability, to each according to his needs," remain as radical as they were in Marx's time. But for the most part, Marx believed that the institutions of a future communist society should be designed and decided democratically by the people living in it; it was not his task, he said, to "write recipes for the kitchens of the future."

FIRST INTERNATIONAL

The International Working Men's Association, or First International, was a federation of workers' groups that, despite ideological divisions within its ranks, had a considerable influence as a unifying force for labour in Europe during the latter part of the 19th century.

The First International was founded under the name International Working Men's Association at a mass meeting in London on Sept. 28, 1864. Its founders were among the most powerful British and French trade-union leaders of the time. Though Karl Marx had no part in organizing the meeting, he was elected one of the 32 members of the provisional General Council and at once assumed its leadership. The International came to assume the character of a highly centralized party, based primarily on individual members and organized in local groups, which were integrated in national federations, though some trade unions and associations were affiliated to it collectively. Its supreme body was the Congress, which met in a different city each year and formulated principles and policies. A General Council elected by the Congress had its seat in London and served as the executive committee, appointing corresponding secretaries for each of the national federations; organizing collections for the support of strikes in various countries; and, in general, advancing the International's goals.

From its beginnings, the First International was riven by conflicting schools of socialist thought—Marxism, Proudhonism (after Pierre-Joseph Proudhon, who advocated only the reform of capitalism), Blanquism (after Louis-Auguste Blanqui, who advocated radical methods and a sweeping revolution), and Mikhail Aleksandrovich Bakunin's version of anarchism, which dominated the International's Italian, Spanish, and French-Swiss federations. The First International split at its Hague Congress in 1872 over the clash between Marx's centralized socialism and Bakunin's anarchism. In order to prevent the Bakuninists from gaining control of the association, the General Council, prompted by Marx, moved its headquarters to New York City, where it lingered until it was formally disbanded at the Philadelphia Conference in July 1876. The Bakuninists, assuming leadership of the International, held annual congresses from 1873 to 1877. At the Ghent Socialist World Congress in 1877, the Social Democrats broke away because their motion to restore the unity of the First International was rejected by the anarchist majority. The anarchists failed, however, to keep the International alive. After the London anarchist congress of 1881, it ceased to represent an organized movement. The International was early proscribed in such countries as Germany, Austria, France, and Spain. French and German proposals that it be outlawed by concerted European action failed, however, because of British reluctance to suppress the General Council in London.

It should be noted that the International's renown at the time as a formidable power with millions of members and almost unlimited resources was out of proportion with the association's actual strength; the hard core of its individual members probably seldom exceeded 20,000. Although so accused, it did not organize the wave of strikes that swept France, Belgium, and Switzerland in 1868, but its support and rumoured support of such strikes was very influential.

BOLSHEVISM

Russia in the early 20th century was an unlikely setting for the proletarian revolution that Karl Marx had predicted. Its economy was primarily agricultural; its factories were few and inefficient; and its industrial proletariat was small. Most Russians were peasants who farmed land owned by wealthy nobles. Russia, in short, was nearer feudalism than capitalism. There was, however, growing discontent in the countryside, and Vladimir Ilich Lenin's Russian Social-Democratic Workers' Party saw an opportunity to harness that discontent to overthrow the autocratic tsarist regime and replace it with a radically different economic and political system.

Lenin was the chief architect of this plan. As head of the revolutionary Bolshevik faction of the party, Lenin made two important changes to the theory and practice of communism as Marx had envisioned it—changes so significant that the party's ideology was later renamed Marxism-Leninism. The first, set out in *What Is to Be Done?* (1902), was that revolution could not and should not be made spontaneously by the proletariat, as Marx had expected, but had to be made by workers and peasants led by an elite "vanguard" party composed of radicalized middle-class intellectuals like himself. Secretive, tightly organized, and highly disciplined, the communist party would educate, guide, and direct the masses. This was necessary, Lenin claimed, because the masses, suffering from false consciousness and unable to discern their true interests, could not be trusted to govern themselves. Democracy was to be practiced only within the party, and even then it was to be constrained by the policy of democratic centralism. That is, full and vigorous debate would lead to a decision that would determine the party's "line" on an issue, whereupon the party's central leadership would close off debate and require adherence to the party line. Such strict discipline was necessary, Lenin maintained, if the party was to guide the masses to revolution and establish the socialist workers' state that would follow. In short, the revolutionary dictatorship of the proletariat had to be a dictatorship of the communist party in the name of the proletariat.

A second and closely related change appears in Lenin's *Imperialism, the Highest Stage of Capitalism* (1916), in which he implied that communist revolution would not begin in advanced capitalist countries such as Germany and Britain because workers there were imbued with reform-minded "trade-union consciousness" instead of revolutionary class consciousness. This, he argued, was because the most direct and brutal exploitation of workers had shifted to the colonies of imperialist nations such as Britain. The capitalists reaped "superprofits" from the cheap raw materials and labour available in these colonies and were thus able to "bribe" workers at home with slightly higher wages, a shorter workweek, and other reforms. So, contrary to Marx's expectations, communist revolution would begin in economically backward countries such as Russia and in the oppressed and exploited colonial countries of the capitalist periphery (later to be called the Third World).

The Russian Revolution of 1917 came about in a way that no one, not even Lenin, had predicted. Its immediate impetus was World War I, which was taking a heavy toll on Russian soldiers at the front and on peasants at home. Riots broke out in several Russian cities. When Tsar Nicholas II ordered soldiers to put them down, they refused. Nicholas abdicated, and his government was replaced by one led by Aleksandr Kerensky. Committed

VLADIMIR ILICH LENIN

(b. April 22, 1870, Simbirsk, Russia—d. Jan. 21, 1924, Gorki,
near Moscow)

Vladimir Ilich Lenin was the founder of the Russian
Communist Party, leader of the Russian Revolution of 1917,
and architect and builder of the Soviet state. Born to a
middle-class family, he was strongly influenced by his eldest
brother, Aleksandr, who was hanged in 1887 for conspiring
to assassinate the tsar. He became a Marxist in 1889 while
practicing law. He was arrested as a subversive in 1895 and
exiled to Siberia, where he married Nadezhda Krupskaya.
They lived in Western Europe after 1900.

At the 1903 meeting in London of the Russian Social-
Democratic Workers' Party, he emerged as the leader of the
Bolshevik faction. In several revolutionary newspapers that
he founded and edited, he put forth his theory of the party
as the vanguard of the proletariat, a centralized body organized around a core of professional revolutionaries; his
ideas, later known as Leninism, would be joined with Karl
Marx's theories to form Marxism-Leninism, which became
the communist worldview.

With the outbreak of the Russian Revolution of 1905,
Lenin returned to Russia, but he resumed his exile in 1907
and continued his energetic agitation for the next 10 years.
He saw World War I as an opportunity to turn a war of
nations into a war of classes, and he returned to Russia with
the Russian Revolution of 1917 to lead the Bolshevik coup
that overthrew the provisional government of Aleksandr
Kerensky. As revolutionary leader of the Soviet state, he
signed the Treaty of Brest-Litovsk with Germany (1918) and
repulsed counterrevolutionary threats in the Russian Civil
War. He founded the Comintern in 1919. In ill health from
1922, he died of a stroke in 1924.

to continuing the war against Germany, Kerensky's provisional government was almost as unpopular as the tsar's. Lenin returned to Russia from exile in Switzerland barely in time to lead the Bolsheviks in seizing state power in October (November, according to the current calendar) 1917. He then became premier of a new government based on soviets, or workers' councils.

The Soviet government moved quickly to withdraw from the war in Europe and to nationalize private industry and agriculture. In the name of the people and under the banner of War Communism, it seized mines, mills, factories, and the estates of wealthy landowners, which it redistributed to peasants. The landowners and aristocrats, aided by troops and supplies from capitalist countries, including Britain and the United States, mounted a "White" counterrevolution against the "Red" government. The Russian Civil War ended in 1920 with the victory of the Reds, but the war in Europe and the war at home left the Soviet Union in shambles, its economic productivity meagre and its people hungry and discontented. Desperate for room to maneuver, Lenin in 1921 announced the New Economic Policy (NEP), whereby the state retained control of large industries but encouraged individual initiative, private enterprise, and the profit motive among farmers and owners of small businesses.

During Lenin's rule, the Communist Party adopted democratic centralism as its decision-making and disciplinary policy. Democratic centralism purported to combine two opposing forms of party leadership: democracy, which allows for free and open discussion, and central control, which ensures party unity and discipline. In 1921 Lenin declared that the party was not a debating society in which all opinions were tolerated and freely expressed; it was a "vanguard" party whose role as leader of the revolution

COMMUNIST PARTY
OF THE SOVIET UNION

The Communist Party of the Soviet Union (CPSU) was the major political party of Russia and the Soviet Union from the Russian Revolution of 1917 to 1991. It arose from the Bolshevik wing of the Russian Social-Democratic Workers' Party. From 1918 through the 1980s it was a monolithic, monopolistic ruling party that dominated the Soviet Union's political, economic, social, and cultural life. The constitution and other legal documents that supposedly regulated the government were actually subordinate to the CPSU, which also dominated the Comintern and the Cominform. Mikhail Gorbachev, leader of the Soviet Union from 1985 to 1991, made efforts to reform the country's economy and political structure, which weakened the party. In 1990 the party voted to surrender its constitutionally guaranteed monopoly of power. The Soviet Union's dissolution in 1991 marked the party's formal demise.

demanded extreme discipline and a high level of organization. Unrestrained discussion, he insisted, would produce intraparty disagreements and factions and prevent the party from acting effectively. On the other hand, absolute control by a centralized leadership would discourage new ideas from lower-level party members. Therefore, Lenin argued, free discussion within the party should be tolerated and even encouraged up to a point, but, once a vote was taken, all discussion had to end. The decision of the majority should constitute the current party "line" and be binding upon all members. In practice, particularly under the leadership of Joseph Stalin from 1928, democratic centralism was much more "centralist" than "democratic," as party congresses became infrequent occasions for rubber-stamping decisions made by the top party leadership.

STALINISM

Lenin's death in 1924 left Joseph Stalin, Leon Trotsky, and Nikolay Bukharin as the leaders of the All-Russian Communist Party. Before he died, Lenin warned his party comrades to beware of Stalin's ambitions. The warning proved prophetic. Ruthless and cunning, Stalin—born Iosif Djugashvili—seemed intent on living up to his revolutionary surname (which means "man of steel"). In the late 1920s, Stalin began to consolidate his power by intimidating and discrediting his rivals. In the mid-1930s, claiming to see spies and saboteurs everywhere, he purged the party and the general populace, exiling dissidents to Siberia or summarily executing them after staged show trials. Bukharin was convicted on trumped-up charges and was executed in 1938. Trotsky, who had fled abroad, was condemned in absentia and was assassinated in Mexico in 1940 by one of Stalin's agents. Those who remained lived in fear of the NKVD (a forerunner of the KGB), Stalin's secret police.

As a variant of Marxism-Leninism, Stalinism had three key features. The first was its reliance on dialectical materialism as a way of justifying almost any course of action that Stalin wished to pursue. For example, in a report to the 16th Congress of the Communist Party in June 1930, Stalin justified the rapid growth of centralized state power as follows:

> *We stand for the withering away of the state. At the same time we stand for the strengthening of the . . . strongest state*

*power that has ever existed . . . Is this "contradictory"? Yes,
it is contradictory. But this contradiction . . . fully reflects
Marx's dialectics.*

But Stalin omitted mentioning that Marx believed
that contradictions were to be exposed and overcome, not
accepted and embraced.

A second feature of Stalinism was its cult of personality. Whereas Lenin had claimed that the workers suffered
from false consciousness and therefore needed a vanguard
party to guide them, Stalin maintained that the Communist
Party itself suffered from false consciousness (and from
spies and traitors within its ranks) and therefore needed
an all-wise leader—Stalin himself—to guide it. This effectively ended intraparty democracy and democratic
centralism. The resulting cult of personality portrayed
Stalin as a universal genius in every subject, from linguistics to genetics.

A third feature of Stalinism was the idea of "socialism
in one country"—i.e., building up the industrial base and
military might of the Soviet Union before exporting revolution abroad. To this end, Stalin rescinded Lenin's New
Economic Policy, began the collectivization of Soviet agriculture, and embarked on a national program of rapid,
forced industrialization. Specifically, he insisted that the
Soviet Union had to be quickly, and, if need be, brutally,
transformed from a primarily agricultural nation to an
advanced industrial power. During the collectivization,
millions of kulaks, or prosperous peasants, were deprived
of their farms and forced to labour on large collective
farms; if they resisted (or were even thought likely to do
so), they were shot or sent to forced labour camps in
Siberia to starve or freeze to death. In the food shortages
that resulted, several million people (the precise number

remains unknown) starved, and many more suffered from malnutrition and disease.

In foreign policy, socialism in one country meant putting the interests of the Soviet Union ahead of the interests of the international communist movement. After World War II, as Winston Churchill famously remarked, an Iron Curtain descended across Europe as Stalin installed communist regimes in Poland, Czechoslovakia, Yugoslavia, Hungary, Romania, Albania, and Soviet-occupied East Germany as a buffer zone against an invasion from Western Europe. He also subordinated the interests and aspirations of communist parties there and elsewhere to the interests of the Communist Party of the Soviet Union (CPSU). A few dissident leaders, notably Josip Broz Tito in Yugoslavia, were rather reluctant allies; but most were pliant, perhaps out of fear of Soviet military might. Beyond Europe, the Soviet Union supported anticolonial "wars of national liberation" in Asia, Africa, and Latin America and gave economic and military support to communist regimes in North Korea, North Vietnam, and Cuba.

After Stalin's death in 1953, there was a slow liberalization within the CPSU and in Soviet society at large, though the Cold War with the West continued. Soviet Premier Nikita Khrushchev denounced Stalin's crimes in a secret speech to the 20th Party Congress in 1956. Khrushchev himself was deposed in 1964, after which a succession of Soviet leaders stifled reform and attempted to impose a modified version of Stalinism. In the 1980s, Mikhail Gorbachev's policies of glasnost ("openness") and perestroika ("restructuring") began a new liberalization of Soviet society. Yet the ghost of Stalin was not exorcized completely until the collapse of the Soviet Union and the effective demise of the CPSU in 1991.

EUROCOMMUNISM

The trend among European communist parties toward independence from Soviet Communist Party doctrine during the 1970s and '80s was known as Eurocommunism. With Mikhail Gorbachev's encouragement, all communist parties took independent courses in the late 1980s, and by 1990 the term Eurocommunism had become moot.

The term was coined in the mid-1970s and received wide publicity after the publication of *Eurocommunism and the State* (1977) by the Spanish communist leader Santiago Carrillo. A spirit of independence among nonruling communist parties had already appeared, however, shortly before World War II with the growth of Popular Fronts in socialist politics and was afforded dramatic encouragement by the example of Josip Broz Tito's Yugoslavia from 1948 on. The excesses of Joseph Stalin's regime and such Soviet repressions as the crackdown in Hungary in 1956 and the invasion of Czechoslovakia in 1968 alienated many communists in the Western countries and tended to accelerate the movement toward independent policies and autonomy.

The Eurocommunist movement avowedly rejected the subordination of all communist parties to the once-prevalent Soviet doctrine of one monolithic world communist movement. Instead, every party was expected to base its policies on the traditions and needs within its own country. The promotion of Eurocommunism seemed to coincide with the stagnation or decline of many European communist parties. Notably, in France the once-powerful French Communist Party, which in the early postwar era was able to command about a third of the French popular vote, experienced a severe decline in later years. Its leader Georges Marchais and his comrades briefly flirted with Eurocommunism in the late

1970s—without any popular success. On the other hand, the Italian Communist Party remained Italy's second-largest party, partly by stressing its independence of Moscow. Its foreign contacts and sympathies seemed to lie more with the European social democrats and labour parties, and in 1991 it changed its name to Democratic Party of the Left (shortened to Democrats of the Left during 1998–2007, after which it joined Italy's new Democratic Party). After the democratic revolutions of 1989, almost all the communist parties of Eastern Europe became social democratic parties in spirit or name. Eurocommunism, in effect, had become the norm.

CHINESE COMMUNISM

The People's Republic of China is the only global super-power still ruled by a communist party, the Chinese Communist Party (CCP), as it has been since the communists came to power in 1949. Even so, the official Chinese version of communism—Maoism, or "Mao Zedong thought"—is a far cry from Marx's original vision. Mao Zedong, the founder of the People's Republic and China's first communist leader, claimed to have "creatively" amended Marxist theory and communist practice to suit Chinese conditions. First, he invoked Lenin's theory of imperialism to explain Chinese "backwardness" and to justify a revolution in a poor agricultural society without the sizable industrial proletariat that Marx believed was generally necessary to instigate a workers' revolution. Second, Mao redefined or replaced key concepts of Marx's theory. Most notably, he replaced the Marxist concept of a proletarian "class" of industrial wage labourers exploited by the capitalist ruling class with the idea of a proletarian "nation" of agricultural peasants exploited by capitalist countries such as the United States. Mao envisioned the proletarian countries encircling the capitalist countries and waging wars of national liberation to cut off foreign sources of cheap labour and raw materials, thereby depriving the capitalist countries of the ever-expanding revenues that are the lifeblood of their economies.

Mao planned and oversaw several industrial and agricultural initiatives that proved disastrous for the Chinese people. Among the most important of these was the Great Leap Forward (1958–60), his version of Stalin's policy of rapid, forced industrialization. Aiming to produce steel in backyard blast furnaces and to manufacture other commodities in hastily erected small-scale factories, Mao's initiative was a spectacular failure.

Nevertheless, Mao continued to aspire to being the "great helmsman" who would lead China out of poverty and into a bright communist future. His cult of personality, like Stalin's, portrayed him as larger than life and endowed with unrivaled wisdom—as found, for example, in the sayings and slogans in his "Little Red Book" (*Quotations from Chairman Mao*).

As Mao consolidated his power, he became increasingly concerned with ideological purity, favouring ideologically dedicated cadres of "reds" over technical "experts" in education, engineering, factory management, and other areas. He launched the Cultural Revolution (1966–76) to enforce ideological orthodoxy. During this period, Mao organized China's urban youths into groups called the Red Guards, shut down China's schools, and encouraged the Red Guards to attack all traditional values and "bourgeois things." They soon splintered into zealous rival groups, and in 1968 Mao sent millions of them to the rural hinterland, bringing some order to the cities. Within the government, a coalition of Mao's associates fought with more moderate elements, many of whom were

MAO ZEDONG
(b. Dec. 26, 1893, Shaoshan, Hunan province, China—d.
Sept. 9, 1976, Beijing)

Mao Zedong (also spelled Mao Tse-tung) was the Chinese
Marxist theorist, soldier, and statesman who led China's
communist revolution and served as chairman of the
People's Republic of China (1949–59) and chairman of the
Chinese Communist Party (CCP; 1931–76). The son of a
peasant, Mao joined the revolutionary army that overthrew
the Qing dynasty but, after six months as a soldier, left to
acquire more education. At Beijing University he met Li
Dazhao and Chen Duxiu, founders of the CCP, and in 1921
he committed himself to Marxism. At that time, Marxist
thought held that revolution lay in the hands of urban
workers, but in 1925 Mao concluded that in China it was
the peasantry, not the urban proletariat, that had to be
mobilized. He became chairman of a Chinese Soviet
Republic formed in rural Jiangxi province; its Red Army
withstood repeated attacks from Chiang Kai-shek's
Nationalist army but at last undertook the Long March to
a more secure position in northwestern China. There Mao
became the undisputed head of the CCP. Guerrilla warfare
tactics, appeals to the local population's nationalist sentiments, and Mao's agrarian policies gained the party military
advantages against their Nationalist and Japanese enemies
and broad support among the peasantry. Mao's agrarian
Marxism differed from the Soviet model, but, when the
communists succeeded in taking power in China in 1949,
the Soviet Union agreed to provide the new state with
technical assistance. However, Mao's policies soon alienated the Soviets, who withdrew their aid in 1960. After
Mao's death, Deng Xiaoping began introducing social and
economic reforms.

purged, were verbally attacked, were physically abused, and subsequently died.

From 1973 to Mao's death in 1976, politics shifted between the hard-line Gang of Four, which consisted of the powerful members of a radical political elite, and the moderates headed by Zhou Enlai and Deng Xiaoping. After Mao's death the Cultural Revolution was brought to a close. By that time, nearly three million party members and countless wrongfully purged citizens awaited reinstatement. The Chinese communist leadership began to experiment with limited free-market reforms in the economy but continued to keep a tight lid on political dissent.

NON-MARXIAN COMMUNISM

Although Marx remains the preeminent communist theorist, there have been several varieties of non-Marxist communism. Among the most influential is anarchism, or anarcho-communism, which advocates not only communal ownership of property but also the abolition of the state. Historically important anarcho-communists include William Godwin in England, Mikhail Aleksandrovich Bakunin and Peter Alekseyevich Kropotkin in Russia (though both spent much of their lives in exile), and Emma Goldman in the United States. In different ways they argued that the state and private property are interdependent institutions: the state exists to protect private property, and the owners of private property protect the state. If property is to be owned communally and distributed equally, the state must be smashed once and for all. In *Statism and Anarchy* (1874), for example, Bakunin attacked Marx's view that the transitional state—the dictatorship of the proletariat—would simply wither away after it had served its purpose of preventing a bourgeois counterrevolution. No state, said Bakunin, has ever withered away, and no state ever will. To the contrary, it is in the very nature of the state to extend its control over its subjects, limiting and finally eliminating whatever liberty they once had to control their own lives. Marx's interim state would in fact be a dictatorship "over" the proletariat. In that respect, at least, Bakunin proved to be a better prophet than Marx.

MILITANT COMMUNIST GROUPS

In the second half of the 20th century a number of militant groups employed violent tactics in the name of communism. Among these radical left-wing groups were the Red Brigades of Italy, the Red Army Faction of West Germany, and the Shining Path of Peru.

RED BRIGADES

The Red Brigades (Italian: Brigate Rosse) of Italy gained notoriety in the 1970s for kidnappings, murders, and sabotage. Its self-proclaimed aim was to undermine the Italian state and pave the way for a Marxist upheaval led by a "revolutionary proletariat."

The reputed founder of the Red Brigades was Renato Curcio, who in 1967 set up a leftist study group at the University of Trento dedicated to figures such as Karl Marx, Mao Zedong, and Che Guevara. In 1969 Curcio married a fellow radical, Margherita Cagol, and moved with her to Milan, where they attracted a coterie of followers. Proclaiming the existence of the Red Brigades in November 1970 through the firebombing of various factories and warehouses in Milan, the group began kidnapping the following year and in 1974 committed its first assassination; among its victims that year was the chief inspector of Turin's antiterrorist squad.

Despite the arrest and imprisonment of hundreds of alleged terrorists throughout the country—including Curcio himself in 1976—the random assassinations continued. In 1978 the Red Brigades kidnapped and murdered former prime minister Aldo Moro. In December 1981 a U.S. Army officer with the North Atlantic Treaty Organization (NATO), Brigadier General James Dozier, was abducted and held captive by the Red Brigades for 42 days before Italian police rescued him unharmed from a hideout in Padua. Between 1974 and 1988, the Red Brigades carried out about 50 attacks, in which nearly 50 people were killed. A common nonlethal tactic employed by the group was "kneecapping," in which a victim was shot in the knees so that he could not walk again.

At its height in the 1970s, the Red Brigades was believed to comprise 400 to 500 full-time members, 1,000 members who helped periodically, and a few thousand supporters who provided funds and shelter. Careful, systematic police work led to the arrest and imprisonment of many of the Red Brigades' leaders and ordinary members from the mid-1970s onward, and by the late 1980s the organization was all but destroyed. However, a group claiming to be the Red Brigades took responsibility in the 1990s for various violent attacks, including those against a senior Italian government adviser, a U.S. base in Aviano, and the NATO Defense College.

RED ARMY FACTION

The Red Army Faction was a West German radical leftist group formed in 1968 and popularly named the Baader-Meinhof Gang after two of its early leaders, Andreas Baader (1943–77) and Ulrike Meinhof (1934–76).

From its early years, members of the Red Army Faction supported themselves through bank robberies and engaged in terrorist bombings and arson, especially of West German corporations and businesses and of West German and U.S. military installations in West Germany. They also kidnapped and assassinated prominent political and business figures. By the mid-1970s, the group expanded its scope outside West Germany and occasionally allied itself with militant Palestinian groups. For example, in 1976 two Baader-Meinhof guerrillas took part in a Palestinian hijacking of an Air France jetliner, which eventually ended after the successful Entebbe raid in Uganda by Israeli commandos.

The Red Army Faction included at least 22 core members in the early 1970s, most of whom, including Meinhof, had been jailed by the summer of 1972. Baader, escaping one imprisonment in 1970, was arrested again in 1976. Meinhof hanged herself in her cell in 1976. Three others, including Baader, were found shot dead in their cells on Oct. 18, 1977. Ostensibly suicides, their deaths came one day after West German commandos stormed a hijacked Lufthansa plane in Mogadishu, Somalia, blocking the hijackers' attempt to win the release of their jailed comrades as ransom for their hostages. Thereafter, the Red Army Faction continued its terrorist activities and splintered into a number of groups.

After the collapse of the communist government in East Germany in 1989–90, it was discovered that the Red Army Faction was being supported by the Stasi, the secret police of the former communist regime, who were providing the group with training, shelter, and supplies. Greatly weakened by the demise of communism throughout Eastern Europe, the group announced an end to its terrorist campaign in 1992, and several of its surviving militants were arrested and tried. However, it retained a following among some European radicals, and in 1996 several thousand sympathizers attended a meeting to commemorate the anniversary of Meinhof's death. The group formally disbanded in 1998, though arrests and trials continued.

SHINING PATH

The Shining Path (Spanish: Sendero Luminoso) is a Peruvian revolutionary organization that endorses Maoism and has employed guerrilla tactics and violent terrorism. It was founded in 1970 in a multiple split in the Communist Party of Peru. It took its name from the maxim of the founder of Peru's first communist party, José Carlos Mariátegui: "*El Marxismo-Leninismo abrirá el sendero luminoso hacia la revolución*" ("Marxism-Leninism will open the shining path to revolution"). The leader and principal founder was Abimael Guzmán Reynoso, alias Comrade Gonzalo, a long-time communist and former philosophy teacher (1962–78) at the National University of San Cristóbal de Huamanga, in the city of Ayacucho in the high Andes Mountains. He and his followers, known as Senderistas, sought to restore the "pure" ideology of Mao Zedong and adopted China's Cultural Revolution as a model for their own revolutionary movement. The organization's other models were Stalinist Russia and the Khmer Rouge regime in Cambodia. Envisioning revolution as a long military offensive, the Shining Path relied primarily on the peasantry and made ruthless use of terror and violence.

With a following of young intellectuals he gathered in Ayacucho in the 1960s, Guzmán spent the next decade recruiting armed supporters among the indigenous peoples in the countryside and the poorer urban districts. The Shining Path began its revolutionary campaign in remote areas of the Andes (the group's first act of violence occurred on May 17, 1980, near Ayacucho) and soon was engaged in bombings and assassinations and other terrorist acts in various urban centres, including Lima and Callao. It gained control of poor rural and urban districts in central and southern Peru by violence and intimidation, while attracting sympathizers and supporters through its tight discipline, its organizing ability, and its emphasis on empowering the native population at the expense of Peru's traditional Spanish-speaking elite. It reportedly established cocaine-processing plants in the Huallaga valley to fund its activities.

Guzmán, whose organizational and tactical abilities underlay the Shining Path's success, was captured in a police raid in Lima on Sept. 12, 1992, and in October he was sentenced to life imprisonment on terrorism charges. Despite his conviction, the organization continued to clash with the government throughout the 1990s. In July 1999 its new leader, Oscar Ramirez Durand (alias Comrade Feliciano), was captured and, like Guzmán, sentenced to life imprisonment. In 2003 Peru's Truth and Reconciliation Committee issued a report that estimated some 70,000 people had been killed by Shining Path guerrillas and government forces during the last two decades of the 20th century. The Shining Path's terrorist activities also seriously disrupted the country's economy.

COMMUNIST GOVERNMENTS TODAY

Despite the difficulties and dislocations wrought by the transition to a capitalist market economy, Russia and the former Soviet republics are unlikely to reestablish communist rule. The Communist Party of the Russian

Federation, the successor of the CPSU, attracts some followers, but its ideology is reformist rather than revolutionary; its chief aim appears to be that of smoothing the continuing and sometimes painful transition to a market economy and trying to mitigate its more blatantly inegalitarian aspects. In China, Maoism is given lip service but no longer is put into practice. Some large industries are still state-owned, but the trend is clearly toward increasing privatization and a decentralized market economy. China is now on the verge of having a full-fledged capitalist economy. This raises the question of whether free markets and democracy can be decoupled, or whether one implies the other. The CCP still brooks no opposition, as the suppression of pro-democracy student demonstrations in Tiananmen Square in 1989 made clear. But the views of a new generation of leaders that arose in the early 21st century were unknown, which makes the direction of Chinese policy difficult to predict.

Mao's version of Marxism-Leninism remains an active but ambiguous force elsewhere in Asia, most notably in Nepal. After a decade of armed struggle, Maoist insurgents there agreed in 2006 to lay down their arms and participate in national elections to choose an assembly to rewrite the Nepalese constitution. Claiming a commitment to multiparty democracy and a mixed economy, the Maoists emerged from the elections in 2008 as the largest party in the assembly—a party that now appears to resemble the pragmatic CCP of recent years more closely than it resembles Maoist revolutionaries of the 20th century.

Meanwhile, North Korea, the last bastion of old Soviet-style communism, is an isolated and repressive regime. Long deprived of Soviet sponsorship and subsidies, Cuba and Vietnam have been reaching out diplomatically and seeking foreign investment in their increasingly market-oriented economies, but politically both remain single-party communist states.

Today Soviet-style communism, with its command economy and top-down bureaucratic planning, is defunct. Whether that kind of regime was ever consistent with Marx's conception of communism is doubtful; whether anyone will lead a new movement to build a communist society on Marxist lines remains to be seen.

NORTH KOREA

In 1948, when the Democratic People's Republic of Korea was established, Kim Il-sung became the first premier of the North Korean communist regime. In 1949 he became chairman of the Korean Workers' Party (KWP), created from communist parties founded earlier. Until his death in 1994, Kim ruled the country with an iron hand by promoting a personality cult centred on himself as the "Great Leader" of the Korean people.

Kim Il-sung died on July 8, 1994, and his son Kim Jong Il succeeded him. However, he did not assume the posts of secretary-general of the KWP or president of North Korea. Instead, he consolidated his power over several years. In 1997 he officially became head of the KWP, and in 1998 the post of president was written out of North Korea's constitution—Kim Il-sung was given the posthumous title "eternal president"—and Kim Jong Il was reelected chairman of the National Defense Commission, which became the country's highest office. His regime adopted the basic guideline of "military first politics" (*sŏngun chŏngch'i*) to safeguard it from any unforeseen adverse impact resulting from such events as the collapse of the Soviet Union and Eastern European communist regimes in the late 1980s and early 1990s and the persistent economic hardships at home.

During his reign as the leader of North Korea, one of the world's few remaining communist countries, Kim Jong Il has stressed his nation's military preparedness and might. ITAR-TASS/Getty Images

According to the revised constitution of 1998, the head of government is the premier, assisted by several vice-premiers and a cabinet, the members of which are appointed by the national legislature, the Supreme People's Assembly (SPA). The president of the SPA is North Korea's titular head of state. In practice, however, the government is under the one-man leadership of Kim, who, in addition to being chairman of the National Defense Commission, is also general secretary of the KWP.

CUBA

On New Year's Day, 1959, revolutionary forces led by Fidel Castro overthrew the government of dictator Fulgencio Batista. Two years later Castro proclaimed the Marxist-Leninist nature of the revolution. Cuba became economically isolated from its northern neighbour as it developed close links to the Soviet Union. However, the collapse of the Soviet Union in the early 1990s isolated Cuba still further, bringing on what Cubans euphemistically call the *período económico especial* ("special economic period"), a time of widespread shortages and financial uncertainty. By the early 21st century, Cuba had loosened some of its more restrictive economic and social policies, but the United States continued its decades-long economic embargo against the Castro regime, assuring that economic hardships would persist.

Cuba remains a unitary socialist republic. The government is totalitarian, exercising direct control or influence over most facets of Cuban life. From 1959 to 2008, Fidel Castro was the chief of state and head of government. He also served as first secretary of the Communist Party of Cuba and commander in chief of the armed forces. In February 2008 he formally relinquished power to his brother Raúl Castro. The country is governed under the constitution of 1976, which superseded revolutionary legislation that was enacted after the constitution of 1940 had been suspended. The 1976 constitution was slightly amended in 1992 and 2002.

In the early 1960s the government dissolved political parties and transformed three revolutionary organizations (the 26th of July Movement, Popular Socialist Party, and 13th of March Revolutionary Directorate) into a single national party, which was officially designated the Communist Party of Cuba in 1965. The government also created several mass organizations, notably the ubiquitous Committees for the Defense of the Revolution, which maintain vigilance against ideological "enemies" and intimidate dissenters and are organized in every city, factory, and workplace and in many rural counties. In 1992 modifications in the electoral law permitted direct elections of members of the National Assembly. There is no party slate and candidates need not belong to the official Cuban Communist Party.

VIETNAM

Vietnam experienced a period of prolonged warfare in the mid-20th century, and a partitioning (1954–75), first militarily and later politically, into the Democratic Republic of Vietnam, better known as North Vietnam, and the Republic of Vietnam, usually called South Vietnam. Following reunification in April 1975, the Socialist Republic of Vietnam was established in July 1976.

Both the 1980 and 1992 constitutions institutionalized the Vietnamese Communist Party as the sole source of leadership for the state and society. The 1992 document, however, delegated much more authority to the president and to the cabinet; they were given the task of running the government, while the party became responsible for overall policy decisions. These changes reduced the role of the party. Nonetheless, the Vietnamese Communist Party remains the dominant political institution within Vietnam. It leads the Vietnam Fatherland Front, a coalition of numerous popular political and social associations that disseminates party policies, serves as a training ground for potential party members, and submits lists of candidates for seats in the National Assembly. Members of the National Assembly are chosen through direct election in their individual electoral units. Male members of the Vietnamese Communist Party fill the majority of the seats.

Chapter 5: Anarchism

A narchism is a cluster of doctrines and attitudes centred on the belief that government is both harmful and unnecessary. Derived from the Greek root (*anarchos*) meaning "without authority," *anarchism*, *anarchist*, and *anarchy* are used to express both approval and disapproval. In early usage all these terms were pejorative: for example, during the English Civil Wars (1642–51) the radical Levelers, who called for universal manhood suffrage, were referred to by their opponents as "Switzerising anarchists," and during the French Revolution the leader of the moderate Girondin faction of Parliament, Jacques-Pierre Brissot, accused his most extreme rivals, the Enragés, of being the advocates of "anarchy":

> *Laws that are not carried into effect, authorities without force and despised, crime unpunished, property attacked, the safety of the individual violated, the morality of the people corrupted, no constitution, no government, no justice, these are the features of anarchy.*

These words could serve as a model for the denunciations delivered by all opponents of anarchism. The anarchists, for their part, would admit many of Brissot's points. They deny man-made laws, regard property as a means of tyranny, and believe that crime is merely the product of property and authority. But they would argue that their denial of constitutions and governments leads not to "no justice" but to the real justice inherent in the free development of humans' sociality—their natural inclination, when unfettered by laws, to live according to the principles and practice of mutual aid.

ANARCHISM AS A
MOVEMENT, 1870–1940

A crucial development in the history of anarchism was the emergence of the doctrine of "propaganda of the deed." In 1876 Errico Malatesta expressed the belief held by Italian anarchists that "the *insurrectionary deed* destined to affirm socialist principles by acts, is the most efficacious means of propaganda." The first acts were rural insurrections intended to arouse the illiterate masses of the Italian countryside. After the insurrections failed, anarchist activism tended to take the form of acts of terrorism by individual protesters, who would attempt to kill ruling figures to make the state appear vulnerable and to inspire the masses with their self-sacrifice. Between 1890 and 1901 several such symbolic murders were carried out; the victims included King Umberto I of Italy, the empress consort Elizabeth of Austria, Pres. Sadi Carnot of France, Pres. William McKinley of the United States, and Antonio Cánovas del Castillo, the prime minister of Spain. This dramatic series of terrorist acts established the image of the anarchist as a mindless destroyer, an image that was further strengthened as anarchist attacks on government officials, as well as on restaurants and other public places, became more widespread.

By the mid-1890s, however, the more militant anarchists in France began to realize that an excess of individualism had detached them from the workers they sought to liberate. Anarchists, indeed, have always found it difficult to reconcile the claims of general human solidarity with the demands—equally insistent—of the individual who desires freedom. Some anarchist thinkers, such as the German Max Stirner, refused to recognize any limitation on the individual's right to do as he pleases or any obligation to act socially. Even those who accepted the socially oriented doctrines of anarchist communism, as outlined by the theorist Peter Alekseyevich Kropotkin (1842–1921), have in practice been reluctant to create forms of organization that threatened their freedom of action or seemed likely to harden into institutions.

In consequence, although a number of international anarchist congresses were held—the most celebrated being those in London in 1881 and Amsterdam in 1907—no effective worldwide organization was ever created, even though by the end of the 19th century the anarchist movement had spread to all continents and was united by informal links of correspondence and friendship between leading figures. National federations were weak even in countries where there were many anarchists, such as France and Italy, and the typical unit of organization remained the small group dedicated to propaganda by deed or word. Such groups engaged in a wide variety of activities; in the 1890s many of them set up experimental schools and communities in an attempt to live according to anarchist principles.

REVOLUTIONARY SYNDICALISM

In France, where individualist trends had been most pronounced and public reaction to terrorist acts had imperiled the very existence of the movement, anarchists made an effort to acquire a mass following, primarily by infiltrating the trade unions. They were particularly active in the *bourses du travail* ("labour exchanges"), local groups of unions originally established to find work for their members. In 1892 a national confederation of *bourses du travail* was formed, and by 1895 a group of anarchists, led by Fernand Pelloutier, Émile Pouget, and Paul Delesalle, had gained effective control of the organization and were developing the theory and practice of working-class activism later known as anarcho-syndicalism, or revolutionary syndicalism.

The anarcho-syndicalists argued that the traditional function of trade unions — to struggle for better wages and working conditions — was not enough. The unions should become militant organizations dedicated to the destruction of capitalism and the state. They should aim to take over factories and utilities, which would then be operated by the workers. In this way the union or syndicate would have a double function — as an organ of struggle within the existing political system and as an organ of administration after the revolution. The anarcho-syndicalists' strategy called for sustaining militancy by creating an atmosphere of incessant conflict, which would culminate in a massive general strike. Many anarcho-syndicalists believed that such an overwhelming act of noncooperation would bring about what they called "the revolution of folded arms," resulting in the collapse of the state and the capitalist system. However, although partial general strikes, with limited objectives, were undertaken in France and elsewhere with varying success, the millennial general strike aimed at overthrowing the social order in a single blow was never attempted. Nevertheless, the anarcho-syndicalists acquired great prestige among the workers of France — and later of Spain and Italy — because of their generally tough-minded attitude at a time when working conditions were bad and employers tended to respond brutally to union activity. After the General Confederation of Labour (Confédération Générale du Travail; CGT), the great French trade-union organization, was founded in 1902, the militancy of the anarcho-syndicalists enabled them to retain control of the organization until 1908 and to wield considerable influence on its activities until after World War I (1914–18).

Like anarchism, revolutionary syndicalism proved attractive to certain intellectuals, notably Georges Sorel, whose *Reflections on Violence* (1908) was the most important literary work to emerge from the movement. The more purist anarchist theoreticians were disturbed by the monolithic character of syndicalist organizations, which they feared might create powerful interest structures in a revolutionary society. At the International Anarchist Congress in Amsterdam in 1907, a crucial debate on this issue took place between the young revolutionary syndicalist Pierre Monatte and the veteran anarchist Errico Malatesta. It defined a division of outlook that still lingers in anarchist circles, which have always included individualist attitudes too extreme to admit any kind of large-scale organization.

Revolutionary syndicalism transformed anarchism, for a time at least, from a tiny minority current into a movement with considerable mass support, even though most members of syndicalist unions were sympathizers and fellow travelers rather than committed anarchists. In 1922 the syndicalists set up their own International with its headquarters in Berlin, taking the historic name of the International Workingmen's Association. When it was established, the organizations that formed it could still boast a considerable following. The Italian Trade Union (Unione Sindicale Italiana) had 500,000 members; the Regional Federation of Argentine Workers (Federación Obrera Regional Argentina), 200,000 members; the General Confederation of Labour (Confederação General de Trabalho) in Portugal, 150,000 members; and the Free Workers (Freie Arbeiter) in Germany, 120,000 members. There were also smaller organizations in Chile, Uruguay, Denmark, Norway, Holland, Mexico, and Sweden. In Britain, the influence of syndicalism was shown most clearly in the Guild Socialism movement, which flourished briefly in the early years of the 20th century. In the United

States, revolutionary syndicalist ideas were influential in the Industrial Workers of the World (IWW), which in the years immediately before and after World War I played a vital part in organizing American miners, loggers, and unskilled workers. Only a small minority of IWW militants were avowed anarchists, however.

ANARCHISM AROUND THE WORLD

Spain

The reconciliation of anarchism and syndicalism was most complete and most successful in Spain; for a long period the anarchist movement in that country remained the most numerous and the most powerful in the world. The first known Spanish anarchist, Ramón de la Sagra, a disciple of Pierre-Joseph Proudhon, who advocated a form of socialist anarchism called mutualism, founded the world's first anarchist journal, *El Porvenir*, in La Coruña in 1845, but it was quickly suppressed. Mutualist ideas were later publicized by Francisco Pi y Margall, a federalist leader and the translator of many of Proudhon's books. During the Spanish revolution of 1873, Pi y Margall attempted to establish a decentralized, or "cantonalist," political system on Proudhonian lines. In the end, however, the influence of the anarchist Mikhail Aleksandrovich Bakunin was stronger. In 1868 his Italian disciple, Giuseppe Fanelli, visited Barcelona and Madrid, where he established branches of the International. By 1870 they had 40,000 members, and in 1873 the movement numbered about 60,000, organized mainly in working men's associations. In 1874 the anarchist movement in Spain was forced underground, a phenomenon that recurred often in subsequent decades. Nevertheless, it flourished, and anarchism became the favoured type of radicalism among two very different groups, the factory workers of Barcelona and other Catalan towns and the impoverished peasants who toiled on the estates of absentee owners in Andalusia.

As in France and Italy, the movement in Spain during the 1880s and '90s was inclined toward insurrection (in Andalusia) and terrorism (in Catalonia). It retained its strength in working-class organizations because the courageous and even ruthless anarchist militants were often the only leaders who would stand up to the army and to the employers, who hired squads of gunmen to engage in guerrilla warfare with the anarchists in the streets of Barcelona. The workers of Barcelona were finally inspired by the success of the French CGT to set up a syndicalist organization, Workers' Solidarity (Solidaridad Obrera), in 1907. Solidaridad Obrera quickly spread throughout Catalonia, and, in 1909, when the Spanish army tried to conscript Catalan reservists to fight against the Riffs in Morocco, it called a general strike. The work was followed by a week of largely spontaneous violence ("La Semana Tragica," or the Tragic Week) that left hundreds dead and 50 churches and monasteries destroyed and that ended in brutal repression. The torture of anarchists in the fortress of Montjuich and the execution of the internationally celebrated advocate of free education Francisco Ferrer led to worldwide protests and the resignation of the conservative government in Madrid. These events also resulted in a congress of Spanish trade unionists at Sevilla in 1910, which founded the National Confederation of Labour (Confederación Nacional del Trabajo; CNT).

The CNT, which included the majority of organized Spanish workers, was dominated throughout its existence by the anarchist militants, who in 1927 founded their own activist organization, the Iberian Anarchist Federation (Federación Anarquista Iberica; FAI). While there was recurrent conflict within the CNT between moderates and FAI activists, the atmosphere of violence and urgency in which radical activities were carried on in Spain ensured that the more extreme leaders, such as Garcia Oliver and Buenaventura Durutti, tended to wield decisive influence. The CNT was a model of anarchist decentralism and antibureaucratism: its basic organizations were not national unions but *sindicatos únicos* ("special unions"), which brought together the workers of all trades and crafts in a certain locality; the national committee was elected each year from a different locality to ensure that no individual served more than one term; and all delegates were subject to immediate recall by the members. This enormous organization, which claimed 700,000 members in 1919, 1.6 million in 1936, and more than 2 million during the Spanish Civil War (1936–39), employed only one paid secretary. Its day-to-day operation was carried on in their spare time by workers chosen by their comrades. This approach ensured that the Spanish anarchist movement would not be dominated by the déclassé intellectuals and self-taught printers and shoemakers who were so influential in other countries.

The CNT and the FAI, which remained clandestine organizations under the dictatorship of Miguel Primo de Rivera, emerged into the open with the abdication of King Alfonso XIII in 1931. Their antipolitical philosophy led them to reject the Republic as much as the monarchy it had replaced, and between 1931 and the military rebellion led by Francisco Franco in 1936 there were several unsuccessful anarchist risings. In 1936 the anarchists, who over the decades had become expert urban guerrillas, were mainly responsible for the defeat of the rebel generals in both Barcelona and Valencia, as well as in country areas of Catalonia and Aragon; and for many early months of the Civil War they were in virtual control of eastern Spain, where they regarded the crisis as an opportunity to carry through the social revolution of which they had long dreamed. Factories and railways in Catalonia were taken over by workers' committees, and in hundreds of villages in Catalonia, Levante, and Andalusia the peasants seized the land and established libertarian communes like those described by the anarchist theorist Kropotkin in *The Conquest of Bread*, which describes in great detail how an ideal society can be achieved through social revolution. The internal use of money was abolished, the land was tilled in common, and village products were sold or exchanged on behalf of the community in general, with each family receiving an equitable share of food and other necessities. An idealistic Spartan fervour characterized these communities, which often consisted of illiterate labourers; intoxicants, tobacco, and sometimes even coffee were renounced; and millenarian enthusiasm took the place of religion, as it has often done in Spain. The reports of critical observers suggest that at least some of these communes were efficiently run and more productive agriculturally than the villages had been previously.

The Spanish anarchists failed during the Civil War largely because, expert though they were in spontaneous street fighting, they did not have the discipline necessary to carry on sustained warfare; the columns they sent to various fronts were unsuccessful in comparison with the communist-led International Brigades. The collectivized factories were taken over by the central government, and many agricultural communes were destroyed by Franco's advance into Andalusia and by the hostile action of General Enrique Lister's communist army in Aragon. In January 1939 the Spanish anarchists were so demoralized by the compromises of the Civil War that they were unable to mount a resistance when Franco's forces marched into Barcelona. The CNT and the FAI became phantom organizations in exile.

The Americas

In the United States, a native and mainly nonviolent tradition of anarchism developed during the 19th century in the writings of Henry David Thoreau, Josiah Warren, Lysander Spooner, Joseph Labadie, and above all Benjamin Tucker. An early advocate of women's suffrage, religious tolerance, and fair labour legislation, Tucker combined Warren's ideas on labour egalitarianism with elements of Proudhon's and Bakunin's antistatism. The result was the most sophisticated exposition to date of anarchist ideas in the United States. Much of Tucker's political influence, especially during the 1880s, derived from his journal *Liberty*, which he published in both Boston and New York City.

Anarchist activism in the United States was mainly sustained by immigrants from Europe, including Johann Most (editor of *Die Freiheit*; "Freedom"), who justified acts of terrorism on anarchist principles; Alexander Berkman, who attempted to assassinate steel magnate Henry Clay Frick in 1892; and Emma Goldman, whose *Living My Life* gives a picture of radical activity in the United States at the turn of the century. Goldman, who had immigrated to the United States from tsarist Russia in 1885, soon became a preeminent figure in the American anarchist movement. A follower of Kropotkin, she lectured widely and published numerous essays on anarchist theory and practice in her journal *Mother Earth*. Most of her campaigns were controversial. She argued on behalf of birth control, defended the bomb throwers of her era as victims of a ruthless capitalist system, opposed women's suffrage— because, in her view, it would only further bind women to bourgeois reformism—and spoke out against American entry into World War I, which she believed was an imperialist war that was sacrificing ordinary people as cannon fodder.

Although anarchists were more often the victims of violence than its perpetrators, the cartoonists' stereotype of the long-haired, wild-eyed anarchist assassin emerged in the 1880s and was firmly established in the public mind during the Chicago Haymarket Riot of 1886. Anarchists—many of them German immigrants—were prominent figures in Chicago's labour movement. After police killed two strikers at a rally at the McCormick Harvesting Machine Company on May 3, 1886, a protest meeting was called for Haymarket Square the next day. Mayor Carter Harrison, who attended the demonstration as an observer, pronounced the gathering peaceful. After Harrison and most of the demonstrators had departed, a contingent of police arrived and demanded that the crowd disperse. At that point a bomb exploded among the police, killing one, and the police responded with random gunfire. In the ensuing melee, several people (including six police) were killed and many more injured.

The incident created widespread hysteria against immigrants and labour leaders and led to renewed suppression by police. Although the identity of the bomb thrower was never determined, eight anarchist leaders were arrested and charged with murder and conspiracy. Four members of the "Chicago Eight" were hanged on Nov. 11, 1887; one committed suicide in his cell; and three others were given long prison sentences. Excoriating the trial as unjust, Illinois Governor John Peter Altgeld pardoned the three surviving Haymarket prisoners in 1893. May Day—international workers' day—was directly inspired by the Haymarket affair, and anarchists such as Goldman, Berkman, and Voltairine de Cleyre, as well as socialist Eugene V. Debs, traced their political awakenings to the events at Haymarket.

A deadly explosion in Chicago's Haymarket Square during an 1886 labour union protest was traced to anarchists. The ensuing uproar negated many union gains and cemented the impression of anarchy as a violent movement.
MPI/Hulton Archive/Getty Images

In 1901 an immigrant Polish anarchist, Leon Czolgosz, assassinated President McKinley. In 1903 Congress passed a law barring all foreign anarchists from entering or remaining in the country. In the repressive mood that followed World War I, anarchism in the United States was suppressed. Berkman, Goldman, and many others activists were imprisoned and deported. In a sensational trial in the spring of 1920, two immigrant Italian anarchists, Nicola Sacco and Bartolomeo Vanzetti, were convicted of killing a payroll clerk and a guard during a robbery at a Massachusetts shoe factory. In apparent retaliation for the conviction, a bomb was set off in the Wall Street area of New York City, killing more than 30 people and injuring

200 others. Despite worldwide protests that raised serious questions about the guilt of the defendants, Sacco and Vanzetti were executed in 1927.

In Latin America, strong anarchist elements were involved in the Mexican Revolution. The syndicalist teachings of Ricardo Flores Magon influenced the peasant revolutionism of Emiliano Zapata. After the deaths of Zapata in 1919 and Flores Magon in 1922, the revolutionary image in Mexico, as elsewhere, was taken over by communists. In Argentina and Uruguay there were significant anarcho-syndicalist movements early in the 20th century, but they too were greatly reduced by the end of the 1930s through intermittent repression and the competition of communism.

Japan

The first self-described anarchist in East Asia was the Japanese writer and activist Kotoku Shusui. In 1901 Kotoku, an early advocate of Japanese socialism, helped to found the Social Democratic Party, which was immediately banned by the government. Early in 1905, after the newspaper he published, the *Heimin shimbun* ("Commoner's Newspaper"), denounced the Russo-Japanese War, the paper was closed and Kotoku was imprisoned. While in prison he was profoundly influenced by anarchist literature—especially Kropotkin's *Fields, Factories, and Workshops*—and adopted anarchism wholeheartedly. As he wrote to a friend at the time, he had "gone [to prison] as a Marxian socialist and returned a radical anarchist." After five months in prison Kotoku traveled to the United States, where he collaborated with members of the IWW. His experiences in the United States led him to abandon parliamentary politics in favour of a violent strategy of "direct action."

After his return to Japan in June 1906, Kotoku began organizing workers for radical activities. He also managed to persuade the newly founded Socialist Party of Japan to adopt his views on direct action. In 1910 Kotoku was among hundreds arrested for involvement in a conspiracy to assassinate the Meiji emperor. Although he had withdrawn from the conspiracy before his arrest, Kotoku was tried for treason and was executed in 1911. His death marked the beginning of a "winter period" for anarchism in Japan, which was to last until the end of World War I.

China

Shortly after 1900, as part of the reforms that followed the unsuccessful Boxer Rebellion (a peasant uprising that attempted to drive all foreigners from China), the Qing (Ch'ing) Dynasty began to send many young Chinese to study abroad, especially in France, Japan, and the United States. In these places and elsewhere, Chinese students established nationalist and revolutionary organizations dedicated to overthrowing the imperial regime. Two of the most important of these groups—the World Association, founded in Paris in 1906, and the Society for the Study of Socialism, founded in Tokyo in 1907—adopted explicitly anarchist programs.

Between 1907 and 1910 the World Association published a journal, *The New Century*, which was a major source of information, written in Chinese, on anarchist theory and the European anarchist movement. The journal promoted an individualistic and "futuristic" anarchism and was among the first Chinese-language publications to openly attack native traditions, in particular Confucianism. The Society for the Study of Socialism, on the other hand, favoured an antimodern anarchism influenced by the

During the Boxer Rebellion, many imperial troops sympathized with the young Chinese nationalists (Boxers) they had been sent to suppress. Subsequently, several groups with an anarchist bent were able to spring up throughout China. Popperfoto/Getty Images

pacifist radicalism of Russian novelist Leo Tolstoy, and it stressed the affinity between anarchism and philosophical currents in the Chinese past, especially Daoism (Taoism). Through its publications, *Natural Justice* and *Balance*, the Society advocated Kropotkin's programs for combining agriculture with industry and mental with manual labour, ideas that were to have a lasting influence on Chinese radicalism.

Significant anarchist activity in China itself did not begin until after the Chinese Revolution (1911–12). Chinese anarchists educated in Paris (the so-called "Paris anarchists") returned to Beijing and immediately became involved in the reform of education and culture. Convinced of the need for social revolution, the Paris anarchists argued in favour of Western science against religion and superstition, called for the emancipation of women and youth, rejected the traditional family and the Confucian values on which it was based, and organized experimental work-study communities as alternatives to traditional forms of family and working life. These ideas and practices were extremely influential in the New Culture movement of the late 1910s and early 1920s. Led by the generation of intellectuals sent to study abroad, the movement was critical of all aspects of traditional Chinese culture and ethics and called for sweeping reforms in existing political and social institutions.

CONTEMPORARY ANARCHISM

After World War II (1939–45), anarchist groups and federations reemerged in almost all countries where they had formerly flourished—the notable exceptions being Spain and the Soviet Union—but these organizations wielded little influence compared to that of the broader movement inspired by earlier ideas. This development is not surprising, since anarchists never stressed the need for organizational continuity, and the cluster of social and moral ideas that are identifiable as anarchism always spread beyond any clearly definable movement.

Anarchist ideas emerged in a wider frame of reference beginning with the American civil rights movement of the 1950s, which aimed to resist injustice through the tactic of civil disobedience. In the 1960s and '70s a new radicalism took root among students and the left in general in the United States, Europe, and Japan, embracing a general criticism of "elitist" power structures and the materialist values of modern industrial societies—both capitalist and communist. For these radicals, who rejected the traditional parties of the left as strongly as they did the existing political structure, the appeal of anarchism was strong.

The general anarchist outlook—with its emphasis on spontaneity, theoretical flexibility, simplicity of life, and the importance of love and anger as complementary and necessary components in both social and individual action—attracted those who opposed impersonal political institutions and the calculations of older parties. The anarchist rejection of the state, and the insistence on decentralism and local autonomy, found strong echoes among those who advocated participatory democracy. The anarchist insistence on direct action was reflected in calls for extraparliamentary action and violent confrontation by some student groups in France, the United States, and Japan. And the recurrence of the theme of workers' control of industry in so many manifestos of the 1960s—especially during the student uprisings in Paris in May 1968—showed the enduring relevance of anarcho-syndicalist ideas.

Beginning in the 1970s, anarchism became a significant factor in the radical ecology movement in the United States and Europe. Anarchist ideas in works by the American novelist Edward Abbey, for example, inspired a generation of eco-anarchists in the United States, including the radical Earth First! organization, to protest urban sprawl and the destruction of old-growth forests. Much influential work in anarchist theory during this period and afterward, such as that of Murray Bookchin, was noteworthy for its argument that statism and capitalism were incompatible with environmental preservation.

Anarchists also took up issues related to feminism and developed a rich body of work, known as anarcha-feminism, that applied anarchist principles to the analysis of women's oppression, arguing that the state is inherently patriarchal and that women's experience as nurturers and care-givers reflects the anarchist ideals of mutuality and the rejection of hierarchy and authority.

The most prevalent current in anarchist thinking during the last two decades of the 20th century (at least in the United States) was an eclectic, countercultural mixture of theories reflecting a wide range of artistic, literary, political, and philosophical influences, including the Frankfurt School of Marxist-oriented social and political philosophers—especially Herbert Marcuse. African American anarchism, as represented in the writings of former Black Panther Lorenzo Kom'boa Ervin in the late 1970s, was a major influence in the United States and in many other parts of the world.

Although some older varieties of anarchism, such as Proudhonian mutualism, had faded away by the end of the 20th century, others persisted, including the anarchist individualism of Josiah Warren, Lysander Spooner, and others in the United States, as well as anarchist communism in Europe and Latin America. Anarcho-syndicalism remained a significant movement in Spain, France, Sweden, and parts of Africa and Latin America. As in the 1960s, anarchism continued to exert a strong appeal among students and young people, and a large percentage of those who considered themselves anarchists were in their teens and twenties. From the early 1970s the anarchist emblem consisting of a circled A was an established part of the iconography of global youth culture.

In 1999 anarchist-led demonstrations against the World Trade Organization (WTO) in Seattle provoked wide media attention, as did later related protests against the World Bank and the International Monetary Fund (IMF). The unprecedented publicity given to the anarchists' explicitly revolutionary viewpoint inspired a proliferation of new anarchist groups, periodicals, and Internet sites. Anarchists were also a significant—and in some cases a predominating—influence in many other political movements, including campaigns against police brutality and capital punishment, the gay rights movement, and diverse movements promoting animal rights, vegetarianism, abortion rights, the abolition of prisons, the legalization of marijuana, and the abolition of automobiles.

At the beginning of the 21st century, no anarchist movement posed a serious threat to state power, and anarchists were no closer to achieving their dream of a society without government than they were a century before. Nevertheless, the perceived failure of governments to solve enduring social problems such as racial and gender inequality, poverty, environmental destruction, political corruption, and war increased the appeal of anarchist ideas among many groups. Young people in particular were attracted to the anarchist priorities of creativity and spontaneity—the importance of living the "new society" here and now rather than postponing it indefinitely until "after the Revolution." For these people and many others around the world, anarchism remained an active and vibrant ferment of criticism, protest, and direct action.

Chapter 6: Fascism

F ascism arrived on the political scene in the 20th century and came to dominate many parts of central, southern, and eastern Europe between 1919 and 1945. Europe's first fascist leader, the Italian dictator Benito Mussolini, took the name of his party from the Latin word *fasces*, which referred to a bundle of elm or birch rods (usually containing an ax) used as a symbol of penal authority in ancient Rome. Although fascist parties and movements differed significantly from each other, they had many characteristics in common, including extreme militaristic nationalism, contempt for electoral democracy and political and cultural liberalism, a belief in natural social hierarchy and the rule of elites, and the desire to create a *Volksgemeinschaft* (German: "people's community"), in which individual interests would be subordinated to the good of the nation. At the end of World War II (1939–45), the major European fascist parties were broken up, and in some countries (such as Italy and West Germany) they were officially banned. Beginning in the late 1940s, however, many fascist-oriented parties and movements were founded in Europe as well as in Latin America and South Africa. Although some European "neofascist" groups attracted large followings, especially in Italy and France, none were as influential as the major fascist parties of the interwar period.

NATIONAL FASCISMS

Fascist parties and movements came to power in several countries between 1922 and 1945: the National Fascist Party (Partito Nazionale Fascista) in Italy, led by Mussolini;

TOTALITARIANISM

Totalitarianism is closely related to fascism. It is a political system that subordinates all aspects of its citizens' lives to the authority of the state, with a single charismatic leader as the ultimate authority. Benito Mussolini coined the term in the early 1920s, but totalitarianism has existed throughout history and throughout the world (e.g., the Qin dynasty of China, 221–207 BCE). It is distinguished from dictatorship and authoritarianism by its supplanting of all political institutions and all old legal and social traditions with new ones to meet the state's needs, which are usually highly focused. Large-scale, organized violence may be legitimized. The police operate without the constraint of laws and regulations. Where pursuit of the state's goal is the only ideological foundation for such a government, achievement of the goal can never be acknowledged.

the National Socialist German Workers' Party (Nationalsozialistische Deutsche Arbeiterpartei), or Nazi Party, led by Adolf Hitler and representing his National Socialism movement; the Fatherland Front (Vaterländische Front) in Austria, led by Engelbert Dollfuss and supported by the Heimwehr (Home Defense Force), a major right-wing paramilitary organization; the National Union (União Nacional) in Portugal, led by António de Oliveira Salazar (which became fascist after 1936); the Party of Free Believers (Elefterofronoi) in Greece, led by Ioannis Metaxas; the Ustaša ("Insurgence") in Croatia, led by Ante Pavelić; the National Union (Nasjonal Samling) in Norway, which was in power for only a week—though its leader, Vidkun Quisling, was later made minister president under the German occupation; and the military dictatorship of Admiral Tojo Hideki in Japan.

Spain's fascist movement, the Falange ("Phalanx"), founded in 1933 by José Antonio Primo de Rivera, never came to power, but many of its members were absorbed into the military dictatorship of Francisco Franco, which itself displayed many fascist characteristics. In Poland the anti-Semitic Falanga, led by Boleslaw Piasecki, was influential but was unable to overthrow the conservative regime of Józef Piłsudski. Vihtori Kosola's Lapua Movement in Finland nearly staged a coup in 1932 but was checked by conservatives backed by the army. The Arrow Cross Party (Nyilaskeresztes Párt) in Hungary, led by Ferenc Szálasi, was suppressed by the conservative regime of Miklós Horthy until 1944, when Szálasi was made a puppet ruler under the German occupation. In Romania the Iron Guard (Garda de Fier)—also called the League of Christian Defense, the Legion of the Archangel Michael, and All for the Fatherland—led by Corneliu Codreanu, was dissolved by the dictatorial regime of King Carol II in 1938. In 1939 Codreanu and several of his legionaries were arrested and "shot while trying to escape." In 1940 remnants of the Iron Guard reemerged to share power but were finally crushed by Romanian conservatives in February 1941.

In France the Cross of Fire (Croix de Feu), later renamed the French Social Party (Parti Social Français), led by Col. François de La Rocque, was the largest and fastest-growing party on the French right between 1936 and 1938. In 1937 it was larger than the French communist and socialist parties combined (one scholar estimated its membership between 700,000 and 1.2 million), and by 1939 it included some 3,000 mayors, about 1,000 municipal councilmen, and 12 parliamentary deputies. Other fascist movements in France included the short-lived

Faisceau (1925–28), led by Georges Valois; the Young Patriots (Jeunesses Patriotes), led by Pierre Taittinger; French Solidarity (Solidarité Française), founded and financed by François Coty and led by Jean Renaud; the Franks (Francistes), led by Marcel Bucard; the French Popular Party (Parti Populaire Français), led by Jacques Doriot; and French Action (Action Française), led by Charles Maurras. After the German invasion in 1940, a number of French fascists served in the Vichy regime of Marshal Philippe Pétain.

The British Union of Fascists, led by Oswald Mosley, had some 50,000 members. In Belgium the Rexist Party, led by Léon Degrelle, won about 10 percent of the seats in the parliament in 1936. Russian fascist organizations were founded by exiles in Manchuria, the United States, and elsewhere; the largest of these groups were the Russian Fascist Party (VFP), led by Konstantin Rodzaevsky, and the All Russian Fascist Organization (VFO), led by Anastasy Vonsiatsky.

Outside Europe, popular support for fascism was greatest in South Africa and the Middle East. Several fascist groups were founded in South Africa after 1932, including the Gentile National Socialist Movement (the "Greyshirts") and its splinter group, the South African Fascists; the South African National Democratic Party, known as the Blackshirts; and the pro-German Ox-Wagon Sentinel (Ossewabrandwag). By 1939 there were at least seven Arab "shirt" movements, including the Syrian People's Party, also called the Syrian National Socialist Party; the Iraqi Futuwa movement; and the Young Egypt movement, also called the Green Shirts.

Several rival protofascist and fascist movements operated in Japan after 1918, and their activities helped to increase the influence of the military on the Japanese government. Among the most important of these groups were the Taisho Sincerity League (Taisho Nesshin'kai), the Imperial Way Faction (Kodo-ha), the Greater Japan National Essence Association (Dai Nippon Kokusui-kai), the Anti-Red Corps (Bokyo Gokoku-Dan), the Great Japan Political Justice Corps (Dai Nippon Seigi-Dan), the Blood Brotherhood League (Ketsumei-Dan), the Jimmu Association (Jimmu-Kai), the New Japan League (Shin-Nihon Domei), the Eastern Way Society (Towo Seishin-Kai), and the Great Japan Youth Party (Da-nihon Seinen-dan).

Following the Mukden Incident (the seizure of the Manchurian city of Mukden [now Shenyang, Liaoning province, China] by Japanese troops) and the wider invasion of Manchuria by Japanese troops in 1931, several fascist-oriented patriotic societies were formed in China; the largest of these groups, the Blue Shirts, formed an alliance with the Kuomintang (National People's Party) under Chiang Kai-shek. At Chiang's order in 1934, the Blue Shirts were temporarily put in charge of political indoctrination in the army and given limited control of its educational system.

European fascism had a number of imitators in Latin America, including the Nacis, founded in Chile by Jorge González von Mareés; the Gold Shirts, founded in Mexico by Nicolás Rodríguez; and the Revolutionary Union (Unión Revolucionaria) of Peruvian dictator Luis Sánchez Cerro. After a failed coup attempt in 1938, the Brazilian Integralist Action party (Ação Integralista Brasileira), which had some 200,000 members in the mid-1930s, was suppressed by the Brazilian government.

In the United States the Ku Klux Klan, a white supremacist organization founded at the end of the Civil War and revived in 1915, displayed some fascist characteristics. One of its offshoots, the Black Legion, had some 60,000 members in the early 1930s and committed

KU KLUX KLAN

The Ku Klux Klan (KKK) refers to either of two racist terrorist organizations in the United States. The first, organized by veterans of the Confederate army, began as a social club and then as a secret means of resisting Reconstruction and restoring white domination over newly enfranchised blacks. Dressed in white robes and sheets, Klansmen whipped and killed freedmen (former slaves) and their white supporters in nighttime raids. It had largely accomplished its goals by the 1870s before gradually fading away. The second KKK arose in 1915, partly out of nostalgia for the Old South and partly out of fear of the rise of communism in Russia and the changing ethnic character of U.S. society. It counted Catholics, Jews, foreigners, and labour unions among its enemies. Its membership peaked in the 1920s at more than four million, but during the Great Depression the organization gradually declined. It became active again during the civil rights movement of the 1960s, attacking blacks and white civil rights workers with bombings, whippings, and shootings. By the end of the 20th century, growing racial tolerance had reduced its numbers to a few thousand.

There have been two iterations of the Ku Klux Klan in the United States. Both centred around the concept of race and fierce national pride. MPI/ Hulton Archive/ Getty Images

numerous acts of arson and bombing. In 1930 Catholic priest Charles E. Coughlin began national radio broadcasts of sermons on political and economic subjects; his talks became increasingly antidemocratic and anti-Semitic, as did the journal he founded, *Social Justice*. After running unsuccessfully for the U.S. presidency in 1936, Coughlin became an apologist for Hitler, Mussolini, and Franco. In 1942 *Social Justice* was banned from the U.S. mails for violating the Espionage Act, and in the same year the American Catholic church ordered Coughlin to stop his broadcasts. The pro-Nazi German-American Bund, founded in 1933, staged military drills and mass rallies until it disintegrated with the U.S. entry into the war in 1941.

NATIONAL SOCIALISM

National Socialism, or Nazism, was a totalitarian movement led by Adolf Hitler as head of the Nazi Party in Germany. In its intense nationalism, mass appeal, and dictatorial rule, National Socialism shared many elements with Italian fascism. However, Nazism was far more extreme both in its ideas and in its practice. In almost every respect it was an anti-intellectual and atheoretical movement, emphasizing the will of the charismatic dictator as the sole source of inspiration of a people and a nation, as well as a vision of annihilation of all enemies of the Aryan *Volk* ("people") as the one and only goal of Nazi policy.

National Socialism had peculiarly German roots. It can be partly traced to the Prussian tradition as developed under Prussian kings Frederick William I (1688–1740) and Frederick the Great (1712–68) and Prussian Prime Minister (and founder of the German Empire) Otto von Bismarck (1815–98), which regarded the militant spirit and the discipline of the Prussian army as the model for all individual and civic life. To it was added the tradition of political romanticism, with its sharp hostility to rationalism and to the principles underlying the French Revolution, its emphasis on instinct and the past, and its proclamation of the rights of German philosopher Friedrich Nietzsche's exceptional individual (the *Übermensch*, or "Superman") over all universal law and rules. These two traditions were later reinforced by the 19th-century adoration of science and of the laws of nature, which seemed to operate independently of all concepts of good and evil. Further reinforcements came from such 19th-century intellectual figures as Joseph-Arthur, comte de Gobineau (1816–82), Richard Wagner (1813–83), and Houston Stewart Chamberlain (1855–1927), all of whom greatly influenced early National Socialism with their claims of the racial and cultural superiority of the "Nordic" (Germanic) peoples over all other Europeans and all other races.

Hitler's intellectual viewpoint was influenced during his youth not only by these currents in the German tradition but also by specific Austrian movements that professed various political sentiments, notably those of pan-Germanic expansionism and anti-Semitism. Hitler's ferocious nationalism, his contempt of the Slavs, and his hatred of the Jews can largely be explained by his bitter experiences as an unsuccessful artist living a threadbare existence on the streets of Vienna, the capital of the multiethnic Austro-Hungarian Empire.

This intellectual preparation would probably not have been sufficient for the growth of National Socialism in Germany but for that country's defeat in World War I (1914–18). The defeat and the resulting disillusionment, pauperization, and frustration—particularly among the lower middle classes—paved the way for the success of the propaganda of Hitler and the Nazis. The Treaty of Versailles (1919), the formal settlement of World War I drafted without German participation, alienated many Germans with its imposition of harsh monetary and territorial reparations. The significant resentment expressed toward the peace treaty gave Hitler a starting point. Because German representatives (branded the "November criminals" by National Socialists) agreed to cease hostilities and did not unconditionally surrender in the armistice of Nov. 11, 1918, there was a widespread feeling—particularly in the military—that Germany's defeat had been orchestrated by diplomats at the Versailles meetings. From the beginning, Hitler's propaganda of revenge for this "traitorous" act, through which the German people had been "stabbed in the back," and his call for rearmament had strong appeal within military circles, which regarded the peace only as a temporary setback in Germany's expansionist program. The ruinous inflation of the German currency in 1923 wiped out the savings of many middle-class households and led to further public alienation and dissatisfaction.

Hitler added to pan-Germanic aspirations the almost mystical fanaticism of a faith in the mission of the German race and the fervour of a social revolutionary gospel. This gospel was most fully expressed in Hitler's personal testament *Mein Kampf* (1925–27; "My Struggle"), in which he outlined both his practical aims and his theories of race and propaganda.

Posing as a bulwark against communism, Hitler exploited the fears aroused in Germany and worldwide by the Bolshevik Revolution in Russia and the consolidation of communist power in the Soviet Union. Thus, he was able to secure the support of many conservative elements that misunderstood the totalitarian character of his movement.

*Mein Kampf is part autobiography, part political agenda. In the book,
Adolf Hitler clearly outlines a political movement that was to become the
Nazi Party.* David Silverman/Getty Images

Hitler's most important individual contribution to the theory and practice of National Socialism was his deep understanding of mass psychology and mass propaganda. He stressed the fact that all propaganda must hold its intellectual level at the capacity of the least intelligent of those at whom it is directed and that its truthfulness is much less important than its success. According to Hitler,

> *It is part of a great leader's genius to make even widely separated adversaries appear as if they belonged to but one category, because among weakly and undecided characters the recognition of various enemies all too easily marks the beginning of doubt of one's own rightness.*

Hitler found this common denominator in the Jews, whom he identified with both Bolshevism and a kind of cosmic evil. The Jews were to be discriminated against not according to their religion but according to their "race." National Socialism declared the Jews—whatever their educational and social development—to be forever fundamentally different from and inimical to Germans.

National Socialism attempted to reconcile conservative, nationalist ideology with a socially radical doctrine. In so doing, it became a profoundly revolutionary movement—albeit a largely negative one. Rejecting rationalism, liberalism, democracy, the rule of law, human rights, and all movements of international cooperation and peace, it stressed instinct, the subordination of the individual to the state, and the necessity of blind and unswerving obedience to leaders appointed from above. It also emphasized the inequality of men and races and the right of the strong to rule the weak; sought to purge or suppress competing political, religious, and social institutions; advanced an ethic of hardness and ferocity; and partly destroyed class distinctions by drawing into the movement misfits and failures from all social classes. Although socialism was traditionally an internationalist creed, the radical wing of National Socialism knew that a mass base existed for policies that were simultaneously anticapitalist and nationalist. However, after Hitler secured power, this radical strain was eliminated.

Working from these principles, Hitler carried his party from its inauspicious beginnings to a dominant position in world politics within 20 years. The Nazi Party originated in 1919 and was led by Hitler from 1920. Through both successful electioneering and intimidation, the party came to power in Germany in 1933 and governed through totalitarian methods until 1945, when Hitler committed suicide and Germany was defeated and occupied by the Allies at the close of World War II.

The history of National Socialism after 1934 can be divided into two periods of about equal length. Between 1934 and 1939 the party established full control of all phases of life in Germany. With many Germans weary of party conflicts, economic and political instability, and the disorderly freedom that characterized the last years of the Weimar Republic (1919–33), Hitler and his movement gained the support and even the enthusiasm of a majority of the German population. In particular, the public welcomed the strong, decisive, and apparently effective government provided by the Nazis. Germany's endless ranks of unemployed rapidly dwindled as the jobless were put to work in extensive public-works projects and in rapidly multiplying armaments factories. Germans were swept up in this orderly, intensely purposeful mass movement bent on restoring their country to its dignity, pride, and grandeur, as well as to dominance on the European stage. Economic recovery from the effects of the Great

Depression and the forceful assertion of German nationalism were key factors in National Socialism's appeal to the German population. Further, Hitler's continuous string of diplomatic successes and foreign conquests from 1934 through the early years of World War II secured the unqualified support of most Germans, including many who had previously opposed him.

Despite its economic and political success, National Socialism maintained its power by coercion and mass manipulation. The Nazi regime disseminated a continual outpouring of propaganda through all cultural and informational media. Its rallies—especially its elaborately staged Nürnberg rallies—its insignia, and its uniformed cadres were designed to impart an aura of omnipotence. The underside of its propaganda machine was its apparatus of terror, with its ubiquitous secret police and concentration camps. It fanned and focused German anti-Semitism to make the Jews a symbol of all that was hated and feared. By means of deceptive rhetoric, the party portrayed the Jews as the enemy of all classes of society.

National Socialism's principal instrument of control was the unification, under Heinrich Himmler and his chief lieutenant, Reinhard Heydrich, of the SS (the uniformed police force of the Nazi Party) and all other police and security organizations. Opposition to the regime was destroyed either by outright terror or, more frequently, by the all-pervading fear of possible repression. Opponents of the regime were branded enemies of the state and of the people, and an elaborate web of informers—often members of the family or intimate friends—imposed utmost caution on all expressions and activities. Justice was no longer recognized as objective but was completely subordinated to the alleged needs and interests of the *Volk*. In addition to the now-debased methods of the normal judicial process, special detention camps were erected.

In these camps the SS exercised supreme authority and introduced a system of sadistic brutality unrivaled in modern times.

Between 1938 and 1945 Hitler's regime attempted to expand and apply the Nazi system to territories outside the German Reich ("Empire"). This endeavour was confined, in 1938, to lands inhabited by German-speaking populations, but in 1939 Germany began to subjugate non-German-speaking nationalities as well. Germany's invasion of Poland on September 1, which initiated World War II, was the logical outcome of Hitler's plans. His first years were spent in preparing the Germans for the approaching struggle for world control and in forging the military and industrial superiority that Germany would require to fulfill its ambitions. With mounting diplomatic and military successes, his aims grew in quick progression. The first was to unite all people of German descent within their historical homeland on the basis of "self-determination." His next step foresaw the creation, through the military conquest of Poland and other Slavic nations to the east, of a *Grosswirtschaftsraum* ("large economic unified space") or a *Lebensraum* ("living space"), which thereby would allow Germany to acquire sufficient territory to become economically self-sufficient and militarily impregnable. There the German master race, or *Herrenvolk*, would rule over a hierarchy of subordinate peoples and organize and exploit them with ruthlessness and efficiency. With the initial successes of the military campaigns of 1939–41, his plan was expanded into a vision of a hemispheric order that would embrace all of Europe, western Asia, Africa, and eventually the entire world.

The extravagant hopes of Nazism came to an end with Germany's defeat in 1945, after nearly six years of war. To a certain extent World War II had repeated the pattern of World War I: great initial German military successes, the forging of a large-scale coalition against Germany as the result of German ambitions and behaviour, and the eventual loss of the war because of German overreaching. National Socialism as a mass movement effectively ended on April 30, 1945, when Hitler committed suicide to avoid falling into the hands of Soviet troops completing the occupation of Berlin.

Out of the ruins of National Socialism arose a Germany that was divided until 1990. Remnants of National Socialist ideology remained in Germany after Hitler's suicide, and a small number of Nazi-oriented political parties and other groups were formed in West Germany from the late 1940s, though some were later banned. In the 1990s gangs of neo-Nazi youths in eastern Germany staged attacks against immigrants, desecrated Jewish cemeteries, and engaged in violent confrontations with leftists and police.

VARIETIES OF FASCISM

Just as Marxists, liberals, and conservatives differed within and between various countries, so too did fascists. In some countries there were rivalries between native fascist movements over personal, tactical, and other differences. Fascist movements also displayed significant differences with respect to their acceptance of racism and particularly anti-Semitism, their identification with Christianity, and their support for Nazi Germany.

ACCEPTANCE OF RACISM

Although not all fascists believed in biological racism, it played a central role in the actions of those who did. Nazism was viciously racist, especially in its attitude toward Jews. The Nazis blamed the Jews for almost everything wrong with Germany, from the Great Depression and the rise of Marxism to the evils of international capitalism and decadence in art. The Holocaust, culminating in the "final solution to the Jewish question," was the immensely cruel outcome of this hatred. During a 12-year period, from 1933 to 1945, some six million Jewish men, women, and children were exterminated by horrific means (gassings, shootings, hangings, and clubbings). In addition, about three million Slavs (whom the Nazis regarded as only slightly less racially inferior than Jews), as well as approximately 400,000 Gypsies (Roma), were murdered.

Croatian fascists preached the racial inferiority of Serbs, and in the late 1930s they became increasingly anti-Semitic. When Germany invaded Yugoslavia in 1941, Ante Pavelić, the Ustaša's leader, became head of a German puppet state, the Independent State of Croatia (NDH), and established a one-party regime. The NDH moved against the more than one million Orthodox Serbs in Croatia, forcing some to convert and expelling or killing others in campaigns of genocide. About 250,000 Serbs in Croatia were eventually liquidated, many in village massacres. The regime also murdered some 40,000 Jews in concentration camps, such as the one at Jasenovac.

Elsewhere in Europe and in South Africa, Latin America, and the United States, fascist movements were racist, and sometimes specifically anti-Semitic, to varying degrees. In Poland members of the Falanga attacked Jews in the streets and created "ghetto benches" for Jewish students in the lecture rooms of the University of Warsaw. In the United States, the Ku Klux Klan and other groups preached the supremacy of the white race. Some fascists in Japan taught that the Japanese were a superior race, and Syrian fascists claimed superiority for their people as well.

In contrast to fascists in most other European countries, Mussolini opposed anti-Semitism during the first 12 years of his rule. After 1933, however, he sometimes allowed anti-Semites within his party to condemn "unpatriotic" Jews in the press. In 1938 the Italian government passed anti-Semitic legislation, and later it abetted the Holocaust. France's largest fascist parties—the Faisceau, the Young Patriots, the Cross of Fire, and the French Popular Party—rejected anti-Semitism, and right-wing Jews were accepted into these movements until at least 1936. Although British fascism was not anti-Semitic at the outset—Mosley's Blackshirts were trained by the British boxer Ted ("Kid") Lewis, who was Jewish—it became so by 1936.

IDENTIFICATION WITH CHRISTIANITY

Most fascist movements portrayed themselves as defenders of Christianity and the traditional Christian family against atheists and amoral humanists. This was true of Catholic fascist movements in Poland, Spain, Portugal, France, Austria, Hungary, Croatia, Bolivia, Argentina, Chile, Brazil, and Romania.

Although fascists in Germany and Italy also posed as protectors of the church, their ideologies contained many elements that conflicted with traditional Christian beliefs, and their policies were sometimes opposed by church leaders. The Nazis criticized the Christian ideals of meekness and guilt on the grounds that they repressed the violent instincts necessary to prevent inferior races from dominating Aryans. Hitler ultimately wished to replace Christianity with a racist form of warrior paganism. In Italy, many practicing Catholics joined the conservative wing of the Fascist Party. In 1931, however, Pope Pius XI denounced fascism's "pagan worship of the State."

SUPPORT FOR GERMANY

Many non-German fascists were just as nationalistic toward their countries as Hitler was toward his. Many Polish fascists fell resisting the German invasion of 1939, and others were later condemned to Nazi concentration camps—as were some Hungarian fascists after 1942. Before he was assassinated in 1934, the Austrian fascist Engelbert Dollfuss sought Mussolini's support to create a fascist government in Austria that would resist the Germans. Before 1940 all French fascists opposed a German invasion of France. Portugal and Spain remained officially neutral or nonbelligerent during World War II, despite the fascist characteristics of their own regimes.

Fascist Italy and fascist Japan were allies of Germany during the war, though Mussolini's autonomy in this alliance was lost when German divisions occupied Italy in 1942 following the landing of American and British troops in North Africa. In the mid-1930s, other non-German fascists, including members of the British Union of Fascists and the German-American Bund, expressed admiration for Hitler's forceful leadership without inviting a German invasion of their countries.

NEOFASCISM

Although fascism was largely discredited in Europe at the end of World War II, fascist-inspired movements were founded in several European countries beginning in the late 1940s. Similar groups were created outside Europe as well. Like their fascist predecessors, the "neofascists" advocated militant nationalism and authoritarian values, opposed the liberal individualism of the Enlightenment, attacked Marxist and other left-wing ideologies, indulged in racist and xenophobic scapegoating, portrayed themselves as protectors of traditional national culture and religion, glorified violence and military heroism, and promoted populist right-wing economic programs.

Despite these similarities, however, neofascism was not simply a revival of fascism. Neofascist parties differed from earlier fascist movements in several significant respects, many of them having to do with the profound political, economic, and social changes that took place in Europe in the first decades after the end of the war. For example, whereas fascists assigned much of the blame for their countries' economic problems to the machinations of communists, liberals, and Jews, neofascists tended to focus on non-European immigrants—such as Turks, Pakistanis, and Algerians—who arrived in increasing numbers beginning in the 1970s. After decades of postwar decolonization, neofascists in Western Europe lost interest in military conquest of other states. Instead, they fought battles for "urban space," which in Germany involved conflicts over government-subsidized housing for immigrants. With increasing urbanization also came a shift in the electoral bases of fascist-oriented movements and a consequent decline in the importance of rural romanticism ("blood and soil") in neofascist political rhetoric. Finally, the gradual acceptance of democratic norms by the vast majority of western Europeans reduced the appeal of authoritarian ideologies and required that neofascist parties make a concerted effort to portray themselves as democratic and "mainstream." Some neofascists even included words like "democratic" and "liberal" in the titles of their movements.

Most neofascists abandoned the outward trappings of earlier fascist parties, such as paramilitary uniforms and Roman salutes, and many explicitly denounced fascist policies or denied that their parties were fascist. Noting this transformation, in 1996 Roger Eatwell cautioned: "Beware of men—and women—wearing smart Italian suits: the colour is now gray, the material is cut to fit the times, but the aim is still power... Fascism is on the move once more, even if its most sophisticated forms have learned to dress to suit the times." Similarly, historian Richard Wolin described these movements as "designer fascism."

As with fascist movements of the interwar period, neofascist movements differed from one another in various respects. The rhetoric of neofascists in Russia and the Balkans, for example, tended to be more openly brutal and militaristic than that of the majority of their Western counterparts. Most neofascist movements in Europe pandered to anti-Semitism, though neofascists in Italy and Spain generally did not. Spanish neofascists also differed from most other neofascists in Europe in that they did not make a major issue of immigration. Portuguese, British, and (for a time) Italian neofascists advocated corporatism (the organization of society into industrial and professional corporations, as practiced under Mussolini), in contrast to French and many other Western neofascists, who promoted free-market capitalism and lower taxes. In the 1990s in Russia and Eastern Europe, neofascist movements were generally more leftist than their counterparts in Western Europe, emphasizing the interests of workers and peasants over those of the urban middle class and calling for "mixed" socialist and capitalist economies.

As mentioned, some of the most notable neofascist movements appeared in European countries where fascist parties had once enjoyed widespread popular support— e.g., Italy, Germany, Austria, France, and Croatia. Yet groups and governments with neofascist tendencies also developed in many other places, particularly in Russia and Serbia, as well as in Argentina, South Africa, Libya, Iraq, and the United States.

ITALY

One of the largest neofascist movements in Western Europe in the 1990s was the Italian Social Movement (Movimento Sociale Italiano [MSI]; renamed the National Alliance [Alleanza Nazionale] in 1994). Founded in 1946, it was led at various times by Giorgio Almirante, Augusto De Marsanich, Arturo Michelini, and Gianfranco Fini. As an official in Mussolini's Italian Social Republic, a puppet state established by the Germans in northern Italy in 1944, Almirante oversaw the regime's propaganda machinery. When the MSI was launched in 1946, Almirante sought to give it a modern image, urging its members to "beware of representing fascism in a grotesque way, or at any rate, in an outdated, anachronistic, and stupidly nostalgic way."

Although Italy's postwar constitution forbade the reorganization of a fascist party, and although Almirante discouraged MSI members from wearing paramilitary black shirts and performing the Roman salute, the propaganda of the MSI echoed a number of themes dear to interwar fascism. First and foremost was its call for the "vital forces" of the nation to resist the communist menace. The MSI contended that not only were communists gaining footholds in the press, in the schools, among intellectuals, and in the trade unions, but they were behind the breakdown of law and order and left-wing terrorism. In the 1950s MSI members entered schools to assault leftists and provoked violent confrontations with socialist and communist activists during election campaigns and strikes.

The MSI extolled the virtues of virility, courage, action, and patriotism. Like the National Fascist Party before it, the MSI also called for a corporatist solution to class conflict and the subordination of individual interests to the

good of the nation. As a defender of "Christian civilization," it supported the Lateran Treaty, which made Roman
Catholicism the state religion of Italy (Catholicism ceased
to be the official religion with the signing of the concordat
of 1984), and the legal prohibition of divorce.

Although at times the MSI cultivated a benign image
and obscured its fascist imagery, at other times it called
attention to its continuity with the fascist past. The practice of avoiding direct references to fascism virtually
disappeared from MSI propaganda in the 1980s and '90s,
as illustrated by the declaration of Fini, elected party secretary in 1987: "Fascism was part of the history of Italy and
the expression of permanent values." At a campaign rally
in October 1992, Alessandra Mussolini, the granddaughter
of Benito Mussolini, stood in the balcony of the 15th-
century Palazzo Venezia (Venice Palace) shouting, "*Grazie
nonno!*" ("Thanks, Granddad!") as thousands of MSI supporters, many wearing black shirts and giving the fascist
salute, marched below her and chanted, "Duce! Duce!"
(Mussolini had been known as Il Duce, "The Leader.")

MSI electoral fortunes varied greatly according to circumstances, ranging from about 2 percent of the vote in
1948 to 13.5 percent in 1994. In local elections in 1993, Fini
and Mussolini were nearly elected mayor of Rome and
mayor of Naples, respectively, and the party won almost a
third of the vote in both cities.

Immediately after these elections, Fini subsumed the
MSI into a new and allegedly more respectable party, the
National Alliance (AN). Officially rejecting "any form of
dictatorship or totalitarianism," he replaced the old slogan of a "third way" between capitalism and communism
with praise for the free market and individual initiative. In
March 1995 the AN won about 14 percent of the vote and
five ministerial posts in a coalition government led by
Silvio Berlusconi. Later that year the AN led an attempt to

repeal the clause in the Italian constitution forbidding the reorganization of a fascist party, but the effort failed. Although Fini described the AN as "postfascist," following the 1994 elections, he declared that Mussolini was the greatest Italian statesman of the 20th century and that fascism before 1938—i.e., before Mussolini formed a military alliance with Hitler—was "mostly good." Fini later disowned his statement about Mussolini and referred to fascism as an "absolute evil."

GERMANY

In 1949 Fritz Dorls and Otto Ernst Remer, a former army general who had helped to crush an attempted military coup against Hitler in July 1944, founded the Socialist Reich Party (Sozialistische Reichspartei; SRP), one of the earliest neofascist parties in Germany. Openly sympathetic to Nazism, the SRP made considerable gains in former Nazi strongholds, and in 1951 it won 11 percent of the vote in regional elections in Lower Saxony. The party was banned as a neo-Nazi organization in 1952.

Among legal neofascist parties in Germany, the most important were the National Democratic Party of Germany (Nationaldemokratische Partei Deutschlands; NPD), founded in 1964 by Waldemar Schütz, a former member of the Nazi Party and the Waffen-SS (the elite military wing of the Nazi Party, which served in combat alongside the regular German army); the German People's Union (Deutsche Volksunion; DVU), founded in 1971; and the Republicans (Die Republikaner; REP), founded in 1983 by another former Waffen-SS member, Franz Schönhuber. Like Almirante in Italy, Schönhuber strove to give his party a more respectable image, and his efforts extended to denying his own previous connection with the Waffen-SS. "I have no Nazi past," he said. "I regard the

National Socialist state as absolutely incompatible with the rule of law. Racism and fascism led us into the most horrible catastrophe in our national history."

Neofascist parties in Germany focused much of their energies on campaigns against immigrants, and they were most successful in areas where immigrant communities were large. Running on slogans such as "Germany for the Germans, the boat is full," the REP gained 7.5 percent of the vote in West German elections in 1989 and more than 7 percent of the vote in elections for the European Parliament in the same year. Neofascist parties also won significant support among disaffected youth in parts of the former East Germany, where there were high levels of unemployment, poor housing, and severe environmental problems in the years immediately following unification.

In 1992–93 gangs of neo-Nazi youth in eastern Germany, most of whom did not belong to political parties, staged attacks on Turkish and other immigrants and desecrated Jewish cemeteries. Public revulsion at the attacks contributed to a temporary dip in the far-right vote in 1993. At the turn of the 21st century, the REP was torn by personal, generational, and tactical divisions, with some members favouring a blatantly pro-Nazi platform and others urging more moderate and mainstream positions.

AUSTRIA

In 1999–2000 a series of electoral successes by the far-right Freedom Party of Austria (Freiheitlichen Partei Österreichs; FPÖ), founded in 1956 and led from 1986 by Jörg Haider, created a storm of controversy and produced widespread protests in Austria and abroad, largely because of perceptions that the leadership of the party, including Haider himself, was sympathetic to Nazism. Haider, whose father had been a leading member of the Austrian Nazi Party before and during World War II, became notorious for his praise of Hitler's employment policies and his remark, made to a group of Austrian veterans of World War II, that the Waffen-SS deserved "honour and respect." Arguing for stricter controls on immigration, he warned against the "over-foreignization" of Austrian society, pointedly borrowing a term—*Überfremdung*—used by Joseph Goebbels, Hitler's minister of propaganda.

Haider became governor of Carinthia, his home province, in March 1999, when the FPÖ won regional elections there with 42 percent of the vote. In general elections in October, the FPÖ narrowly outpolled the conservative Austrian People's Party (Österreichische Volkspartei; ÖVP) with 27 percent of the vote and thereby became the second-largest party in Austria. (The Social-Democratic Party of Austria [Sozialdemokratische Partei Österreichs; SPÖ] finished first, with more than 33 percent.) The prospect that the FPÖ would be included in a new Austrian government prompted a threat by the other member states of the European Union (EU) to suspend all bilateral political contacts with Austria. Despite the warning, the ÖVP, with considerable reluctance, formed a government with the FPÖ in February 2000, granting the party five cabinet ministries (Haider himself was not given a cabinet post).

The new government was greeted by widespread demonstrations, diplomatic protests, and calls for boycotts on travel to Austrian tourist destinations. Facing intense international pressure, Haider resigned his leadership of the FPÖ at the end of February, only three weeks after his party entered the government. His final split with the FPÖ occurred when he announced he was forming a new party, the Alliance for the Future of Austria (Bündnis Zukunft Österreich; BZÖ), in 2005. In 2008 the new party showed strong gains, and Haider seemed poised for a comeback on the national stage. On Oct. 11, 2008, however, he died from injuries sustained in a car accident.

FRANCE

In the 1980s and '90s, neofascism in France was dominated by the National Front (Front National; FN), founded in 1972 by François Duprat and François Brigneau and led beginning later that year by Jean-Marie Le Pen. After 10 years on the margins of French politics, the FN began a period of spectacular growth in 1981. Campaigning on the slogan "France for the French" (as had French fascists in the 1930s) and linking high unemployment and increased crime to the presence of immigrants, the FN increased its support from 1 percent of the vote in 1981 to 14 percent in 1988. In 1984 the FN gained 11 percent of the vote in elections for the European Parliament and thereby became the largest extreme-right group within that body. In municipal elections in 1989 the FN won city council seats in more than one-third of cities exceeding 20,000 inhabitants, and in 1995–97 it gained control of four southern cities—Marignane, Orange, Toulon, and Vitrolles. Le Pen won 15 percent of the vote in presidential elections in 1995, and the FN also took 15 percent in legislative elections in May–June 1997. In areas of its greatest strength—southern and eastern France—the FN won more than 20 percent.

The FN's rapid increase in popularity occurred despite Le Pen's previous association with extreme right-wing causes, his cavalier remarks about the Holocaust (in 1987 he told a television interviewer that the Holocaust was only "a detail of history"), the presence of former fascists in his organization, and other neofascist aspects of his movement.

The FN's popular anti-immigrant themes included the claim that non-French immigrants, especially Muslims, threatened French national identity and culture—a threat that had been compounded, according to the FN, by the huge influx of films, music, and television programs from the United States. The FN also called for a return to traditional values—family, law and order, hard work, and patriotism—and claimed that these values had been eroded by liberal permissiveness and multiculturalism.

Although Le Pen described himself as a "Churchillian democrat," his commitment to political democracy was similar to that of La Rocque in the 1930s and '40s—more tactical than principled. "We must be respectful of legality while it exists," he declared in 1982. Just as La Rocque had admired Mussolini, so Le Pen admired Francisco Franco in Spain and Augusto Pinochet in Chile. Le Pen praised Pinochet's overthrow of socialist president Salvador Allende in 1973, and he declared that the French army should follow Pinochet's example if a similar leftist government were to arise in France.

The FN imposed censorship when it had the power to do so. Mayors of cities governed by the FN removed left-wing journals from municipal libraries, forbade librarians to order "internationalist" books, and required the purchase of materials supporting the FN's views. The mayor of Toulon, Jean-Marie Le Chevallier, canceled the award of a literary prize to a Jewish writer and tried to shut down a well-known performance festival in the city because of its leftist political orientation.

By the 1990s the FN had acquired a broad-based and diverse following, including small businessmen and self-employed artisans, unemployed white-collar and blue-collar workers, socially conservative Catholics, and young people. In 1998 Le Pen's associate Bruno Mégret split from the FN to form a new party, the National Movement (Mouvement National; MN), taking with him most of the FN's departmental secretaries and city councillors. Nevertheless, Le Pen's style and policies continued to attract significant support, and he served as an elected member of the European Parliament well into the 21st century. He also ran several times for the French presidency; in 1988 and 1995 he won some 15 percent of the vote. In 2002 Le Pen defeated Prime Minister Lionel Jospin in the first round of the presidential election, winning 18 percent. However, with nearly the entire French political establishment—including the Socialist Party and the French Communist Party—endorsing conservative president Jacques Chirac, he was easily defeated in the second round.

RUSSIA

After the end of World War II, few Russians needed to be reminded of the evils of German fascism. Nevertheless, several fascist groups emerged in Russia after the breakup of the Soviet Union in 1991. Resentment over the loss of the Soviet empire, concern for the fate of ethnic Russians in the successor states, bad economic conditions, the breakdown of law and order, the desire for a strong leader, and the fact that democratic institutions were not deeply rooted in Russia all combined to make fascist ideas appealing to some segments of the Russian population.

Some Russian fascists attempted to revive the reactionary ideology of the Black Hundreds, a loose association of extreme right-wing organizations formed in Russia during the early years of the 20th century. Black Hundred ideology was highly nationalistic, anticosmopolitan, anti-Semitic, anti-Masonic, anti-Western, antidemocratic, antiegalitarian, antiliberal, and anti-"decadence." The

Black Hundreds were strong supporters of the Russian Orthodox church, the army, and authoritarian government (favouring either monarchy or military dictatorship), and they indulged in conspiracy theories that blamed most of Russia's troubles on Jews and Freemasons, a secret fraternal order.

In the 1980s the leading group espousing Black Hundred ideology was Pamyat ("Memory"), whose main spokesman after 1984 was Dmitry Vasiliev. During the communist era Pamyat worked for the restoration of churches and national monuments in Moscow, and Vasiliev generally supported the Communist Party and praised Lenin, Stalin, and the KGB for defending national traditions. After 1989, however, Vasiliev increasingly supported the Russian Orthodox church and began to advocate monarchism. Pamyat writers denounced communists as "godless," "cosmopolitan," and "antipatriotic," and they criticized the neglect of national traditions, anti-Russian sentiment in the Baltic countries, the moral decline of youth, increased crime, the weakening of the family, and alcoholism. Although Pamyat had a near monopoly on the extreme right in 1987–88, by 1991 it had been overtaken by rival movements.

One of these movements was the Liberal-Democratic Party of Russia (Liberalno-Demokraticheskaya Partiya Rossi; LDPR), led by Vladimir Zhirinovsky. Founded in 1990, the party grew rapidly, and in presidential elections in 1991 Zhirinovsky won almost 8 percent of the vote, which placed him third after Boris Yeltsin and Nicolay Ryzhkov. In parliamentary elections in 1993, the LDPR gained nearly 23 percent of the vote, more than the Russian Communist Party (12.4 percent) did. However, by 1996 Zhirinovsky's support had declined precipitously, and in presidential elections that year he managed to win only 6 percent of the vote.

Most neofascists denied that they were "fascists," and Zhirinovsky was no exception. On various occasions he asserted his adherence to democratic values, the rights of man, a multiparty system, and the rule of law. However, in 1991 he declared: "I say quite plainly, when I come to power there will be a dictatorship. Russia needs a dictator now." He added: "I'll be ruthless. I will close down the newspapers one after another. I may have to shoot 100,000 people, but the other 300 million will live peacefully. You want to call it Russian fascism, fine."

Zhirinovsky also indulged in racism and anti-Semitism, even though his own father was apparently Jewish and he himself had been active in a Russian Jewish group in 1989. When asked about his parents in 1993, he replied, "My mother was Russian, my father a lawyer"—a comment that became a popular joke in Russia about people who try to conceal their origins. Zhirinovsky also claimed that the Russian Revolution of 1917 was mainly the work of "baptized Jews" and that the state of Israel and Mossad, the Israeli intelligence agency, were engaged in anti-Russian conspiracies. Although he sometimes complained that the United States was becoming a nonwhite society, he declared that only an alliance between the United States, Germany, and Russia could "preserve the white race on the European and American continents."

The Russian National Unity (Russkoe Natsionalnoe Edinstvo; RNE), a paramilitary organization founded in 1990 by Aleksandr Barkashov, claimed to have an extensive network of local branches, but its electoral support was significantly less than that of the LDPR. Barkashov, a former commando in the Russian army, touted his Blackshirts as a reserve force for the Russian army and the Ministry of Internal Affairs. He blamed many of Russia's economic problems on Jews, claimed that two RNE Blackshirts had been victims of Jewish ritual murder, insisted that only a "few hundred" Jews had perished in German concentration camps, and said that the Holocaust was a "diversion" created to conceal a Jewish-inspired genocide of 100 million Russians. The RNE's symbol was a left-pointed swastika together with a four-pointed star. The RNE emphasized the "primary importance" of Russian blood, accused "internationalists-communists" of undermining the "genetic purity" of the nation with a program of racial mixture, and called for a rebirth of "Russian-Aryan traditions." Although Barkashov denied that he was a fascist, he admired Hitler enormously.

Barkashov insisted in 1994 that he would come to power by "absolutely legal means." Nevertheless, the RNE's program stated that conventional democracy was inefficient, and it called for an "ethnic democracy" in which the right to vote would be restricted to those who had demonstrated their loyalty to the nation. A major plank in the RNE's platform was its defense of ethnic Russians outside Russia proper. Barkashov denounced the oppression of ethnic Russians in Estonia and Latvia and later supported Russian military intervention in Chechnya to protect Russian citizens "from force and arbitrary rule," calling for harsh measures—ranging from temporary internment to deportation—against the 80,000 Chechen "criminals" who lived in Russia.

SERBIA

Following the collapse of communism in the former Yugoslavia and the secession of Croatia and Bosnia and Herzegovina from the Yugoslav federation in 1991–92, units of the Yugoslav army and Serbian paramilitary forces engaged in campaigns of "ethnic cleansing" aimed at driving out non-Serb majorities in northeastern Croatia and parts of northern and eastern Bosnia and establishing nominally independent Serb republics in the vacated territories. The attacks, which were compared in their ferocity and cruelty to the Nazi invasions of eastern Europe and Russia, involved mass executions (mostly of men and boys), forced marches, torture, starvation, and systematic rape. These tactics were aimed at creating irreversible ethnic hatreds that would permanently prevent the development of multiethnic states in the areas under attack. In 1998–99 similar tactics were employed in Kosovo, then a province of Serbia in which 90 percent of the population was ethnically Albanian and predominantly Muslim.

Organized and directed by the regime of Serbian Pres. Slobodan Milošević, leader of the Socialist Party of Serbia (Socijalisticka Partija Srbije; SPS), the campaigns in Croatia and Bosnia were undertaken in part to bolster Milošević's image as a staunch nationalist and to consolidate his power at the expense of Vojislav Seselj's Serbian Radical Party (Srpska Radikalna Stranka; SRS), then the largest neofascist party in Serbia. Although the SPS had won 65 percent of the vote in elections to the Serbian assembly in 1990, deteriorating economic conditions and perceived threats to Serbian enclaves in Croatia and Bosnia (where Serbs constituted 12 percent and 31 percent of the population, respectively) resulted in a significant loss of support for Milošević's SPS and a corresponding growth in the SRS and other extreme nationalist and neofascist groups. In 1992 the SPS won only 40 percent of the vote and was forced to enter into an unofficial "red-brown" alliance with the SRS, which finished with 20 percent. To counter the growing threat from the right, Milošević gradually adopted many of the neofascists' policies, including support for the creation of a "Greater Serbia" that would incorporate Montenegro, Macedonia, and large areas of Croatia and Bosnia.

In May 1993, after a year of severe economic hardship caused by UN-imposed sanctions, Milošević accepted an international agreement for the division of Bosnia into 10 ethnic cantons. The Vance-Owen plan (named after its principal negotiators, former U.S. secretary of state Cyrus Vance and former British foreign minister David Owen) was rejected by the self-styled parliament of the Bosnian Serbs and condemned by Seselj, who attacked Milošević for "selling out" and called for a parliamentary vote of no confidence. Milošević responded by launching an "antifascist" campaign against Seselj and the SRS, charging Seselj with profiteering and committing war crimes in Croatia and Bosnia and arresting several members of the SRS's paramilitary wing, the "Chetniks" (named after the Serbian nationalist guerrilla movement that battled the Nazis and later the communist Partisans in Yugoslavia during World War II). Milošević subsequently attempted to weaken nationalist support for the SRS by allying himself with the notorious paramilitary leader Zeljko Raznjatovic (popularly known by his nom de guerre, Arkan) and his new Serbian Unity Party (Srpska Partja Jedinstva; SJP). In elections in December 1993, the SPS increased its representation in the Serbian assembly at the expense of the SRS, taking 49 percent of the vote, compared with the SRS's 14 percent.

In early 1998 Serbian military and police forces began attacks in Kosovo on alleged strongholds of the Kosovo Liberation Army (KLA), an ethnically Albanian guerrilla movement fighting to end Serbian control of the province. The Serbs' harsh repression of the Albanian civilian population drew international condemnation and resulted in renewed UN sanctions on Yugoslavia. On March 24, 1999, after a Serbian delegation at peace talks in Rambouillet, France, rejected an accord that had been signed by representatives of Kosovar Albanians and the KLA, NATO began an intensive bombing campaign directed at Yugoslav military targets and later also at civilian infrastructure and government buildings in Serbia. In response, Serbian security forces in Kosovo conducted a massive campaign of ethnic cleansing, including large-scale massacres of civilians, and eventually forced more than 850,000 Kosovars to flee to border areas in Albania, Macedonia, and Montenegro. The bombing came to an end in early June after Milošević agreed to the withdrawal of Serbian forces from Kosovo, the deployment of NATO peacekeeping troops, and the repatriation of Albanian refugees. In the meantime, the UN International Criminal Tribunal at The Hague indicted Milošević and four top officials of his government for crimes against humanity. The trial began in February 2002 but experienced numerous delays because of the poor health of Milošević, who was found dead in his prison cell in 2006.

CROATIA

In the early 1990s the main spokesman for neofascism in Croatia was Dobroslav Paraga, founder in 1990 of the Croatian Party of Rights (Hrvatska Stranka Prava; HSP). A former seminary student and dissident under the communist regime in Croatia in the 1980s, Paraga believed that Serbia was a mortal danger to Croatian national survival, and he called for the creation of a "Greater Croatia" that would include much of Serbia and all of Bosnia and Herzegovina. He insisted that war with Serbia was inevitable and had to end in the "total defeat" of the enemy with "nothing left of Serbia except Belgrade and its surroundings."

Paraga's followers openly endorsed the pro-Nazi Ustaša regime, which had carried out large-scale exterminations of Serbs, Jews, and Gypsies (Roma) in Croatia during World War II. Reflecting the enthusiasm for Ustaša symbolism that swept Croatia after the outbreak of the Bosnian war in 1991, HSP members often wore caps marked with a U and donned black shirts in imitation of the former Ustaša paramilitary; they also gave fascist salutes and repeated the old Ustaša slogan "Ready for the homeland." The HSP's paramilitary wing, the Croatian Defense Association (Hrvatska Obrambeni Savez; HOS), was heavily involved in fighting against Serbia.

In elections in 1992, the HSP received only about 7 percent of the parliamentary vote and Paraga only 5 percent of the presidential vote. The party's electoral impact was reduced by its insistence on continuing the unpopular war against Serbia and by Paraga's refusal to join forces with other neofascist parties in Croatia, such as the Croatian Party of Pure Rights (Hrvastska Ci sta Stranka Prava; HCSP), the Croatian Democratic Party (Hrvatgska Demokratska Stranka Prava; HDSZP), and the National Democratic League (Nacionalna Demokratska Liga; NDL).

Like the SRS in Serbia, the HSP was opposed by a larger ruling party—the Croatian Democratic Union (Hrvatska Demokratska Zajednica; HDZ), founded in 1989 by Franjo Tudjman. The HDZ eventually adopted neofascist policies in order to undercut the appeal of its extreme nationalist and neofascist rivals. Like the HSP, the Tudjman regime employed many Ustaša symbols, and it even rehabilitated many Ustaša leaders and nominated some of them to government posts. The HDZ incorporated into its ranks the Croatian National Committee, a group founded by Ranimir Jelic, a close associate of Ante Pavelić, the founder of the original Ustaša. In 1995 Tudjman's troops undertook extensive ethnic cleansing campaigns in western Slavonia and the historically Serbian region of Krajina, forcing the evacuation of some

150,000 Croatian Serbs to Serbia and Serb-held areas of Bosnia.

Beginning in 1991, Tudjman took various repressive measures against the HSP, including the arrest of Paraga on charges of having formed an illegal paramilitary group and the formal incorporation of the HOS into the regular Croatian army. In 1993 the government launched a largely successful "antifascist" campaign aimed at curbing the influence of HSP supporters in the military. In the same year, Paraga was brought to trial for having allegedly plotted a coup, though he was later acquitted.

OUTSIDE EUROPE

The largest neofascist movements outside Europe after World War II emerged in Latin America, South Africa, and the Middle East. Juan Perón, who ruled Argentina as the legally elected president in 1946–55 and again in 1973–74, served as a military attaché to Italy in the 1930s and was a great admirer of Mussolini. Perón won the support of poor industrial workers (the *descamisados*, or "shirtless ones") as well as many wealthy businessmen by promoting higher wages and benefits as well as industrial development. He also had the backing of many middle-class nationalists and a large portion of the army officer corps. His charismatic wife, Eva Perón, popularly known as Evita, attracted a cult following for her charitable activities and her storybook rise from "rags to riches." However, owing to inflation, corruption, and Perón's conflicts with the formerly dominant landowning class and the Catholic church, the military eventually turned against him, and he was ousted in a coup in 1955. After a long exile in Spain, Perón returned to Argentina in 1973 and, in a special election in October of that year, was elected president with his second wife, Isabel Perón, as vice president. Succeeding her husband after his death in 1974, Isabel Perón could not prevent a split between rightist and leftist factions of the Peronist coalition. Having lost all popular support, Isabel Perón was overthrown in a military coup in March 1976.

The most significant neofascist group in South Africa after 1945 was the South African Gentile National Socialist Movement, which changed its name to the White Workers Party in 1949. Although the party did not succeed in creating a mass movement, it did encourage the adoption of policies of white supremacy and apartheid by the dominant National Party of South Africa.

In the Middle East the regimes of Muammar al-Qaddafi in Libya and Ṣaddām Ḥussein in Iraq were neofascist in several respects. A charismatic dictator and devout Muslim, Qaddafi came to power in 1969 in a military coup that overthrew King Idris. He advocated what he called "true democracy," characterized by state ownership of key sectors of the economy, strict adherence to Islamic law, and the mobilization of mass support through "people's congresses," government-controlled labour unions, and other organizations. In Iraq, Ḥussein's Ba'th movement defended an extremely nationalistic brand of socialism that rejected Western liberalism as well as "materialistic communism." Ḥussein's regime, which came to power in a coup in 1968, was essentially a personal dictatorship.

In the 1990s a number of racist "militia" groups were active in the United States, and many of them made use of paramilitary uniforms and neo-Nazi symbolism. However, they lacked the popular support necessary to launch a strong political movement or to engage in electoral politics on their own.

Chapter 7: Democratic Movements of the 20th and 21st Centuries

D uring the 20th century, the number of countries possessing the basic political institutions of representative democracy increased significantly. At the beginning of the 21st century, independent observers agreed that more than one-third of the world's nominally independent countries possessed democratic institutions comparable to those of the English-speaking countries and the older democracies of continental Europe. In an additional one-sixth of the world's countries, these institutions, though somewhat defective, nevertheless provided historically high levels of democratic government. Altogether, these democratic and near-democratic countries contained nearly half the world's population. What accounted for this rapid expansion of democratic institutions?

THE SPREAD OF DEMOCRACY IN THE 20TH CENTURY

A significant part of the explanation is that all the main alternatives to democracy—whether of ancient or of modern origins—suffered political, economic, diplomatic, and military failures that greatly lessened their appeal. With the victory of the Allies in World War I (1914–18), the ancient systems of monarchy, aristocracy, and oligarchy ceased to be legitimate. Following the military defeat of Italy and Germany in World War II

(1939–45), the newer alternative of fascism was likewise discredited, as was Soviet-style communism after the economic and political collapse of the Soviet Union in 1990–91. Similar failures contributed to the gradual disappearance of military dictatorships in Latin America in the 1980s and '90s.

Accompanying these ideological and institutional changes were transformations in economic institutions. Highly centralized economies under state control had enabled political leaders to use their ready access to economic resources to reward their allies and punish their critics. As these systems were displaced by more decentralized market economies, the power and influence of top government officials declined. In addition, some of the conditions that were essential to the successful functioning of market economies also contributed to the development of democracy: ready access to reliable information, relatively high levels of education, ease of personal movement, and the rule of law. As market economies expanded and as middle classes grew larger and more influential, popular support for such conditions increased, often accompanied by demands for further democratization.

The development of market economies contributed to the spread of democracy in other ways as well. As the economic well-being of large segments of the world's population gradually improved, so too did the likelihood that newly established democratic institutions would survive and flourish. In general, citizens in democratic countries with persistent poverty are more susceptible to the appeals of antidemocratic demagogues who promise simple and immediate solutions to their country's economic problems. Accordingly, widespread economic prosperity in a country greatly increases the chances that democratic government will succeed, whereas widespread poverty greatly increases the chances that it will fail.

During the 20th century, democracy continued to exist in some countries despite periods of acute diplomatic, military, economic, or political crisis, such as occurred during the early years of the Great Depression. The survival of democratic institutions in these countries is attributable in part to the existence in their societies of a culture of widely shared democratic beliefs and values. Such attitudes are acquired early in life from older generations, thus becoming embedded in people's views of themselves, their country, and the world. In countries where democratic culture is weak or absent, as was the case in the Weimar Republic of Germany in the years following World War I, democracy is much more vulnerable, and periods of crisis are more likely to lead to a reversion to a nondemocratic regime.

LIBERALIZATION AND STRUGGLE IN COMMUNIST COUNTRIES

Following World War II, the Soviet Union maintained a strong influence over the governments of fellow communist countries in Eastern Europe. Popular discontent with the communist system manifested itself on a few occasions, such as during the Hungarian Revolution of 1956 and the Prague Spring of 1968, a brief period of liberalization in Czechoslovakia; some dissidents within the Soviet Union also made their voices heard. However, widespread, sustained protest did not occur until the 1980s. During that time, pro-democracy protests also occurred in communist-ruled China.

In the late 1980s signs of unmistakable and irreversible liberalization in the Soviet bloc began to appear in the form of popular manifestations in Eastern Europe, which the Soviet government seemed willing to tolerate and even, to some extent, encourage. Czechoslovaks demonstrated against their communist regime on the anniversary of the 1968 Soviet invasion. In Poland, the Solidarity union demanded democratic reforms. The Sejm (parliament) legalized and vowed to return the property of the Roman Catholic church, and the government of Gen. Wojciech Witold Jaruzelski approved partially free elections to be held on June 4, 1989, the first such in over 40 years. Solidarity initially won 160 of the 161 available seats and then took the remaining seat in a runoff election. On May 2 of that year Hungary dismantled barriers on its border with Austria—the first real breach in the so-called Iron Curtain between Eastern and Western Europe.

Soviet leader Mikhail Gorbachev was less tolerant of protests and separatist tendencies in the Soviet Union itself; for instance, he ordered soldiers to disperse 15,000 Georgians demanding independence. He moved ahead, however, with reforms that loosened the Communist Party's grip on power in the Soviet Union, even as his own authority was increased through various laws granting him emergency powers. In March 1989, protesters in Moscow supported the parliamentary candidacy of the dissident communist Boris Yeltsin, who charged Gorbachev with not moving fast enough toward democracy and a market economy. On the 26th of that month, in the first relatively free elections ever held in the Soviet Union, for 1,500 of the 2,250 seats in the new Congress of People's Deputies, various non-communists and ethnic representatives emerged triumphant over Communist Party candidates. Three days later Gorbachev told the Hungarian premier that he opposed foreign intervention in the internal affairs of Warsaw Pact states (i.e., countries within the Soviet bloc)—a loud hint that he did not intend to enforce the Brezhnev Doctrine, which was the assertion of the Soviets' right to intervene to protect communist governments wherever they might be threatened.

In late spring 1989 U.S. Pres. George H.W. Bush spoke out on his hopes for East–West relations in a series of speeches and quietly approved the subsidized sale of 1,500,000 tons of wheat to the Soviets. In a Moscow meeting with Secretary of State James Baker, Gorbachev not only endorsed the resumption of Strategic Arms Reduction Talks (START), with the goal of deep cuts in strategic arsenals, but also stated that he would unilaterally withdraw 500 warheads from Eastern Europe and accept NATO's request for asymmetrical reductions in conventional armaments. In response, Bush announced that the time had come "to move beyond containment" and to "seek the integration of the Soviet Union into the community of nations." Western European leaders were even more eager to end the Cold War between the United States and the Soviet Union and their respective allies. West German chancellor Helmut Kohl and Gorbachev agreed in June to support self-determination and arms reductions and to build a "common European home."

For Gorbachev the policies of glasnost ("openness"), free elections, and warm relations with Western leaders were a calculated risk born of the Soviet Union's severe economic crisis and need for Western help. For other communist regimes, however, Moscow's "new thinking" was an unalloyed disaster. The governments of Eastern Europe owed their existence to the myth of the "world proletarian revolution" and their survival to police-state controls backed by the threat of Soviet military power. Now, however, the Soviet leader himself had renounced the right of intervention, and he urged Eastern European communist parties to imitate his policies of perestroika ("restructuring") and glasnost. Eastern European bosses like Erich Honecker of East Germany and Miloš Jakeš of

Czechoslovakia quietly made common cause with hard-liners in Moscow.

Chinese leaders were in a different position. Ever since the late 1950s the Chinese Communist Party had regularly and officially denounced the Soviets as revisionists — Marxist heretics — and Gorbachev's deeds and words only proved their rectitude. Even so, since the death of Mao Zedong the Chinese leadership had itself adopted limited reforms under the banner of the Four Modernizations (of agriculture, industry, science and technology, and defense) and had permitted a modicum of highly successful free enterprise while retaining a monopoly of political power. When Hu Yaobang, a former leader, died on April 15, 1989, however, tens of thousands of students and other protesters began to gather in Chinese cities to demand democratic reforms. Within a week 100,000 people filled Tiananmen Square in Beijing and refused to disperse despite strong warnings. The 70th anniversary of the May Fourth Movement, the first student movement in modern Chinese history, propelled the protests, as did Gorbachev's own arrival for the first Sino-Soviet summit in 30 years. By May 20 the situation was completely out of control: more than 1,000,000 demonstrators occupied large sections of Beijing, and on the 29th students erected a statue called the "Goddess of Democracy" in Tiananmen Square.

Behind the scenes a furious power struggle ensued between party chiefs advocating accommodation and those calling for the use of force; it remained uncertain whether the Chinese People's Liberation Army could be trusted to act against the demonstration. Finally, military units from distant provinces were called in to move against the crowds; they did so on June 3–4, 1989, killing hundreds of protesters. Thousands more were arrested in the days that followed.

*The iconic image of tanks rolling into China's Tiananmen Square has come
to represent the lengths some countries will go to in order to quash burgeon-
ing pro-democracy movements.* Manuel Ceneta/AFP/Getty Images

The suppression of the democratic movement in
China conditioned the thinking of Eastern European
officials and protesters alike for months. Taking heart
from Gorbachev's reformism, citizens hoped that the
time had finally come when they might expand their narrow political options. They moved cautiously, however,
not wholly trusting that the Soviet Union would stand
aside and fearing that at any moment their local state
security police would opt for a "Tiananmen solution."
Nonetheless, in July 1989, at the annual Warsaw Pact
meeting, Gorbachev called on each member state to pursue "independent solutions [to] national problems" and
said that there were "no universal models of Socialism."
At the same time Bush toured Poland and Hungary, prais-
ing their steps toward democracy and offering aid, but
saying and doing nothing that would embarrass the Soviets

or take strategic advantage of their difficulties. So it was that for the first time both superpower leaders indicated with increasing clarity that they intended to stand aside and allow events in Eastern Europe to take their course independent of Cold War considerations. Gorbachev had indeed repealed the Brezhnev Doctrine, and Bush had done nothing to impel him to reimpose it.

The results were almost immediate. In August a trickle, then a flood of would-be émigrés from East Germany tried the escape route open through Hungary to Austria and West Germany. In the same month the chairman of the Soviet Central Committee admitted the existence of the secret protocols in the German-Soviet Nonaggression Pact (1939) under which Soviet leader Joseph Stalin had annexed Latvia, Lithuania, and Estonia. On the 50th anniversary of the pact, Aug. 23, 1989, an estimated 1,000,000 people in the Baltic states formed a human chain linking their capitals to denounce the annexation as illegal and to demand self-determination. In September the Hungarian government suspended its effort to stave off the flight of East Germans, and by the end of the month more than 30,000 had escaped to the West. Demonstrations for democracy began in East Germany itself in late September, spreading from Leipzig to Dresden and other cities. On October 6–7 Gorbachev, visiting in honour of the German Democratic Republic's 40th anniversary, urged East Germany to adopt Soviet-style reforms and said that its policy would be made in Berlin, not Moscow.

Against this background of massive and spreading popular defiance of communist regimes, Western governments maintained a prudent silence about the internal affairs of Soviet-bloc states, while sending clear signals to Moscow of the potential benefits of continued liberalization. When Boris Yeltsin, Gorbachev's nemesis, visited the United States in September, the administration kept a

discreet distance. Later that month Soviet foreign minister Eduard Shevardnadze held extensive and private talks
with U.S. secretary of state James Baker; he dropped once
and for all the Soviet demand that the American Strategic
Defense Initiative (SDI; "Star Wars") program be included
in the START negotiations. In the first week of October
the European Community, West Germany, and then (at
the insistence of Congress) the United States offered
emergency aid totalling $2 billion to the democratizing
Polish government. The chairman of the U.S. Federal
Reserve Board went to Moscow to advise the Soviets on
how they, too, might make the transition to a market
economy, and Secretary Baker proclaimed, "We want perestroika to succeed." A month later Gorbachev gave the
first indication of the limits to reform, warning that
Western efforts to "export capitalism" or "interfere with
east European politics would be a great mistake." By that
time, however, the collapse of communism in the satellite
states, at least, was irreversible.

Hungary became the second (after Poland) to seize its
independence when the National Assembly, in October
1989, amended its constitution to abolish the Hungarian
Socialist Workers' Party's "leading role" in society,
legalize non-communist political parties, and change the
name of the country from the "People's Republic" to
simply the "Republic of Hungary." East Germany, one
of the most repressive of all Soviet-bloc states, was next.
By late October crowds numbering more than 300,000
rose up in Leipzig and Dresden to demand the ouster
of the communist regime. On November 1 the East
German cabinet bowed before the unrelenting, nonviolent pressure of its people by reopening its border
with Czechoslovakia. On November 3 the ministers in
charge of security and the police resigned. The next day
a reported 1,000,000 demonstrators jammed the streets

of East Berlin to demand democracy, prompting the res-
ignations of the rest of the cabinet.

After 50,000 more people had fled the country in the
ensuing week, the East German government threw in the
towel. On November 9 it announced that exit visas would
be granted immediately to all citizens wishing to "visit the
West" and that all border points were now open. At first,
citizens did not dare believe—hundreds of East Germans
had lost their lives trying to escape after the Berlin Wall
went up in August 1961—but when some did, the news
flowed like electricity that the Berlin Wall had fallen. A
week later the dreaded Stasis, or state security police, were
disbanded. By December 1 the East German Volkskammer
(parliament) renounced the Communist Socialist Unity
Party's "leading role" in society and began to expose the
corruption and brutality that had characterized the
Honecker regime. A new coalition government took control and planned free national elections for May 1990.

Czechoslovaks were the fourth people to carry out a
nonviolent revolution, though at first frustrated by the
hard-line regime's continued will to repress. A demonstration on Nov. 17, 1989, in Wenceslas Square in Prague was
broken up by force. The Czechoslovaks, emboldened by
events in East Germany and the absence of a Soviet reaction, turned out in ever larger numbers, however,
demanding free elections and then cheering the rehabilitated hero of the 1968 Prague Spring, Alexander Dubček.
The entire cabinet resigned, and the Communist Central
Committee promised a special congress to discuss the
party's future. The dissident liberal playwright Václav
Havel denounced the shake-up as a trick, crowds of
800,000 turned out to demand democratic elections,
and Czechoslovak workers declared a two-hour general
strike as proof of their solidarity. The government caved
in, abandoning the Communist Party's "leading role" on

November 29, opening the border with Austria on the 30th, and announcing a new coalition cabinet on December 8. Pres. Gustav Husák resigned on the 10th and free elections were scheduled for the 28th. By the end of the year Havel was president of Czechoslovakia and Dubček was parliamentary chairman.

The fifth and sixth satellite peoples to break out of the 45-year communist lockstep were the Bulgarians and Romanians. The former had an easy time of it after the Communist Party secretary and president, Todor Zhivkov, resigned on Nov. 10, 1989. Within a month crowds in Sofia called for democratization, and the Central Committee leader voluntarily surrendered the party's "leading role." Romania, however, suffered a bloodbath. There the Communist dictator Nicolae Ceauşescu had built a ferocious personal tyranny defended by ubiquitous and brutal security forces. He intended to ride out the anticommunist wave in Eastern Europe and preserve his rule. Thus, when crowds of Romanian citizens demonstrated for democracy in imitation of events elsewhere, the government denounced them as "fascist reactionaries" and ordered its security forces to shoot to kill. Courageous crowds continued to rally and regular army units joined the rebellion, and, when the Soviets indicated their opposition to Ceauşescu, civil war broke out. On Dec. 22, 1989, popular forces captured Ceauşescu while he attempted to flee, tried him on several charges, including genocide, and executed him on the 25th. An interim National Salvation Front Council took over and announced elections for May 1990. By the end of the year the Czechoslovaks and Hungarians had already concluded agreements with Moscow providing for the rapid withdrawal of Soviet military forces from their countries.

Throughout the Cold War, protests against repressive communist regimes drew widespread attention, especially in the West. In particular the events in Hungary,

HUNGARIAN REVOLUTION

The Hungarian Revolution of 1956 was a popular uprising in Hungary following a speech by Soviet leader Nikita Khrushchev in which he attacked the period of Joseph Stalin's rule. Encouraged by the new freedom of debate and criticism, a rising tide of unrest and discontent in Hungary broke out into active fighting in October 1956. Rebels won the first phase of the revolution, and Imre Nagy became premier, agreeing to establish a multiparty system. On Nov. 1, 1956, he declared Hungarian neutrality and appealed to the UN. Western powers failed to respond, and on November 4 the Soviet Union invaded Hungary to stop the revolution. Nevertheless, Stalinist-type domination and exploitation did not return, and Hungary thereafter experienced a slow evolution toward some internal autonomy.

Czechoslovakia, Poland, and Germany captured the interest of many international observers, as did the actions of Soviet dissidents Andrey Sakharov and Yelena Bonner.

SOVIET DISSIDENTS: ANDREY SAKHAROV AND YELENA BONNER

Andrey Dmitriyevich Sakharov (1921–89) was a Soviet nuclear theoretical physicist who became an outspoken advocate of human rights, civil liberties, and reform in the Soviet Union as well as rapprochement with noncommunist nations. In the late 1950s Sakharov became concerned about the consequences of nuclear testing in the atmosphere, forseeing an eventual increased global death toll over time. After years of attempts at private persuasion, in 1961 Sakharov went on record against Soviet premier

Nikita Khrushchev's plan for an atmospheric test of a 100-megaton thermonuclear bomb, fearing the hazards of widespread radioactive fallout. The bomb was tested at approximately half yield (58 megatons) on Oct. 30, 1961. Through these efforts, Sakharov began to adopt strong moral positions about the social responsibilities of scientists.

In 1964 Sakharov successfully mobilized opposition to the spurious doctrines of the still-powerful Stalin-era biologist Trofim D. Lysenko. In May 1968 Sakharov finished his essay *Reflections on Progress, Peaceful Coexistence, and Intellectual Freedom*, which first circulated as typewritten copies (*samizdat*) before being published in the West in *The New York Times* and elsewhere beginning in July. Sakharov warned of grave perils threatening the human race, called for nuclear arms reductions, predicted and endorsed the eventual convergence of communist and capitalist systems in a form of democratic socialism, and criticized the increasing repression of Soviet dissidents. From this point until his death, he became more politically active in support of the human rights movement and other causes. As a consequence of his social activism, he was banned from pursuing further military work.

In 1975 Sakharov was awarded the Nobel Prize for Peace. The Soviet government reacted with extreme irritation and prevented Sakharov from leaving the country to attend the Nobel ceremony in Oslo, Norway. Sakharov's Nobel lecture, "Peace, Progress, and Human Rights," was delivered instead by Yelena G. Bonner, a human rights activist whom he had married in 1972. Sakharov and Bonner continued to speak out against Soviet political repression at home and hostile relations abroad, for which Sakharov was isolated and became the target of official censure and harassment. In January 1980 the Soviet government stripped him of his honours and exiled him to the closed city of Gorky (now Nizhny Novgorod) to silence him following his open denunciation of the Soviet invasion of Afghanistan and his call for a worldwide boycott of the coming Olympic Games in Moscow. In 1984 Bonner was convicted of anti-Soviet activities and was likewise confined to Gorky.

In 1985 Sakharov undertook a six-month hunger strike, eventually forcing the new Soviet leader Mikhail Gorbachev to grant Bonner permission to leave the country to have a heart bypass operation in the United States. During her six-month absence, she also met with Western leaders and others to focus concern on her husband's causes, and she wrote a book about their plight, titled *Alone Together* (1986). Several months after she rejoined her husband, Gorbachev released Sakharov and Bonner from their exile, and in December 1986 they returned to Moscow and to a new Russia.

The final three years of Sakharov's life were filled with meetings with world leaders, press interviews, travel abroad, renewed contacts with his scientific colleagues, and the writing of his memoirs. In March 1989 he was elected to the First Congress of People's Deputies, representing the Academy of Sciences. Sakharov had his honours restored, received new ones, and saw many of the causes for which he had fought and suffered become official policy under Gorbachev and his successors.

PRAGUE SPRING

The Prague Spring was a brief period of liberalization in Czechoslovakia under Alexander Dubček in 1968. Soon after he became first secretary of the Czechoslovak Communist Party on Jan. 5, 1968, Dubček granted the press greater freedom of expression; he also rehabilitated victims of political purges during the Joseph Stalin era. In

April he promulgated a sweeping reform program that included autonomy for Slovakia, a revised constitution to guarantee civil rights and liberties, and plans for the democratization of the government. Dubček claimed that he was offering "socialism with a human face." By June many Czechoslovaks were calling for more rapid progress toward real democracy. Although Dubček insisted that he could control the country's transformation, the Soviet Union and other Warsaw Pact countries viewed the developments as tantamount to counterrevolution. On the evening of Aug. 20, Soviet armed forces invaded the country and quickly occupied it. As hard-line communists retook positions of power, the reforms were curtailed, and Dubček was deposed the following April.

VELVET REVOLUTION AND VELVET DIVORCE

In 1989, despite the momentous events in surrounding countries, the Czechoslovak people took little action until late in the fall that year. On November 16, students in Bratislava gathered for a peaceful demonstration; the next day a student march, approved by the authorities, took place in Prague. The Prague march was intended to commemorate the 50th anniversary of the suppression of a student demonstration in German-occupied Prague, but students soon began criticizing the regime, and the police reacted with brutality.

This incident set off a nationwide protest movement—dubbed the Velvet Revolution—that gained particular strength in the country's industrial centres. Pro-democracy demonstrations and strikes took place under the makeshift leadership of the Civic Forum, an opposition group for which the dissident playwright and Charter 77 coauthor Václav Havel served as chief spokesman. In Slovakia a parallel group named Public Against Violence was founded.

Daily mass gatherings culminated in a general strike on November 27, during which the people demanded free elections and an end to one-party rule.

The communist authorities were forced to negotiate with the opposition, and, as a result, a transition government incorporating members of the Civic Forum and Public Against Violence was formed. Husák resigned in December 1989, and Havel was chosen to succeed him as Czechoslovakia's first noncommunist president in more than 40 years. The former party leader Alexander Dubček returned to political life as the new speaker of the Federal Assembly. In June 1990, in the first free elections held in Czechoslovakia since 1946, the Civic Forum and Public Against Violence won decisive majorities; in July Havel was reelected as president.

The new government undertook the multifarious tasks of the transition from communism to democracy, beginning with privatizing businesses, revamping foreign policy, and writing a new constitution. The last Soviet troops were withdrawn from Czechoslovakia in June 1991, and the Warsaw Pact was disbanded the following month, thus completing Czechoslovakia's separation from the Soviet bloc. However, the drafting of a new constitution was hindered by differences between political parties, Czech-Slovak tensions, and power struggles. Another serious obstacle was the cumbersome federal structure inherited from the communists. When issues dividing Czechs and Slovaks were discussed, the existence of multiple ministerial cabinets and diets made it extremely difficult to achieve the prescribed majority on the federal level. Moreover, the minority bloc of Slovak deputies had disproportionate veto power.

The Czechoslovak federation began to appear increasingly fragile in 1991–92, and separatism became a momentous issue. Parliamentary elections in June 1992 gave the Czech premiership to Václav Klaus, an economist by training and finance minister since 1989. Klaus headed a centre-right coalition that included the Civic Democratic Party, which he had cofounded. The Slovak premiership went to Vladimir Mečiar, a vocal Slovak nationalist and prominent member of Public Against Violence who had served briefly as Slovak prime minister in 1990–91. Mečiar headed his Movement for a Democratic Slovakia party. The parties led by Klaus and Mečiar were supported by about one-third of the electorate in their respective republics, but the differences between the two were so great that a lasting federal government could not be formed.

After Havel's resignation on July 20, 1992, no suitable candidate for the federal presidency emerged; Czechoslovakia now lacked a symbol of unity as well as a convincing advocate. Thus, the assumption was readily made, at least in political circles, that the Czechoslovak state would have to be divided. There was little evidence of public enthusiasm for the split, but neither Klaus nor Mečiar wished to ask the population for a verdict through a referendum. The two republics proceeded with separation negotiations in an atmosphere of peace and cooperation. By late November, members of the National Assembly had voted Czechoslovakia out of existence. Both republics promulgated new constitutions, and at midnight on Dec. 31, 1992, after 74 years of joint existence disrupted only by World War II, Czechoslovakia was formally dissolved. With the completion of this so-called Velvet Divorce, the independent countries of Slovakia and the Czech Republic were created on Jan. 1, 1993.

Solidarity

In the early 1980s Solidarity (Polish: Solidarność) became the first independent labour union in a country belonging to the Soviet bloc. It was founded in September 1980, was forcibly suppressed by the Polish government in December 1981, and reemerged in 1989 to become the first opposition movement to participate in free elections in a Soviet-bloc nation since the 1940s. Solidarity subsequently formed a coalition government with Poland's United Workers' Party (PUWP), after which its leaders dominated the national government.

The origin of Solidarity traces back to 1976, when a Workers' Defense Committee (Komitet Obrony Robotnikow; KOR) was founded by a group of dissident intellectuals after several thousand striking workers had been attacked and jailed by authorities in various cities. The KOR supported families of imprisoned workers, offered legal and medical aid, and disseminated news through an underground network. In 1979 it published a Charter of Workers' Rights.

During a growing wave of new strikes in 1980 protesting rising food prices, Gdańsk became a hotbed of resistance to government decrees. Some 17,000 workers at the Lenin Shipyards there staged a strike and barricaded themselves within the plant under the leadership of Lech Wałęsa, an electrician by trade. In mid-August 1980 an Interfactory Strike Committee was established in Gdańsk to coordinate rapidly spreading strikes there and elsewhere; within a week it presented the Polish government with a list of demands that were based largely on KOR's Charter of Workers' Rights. On August 30, accords reached between the government and the Gdańsk strikers sanctioned free and independent unions with the right to strike, together with greater freedom of religious and political expression.

Solidarity formally was founded on Sept. 22, 1980, when delegates of 36 regional trade unions met in Gdańsk and united under the name Solidarność. The KOR subsequently disbanded, its activists becoming members of the union, and Wałęsa was elected chairman of Solidarity. A separate agricultural union composed of private farmers, named Rural Solidarity (Wiejska Solidarność), was founded in Warsaw on Dec. 14, 1980. By early 1981 Solidarity had a membership of about 10 million people and represented most of the workforce of Poland.

Throughout 1981 the government (led by Gen. Wojciech Witold Jaruzelski) was confronted by an ever stronger and more demanding Solidarity, which inflicted a series of controlled strikes to back up its appeals for economic reforms, for free elections, and for the involvement of trade unions in decision making at the highest levels. Solidarity's positions hardened as the moderate Wałęsa came to be pressured by more militant unionists. Jaruzelski's government, meanwhile, was subjected to severe pressure from the Soviet Union to suppress Solidarity.

On Dec. 13, 1981, Jaruzelski imposed martial law in Poland in a bid to crush the Solidarity movement. Solidarity was declared illegal, and its leaders were arrested. The union was formally dissolved by the Sejm (Parliament) on Oct. 8, 1982, but it nevertheless continued as an underground organization.

In 1988 a new wave of strikes and labour unrest spread across Poland, and prominent among the strikers' demands was government recognition of Solidarity. In April 1989 the government agreed to legalize Solidarity and allow it to participate in free elections to a bicameral Polish parliament. In the elections, held in June of that year, candidates endorsed by Solidarity won 99 of 100 seats in the newly formed Senate (upper house) and all 161 seats (of 460 total) that opposition candidates were entitled to contest in the Sejm (lower house). In August Solidarity agreed to form a coalition government with the PUWP, and on August 24 a longtime Solidarity adviser, Tadeusz Mazowiecki, became the first noncommunist premier to govern Poland since the late 1940s. In December 1990 Wałęsa was elected president of Poland after splitting with Mazowiecki in a dispute over the pace of Poland's conversion to a market economy. The split between Wałęsa and Mazowiecki prevented the formation of a Solidarity-backed coalition to govern the country in the wake of the PUWP's collapse, and the union's direct role in Poland's new parliamentary scene dwindled as many new political parties emerged in the early 1990s.

FALL OF THE BERLIN WALL

The Berlin Wall surrounded West Berlin and prevented access to it from East Berlin and adjacent areas of East Germany during a 28-year period, from 1961 to 1989. In the years between 1949 and 1961, about 2.5 million East Germans had fled from East to West Germany, including steadily rising numbers of skilled workers, professionals, and intellectuals. Their loss threatened to destroy the economic viability of the East German state. In response, East Germany built a barrier to close off East Germans' access to West Berlin (and hence West Germany). This barrier, the Berlin Wall, was first erected on the night of Aug. 12–13, 1961, as the result of a decree passed on August 12 by the East German Volkskammer ("Peoples' Chamber"). The original wall, built of barbed wire and cinder blocks, was subsequently replaced by a series of concrete walls (up to 15 feet [5 metres] high) that were topped with barbed wire and guarded with watchtowers, gun emplacements, and mines. By the 1980s this system of walls, electrified fences, and fortifications extended 28 miles (45 km) through Berlin, dividing the two parts of the city, and extended a further 75 miles (120 km) around West Berlin, separating it from the rest of East Germany.

*Citizens on both sides of the Berlin Wall took great joy in dismantling the
concrete barrier in November 1989. As the wall became a thing of the
past, so, too, did the communist government of the former East Germany.*
Andreas von Lintel/AFP/Getty Images

The Berlin Wall came to symbolize the Cold War's
division of East from West Germany and of Eastern from
Western Europe. About 5,000 East Germans managed to
cross the Berlin Wall (by various means) and reach West
Berlin safely, while another 5,000 were captured by East
German authorities in the attempt and 191 more were
killed during the actual crossing of the wall.

East Germany's hard-line communist leadership was
forced from power in October 1989 during the wave of
democratization that swept through Eastern Europe. On
November 9 the East German government opened the
country's borders with West Germany (including West
Berlin), and openings were made in the Berlin Wall through
which East Germans could travel freely to the West. The

wall henceforth ceased to function as a political barrier between East and West Germany.

OTHER PRO-DEMOCRACY MOVEMENTS

The fall of communism was arguably the most dramatic result of 20th-century pro-democracy movements. However, during the late 20th and early 21st centuries, numerous pro-democracy movements sprang up outside Eastern Europe and China. Movements in Chile, Myanmar, and Tonga highlight the general trends that occurred in other countries.

CHILE

On Sept. 11, 1973, in the South American country of Chile, the Chilean armed forces staged a coup d'état. Chile's first socialist president, Salvador Allende, died during an assault on the presidential palace, and a junta, or administrative council, composed of three generals and an admiral, with Gen. Augusto Pinochet Ugarte as president, was installed. At the outset the junta received the support of the oligarchy and of a sizable part of the middle class. This support by moderate political forces, including many Christian Democrats, can be explained by their belief that a dictatorship represented a transitional stage necessary to restoring the status quo as it had been before Allende's election in 1970. Very soon they were to concede that the military officers in power had their own political objectives, including the repression of all left-wing and centre political forces. The Christian Democratic, National, and Radical Democracy parties were declared to be in "indefinite recess," and the Communists, Socialists, and Radicals were proscribed. In 1977 the traditional parties were dissolved, and a private enterprise economy was instated.

The policies of the military government, though encouraging the development of free enterprise and a new entrepreneurial class, caused unemployment, a decline of real wages, and, as a consequence, a worsening of the standard of living of the lower and middle classes. Large-scale popular protests erupted in 1983, and several opposition parties, the Christian Democratic Party being the largest, formed a new centre-left coalition, the Democratic Alliance (Alianza Democrática; AD). The Roman Catholic Church also began openly to support the opposition. In August 1984, 11 parties of the right and centre signed an accord, worked out by the archbishop of Santiago, Raúl Cardinal Silva Henríquez, calling for elections to be scheduled before 1989.

The economic and political climate continued to be volatile in the late 1980s, with increasing pressure for governmental change, acts of terrorism multiplying, and the economy, though showing some signs of recovery, remaining basically unstable. Although Pinochet made occasional concessions, he showed little sign of relinquishing his control or relaxing his restrictive policies. To organize opposition to Pinochet, who was chosen as the junta's candidate for the 1988 presidential plebiscite, 16 centrist and leftist parties formed the Command for No (Comando por el No). On Oct. 5, 1988, voters rejected Pinochet. As the country prepared for its first free presidential and legislative elections since 1973, Command for No—renamed the Coalition of Parties for Democracy (Concertación de los Partidos por la Democracia; CPD)—and the government negotiated constitutional amendments that were approved in a national referendum in July 1989, among them the revocation of Article Eight, which banned Marxist parties. Two months later the government declared, with some restrictions, that all political exiles were permitted to return to Chile.

In the December 1989 presidential election, Christian Democrat Patricio Aylwin Azócar, leader of the CPD, won by a large margin over his closest opponent, Hernán Büchi Buc, a former finance minister and the government-endorsed candidate. The coalition also gained a majority in the lower chamber and nearly half the seats in the upper chamber.

MYANMAR (BURMA)

Student and worker unrest in the Southeast Asian country of Burma had erupted periodically throughout the 1980s, but the intensity of the protests in the summer of 1988 made it seem as if the country were on the verge of revolution. On Sept. 18, 1988, the armed forces, led by Gen. Saw Maung, seized control of the government. The military moved to suppress the demonstrations, and thousands of unarmed protesters were killed. Martial law was imposed over most of the country, and a new military body called the State Law and Order Restoration Council (SLORC) replaced the constitutional government.

The SLORC changed the name of the country to Myanmar, implemented the economic reforms drafted by the previous government, and called for the election of a new legislature and revision of the 1974 constitution. In May 1990 Myanmar held its first multiparty elections in 30 years. Of the dozens of parties that participated, the two most important were the government's National Unity Party (NUP), successor to the BSPP, and an opposition coalition called the National League for Democracy (NLD). The result was a landslide victory for the opposition NLD, which won some four-fifths of the seats.

The SLORC, however, would not permit the legislature—which it now declared to be a constituent assembly tasked with drafting a new constitution—to convene. Moreover, the military regime did not release the NLD's leaders, Tin U, a former general and colleague of Ne Win, and Aung San Suu Kyi, the daughter of the nationalist leader Aung San, both of whom had been under house arrest since July 1989; another leader, Sein Win, remained in exile in the West. Throughout the 1990s, the military solidified its political and economic hold of the country. In 1997 the military revamped the organizational structure of its ruling body and changed its name from the SLORC to the State Peace and Development Council (SPDC).

The political stalemate carried over into the 21st century, with the SPDC continuing to harass the NLD and the military maintaining stringent control. Late in 2000, however, the SPDC initiated secret talks with Aung San Suu Kyi (during another period of house arrest), and in 2001 it released approximately 200 political prisoners, evidently as a result of its negotiations with her. The potential for further democratic advancement emerged when Gen. Khin Nyunt was named prime minister in 2003. He promised to usher the country toward a new constitution and free elections, but his rule was cut short by allegations of corruption. In late 2004 he too was placed under house arrest and was replaced by Gen. Soe Win.

Despite increased global interaction, Myanmar remained hampered by international sanctions. It was clear that its prospects for further economic growth and acceptance by the international community were contingent on democratic progress and an improved human rights record. When in September 2007 the monastic community staged a large-scale demonstration calling for democratic reforms, the harsh response from the military drew widespread international criticism. In the wake of this unrest, the

National Assembly finally approved a draft of a new constitution, which was ratified by public referendum in May 2008. The SPDC promised elections in 2010.

TONGA

The country of Tonga comprises some 170 islands in the southwestern Pacific Ocean. Tonga's constitution, granted in 1875 by King George Tupou I and amended only slightly since, established a constitutional monarchy. The chief executive is the monarch, who governs in close consultation with the prime minister. The country's unicameral legislature, the Fale Alea, is made up of cabinet members, nobles, and a minority of elected representatives. A pro-democracy movement took shape in the late 20th century, and, from the 1990s, reform advocates won significant representation in the legislature. The government, however, resisted change. Pro-democracy leaders, including 'Akilisi Pohiva, a member of the legislature, were occasionally arrested and imprisoned.

As the reform movement gained momentum, some members of the legislature and some in the royal family were sympathetic. The government, however, responded by attempting to further solidify its authority. In 1999 the first indigenous broadcast television service, government-owned Television Tonga, was established. A newspaper critical of the government and the monarchy, *Taimi 'o Tonga*, was banned at various times for allegedly being seditious. The legislature amended the constitution in 2003 to increase governmental control over the media, despite an earlier large-scale public demonstration in Nuku'alofa, the capital and chief port of Tonga, against the changes; the Supreme Court later invalidated the amendments. From July to September 2005, in the first national strike in the country's history, thousands of public service workers struck successfully for greater pay equity.

The country's first nonnoble prime minister, Feleti (Fred) Sevele, was appointed in March 2006. In September, King Taufa'ahau Tupou IV died and was succeeded by Crown Prince Tupouto'a, who ruled as King George (Siaosi) Tupou V. Later that month a National Committee for Political Reform, whose formation had been approved by King Taufa'ahau Tupou IV, made its report to the legislature. Its recommendations included reducing the size of the legislature and increasing the number of seats for popularly elected representatives. The Fale Alea passed an amended version, which was to take effect within the next several years; following the vote, a demonstration by pro-democracy protesters turned into a riot that went on for several weeks. Arson destroyed most of the capital's business district and left seven people dead; hundreds were arrested. Troops were called in from New Zealand and Australia to reestablish peace.

Following his accession to the throne, King George Tupou V began divesting himself of ownership in many of the state assets that constituted much of the wealth of the monarchy. This process was completed prior to his coronation in August 2008. At the same time, the king announced the cession of much of the monarchy's absolute power; henceforth, most of the monarch's governmental decisions, except those relating to the judiciary, would be made in consultation with the prime minister.

PROBLEMS AND CHALLENGES

For many of the countries that made a transition to democracy in the late 20th and early 21st centuries, the problems and challenges facing democracy were particularly acute. Obstacles in the path of a successful consolidation of democratic institutions included economic problems such as widespread poverty, unemployment, massive inequalities in income and wealth, rapid inflation, and low or negative rates of economic growth. Countries at low levels of economic development also usually lacked a large middle class and a well-educated population. In many of these countries, the division of the population into antagonistic ethnic, racial, religious, or linguistic groups made it difficult to manage political differences peacefully. In others, extensive government intervention in the economy, along with other factors, resulted in the widespread corruption of government officials. Many countries also lacked an effective legal system, making civil rights highly insecure and allowing for abuse by political elites and criminal elements. In these countries the idea of the rule of law was not well established in the prevailing political culture, in some cases because of constant warfare or long years of authoritarian rule. In other respects the political culture of these countries did not inculcate in citizens the kinds of beliefs and values that could support democratic institutions and practices during crises or even during the ordinary conflicts of political life.

In light of these circumstances, it is quite possible that the extraordinary pace of democratization begun in the 20th century will not continue long into the 21st century. In some countries, authoritarian systems probably will remain in place. In some countries that have made the transition to democracy, new democratic institutions probably will remain weak and fragile. Other countries might lose their democratic governments and revert to some form of authoritarian rule.

Yet, despite these adversities, the odds are great that in the foreseeable future a very large share of the world's population, in a very large share of the world's countries, will live under democratic forms of government that continue to evolve in order to meet challenges both old and new.

Chapter 8:
Nationalism

Throughout history people have been attached to their native soil, to the traditions of their parents, and to established territorial authorities; but it was not until the end of the 18th century that nationalism began to be a generally recognized sentiment molding public and private life and one of the great, if not the greatest, single determining factors of modern history. Because of its dynamic vitality and its all-pervading character, nationalism is often thought to be very old; sometimes it is mistakenly regarded as a permanent factor in political behaviour. Actually, the American and French revolutions may be regarded as its first powerful manifestations. After penetrating the new countries of Latin America it spread in the early 19th century to central Europe and from there, toward the middle of the century, to eastern and southeastern Europe. At the beginning of the 20th century nationalism flowered in the ancient lands of Asia and Africa. Thus the 19th century has been called the age of nationalism in Europe, while the 20th century has witnessed the rise and struggle of powerful national movements throughout Asia and Africa. Nationalism, in a nutshell, is based on the premise that the individual's loyalty and devotion to a nation-state—or, in some cases, to a nation of people that lacks its own state—surpasses other individual or group interests.

NATIONALISM IN EUROPE

In the 19th century nationalism, supported by the principles of liberalism, asserted itself and affected more and more people: the rising middle class and the new proletariat. The revolutionary wave of 1848, the year of "the spring of the peoples," seemed to realize the hopes of nationalists such as Giuseppe Mazzini, who had devoted his life to the unification of the Italian nation by democratic means and to the brotherhood of all free nations. Though his immediate hopes were disappointed, the 12 years from 1859 to 1871 brought the unification of Italy and Romania, both with the help of Napoleon III, and of Germany; at the same time the 1860s saw great progress in liberalism, even in Russia and Spain. The victorious trend of liberal nationalism, however, was reversed in Germany by Otto von Bismarck, founder of the German Empire. He unified Germany on a conservative and authoritarian basis and defeated German liberalism. The German annexation of Alsace-Lorraine, a 5,067-square-mile (13,123-square-km) piece of territory that was ceded by France to Germany in 1871 after the Franco-German War, was against the will of the inhabitants and was contrary to the idea of nationalism as based upon the free will of man. The people of Alsace-Lorraine were held to be German by objective factors, by race, independent of their will or of their allegiance to any nationality of their choice.

In the second half of the 19th century, nationalism disintegrated the supranational states of the Habsburgs and the Ottoman sultans, both of which were based upon pre-national loyalties. In Russia, the penetration of nationalism produced two opposing schools of thought. Some nationalists proposed a westernized Russia, associated with the progressive, liberal forces of the rest of Europe. Others stressed the distinctive character of Russia and Russianism, its independent and different destiny based upon its autocratic and orthodox past. These Slavophiles, similar to and influenced by German romantic thinkers, saw Russia as a future saviour of a West undermined by liberalism and the heritage of the American and French revolutions.

One of the consequences of World War I (1914–18) was the triumph of nationalism in central and eastern Europe. From the ruins of the Habsburg and Romanov empires emerged the new nation-states of Austria, Hungary, Czechoslovakia, Poland, Yugoslavia, and Romania. Those states in turn, however, were to be strained and ravaged by their own internal nationality conflicts and by nationalistic disputes over territory with their neighbours.

Russian nationalism was in part suppressed after Vladimir Ilich Lenin's victory in 1917, when the Bolsheviks took over the old empire of the tsars. But the Bolsheviks also claimed the leadership of the world communist movement, which was to become an instrument of the national policies of the Russians. During World War II (1939–45) Joseph Stalin appealed to nationalism and patriotism in rallying the Russians against foreign invaders. After the war he found nationalism one of the strongest obstacles to the expansion of Soviet power in Eastern Europe. National communism, as it was called, became a divisive force in the Soviet bloc. In 1948 Josip Broz Tito, the communist leader of Yugoslavia, was denounced by Moscow as a nationalist and a renegade; nationalism was a strong factor in the rebellious movements in Poland and Hungary in the fall of 1956; and subsequently its influence was also felt in Romania and Czechoslovakia and again in Poland in 1980.

ASIAN AND AFRICAN NATIONALISM

Nationalism began to appear in Asia and Africa after World War I. It produced such leaders as Kemal Atatürk in Turkey, Sa'd Pasha Zaghūl in Egypt, Ibn Sa'ūd in the Arabian peninsula, Mahatma Gandhi in India, and Sun Yat-sen in China. Atatürk succeeded in replacing the medieval structure of the Islamic monarchy with a

Mustafa Kemal (Atatürk) in 1923. UPI/Bettmann Newsphotos

revitalized and modernized secular republic in 1923. Demands for Arab unity were frustrated in Africa and Asia by British imperialism and in Africa by French imperialism. Yet Britain may have shown a gift for accommodation with the new forces by helping to create an independent Egypt (1922; completely, 1936) and Iraq (1932) and displayed a similar spirit in India, where the Indian National Congress, founded in 1885 to promote a liberal nationalism inspired by the British model, became more radical after 1918. Japan, influenced by Germany, used modern industrial techniques in the service of a more authoritarian nationalism.

The progress of nationalism in Asia and Africa is reflected in the histories of the League of Nations after World War I and of the UN after World War II. The Treaty of Versailles, which provided for the constitution of the League of Nations, also reduced the empires of the defeated Central Powers, mainly Germany and Turkey. The league distributed Germany's African colonies as mandates to Great Britain, France, Belgium, and South Africa, and its Pacific possessions to Japan, Australia, and New Zealand under various classifications according to their expectations of achieving independence. Among the League's original members, there were only five Asian countries (China, India, Japan, Thailand, and Iran) and two African countries (Liberia and South Africa), and it added only three Asian countries (Afghanistan, Iraq, and Turkey) and two African countries (Egypt and Ethiopia) before it was dissolved in 1946. Of the mandated territories under the League's control, only Iraq, Lebanon, and Syria achieved independence during its lifetime.

Of the original 51 members of the UN in 1945, eight were Asian (China, India, Iraq, Iran, Lebanon, Saudi Arabia,

Syria, and Turkey) and four were African (the same as in the League). By 1980, 35 years after its founding, the UN had added more than 100 member nations, most of them Asian and African. Whereas Asian and African nations had never totalled even one-third of the membership in the League, they came to represent more than one-half of the membership of the UN. Of these new Asian and African nations, several had been created, entirely or in part, from mandated territories.

After World War II, India, Pakistan, Ceylon (Sri Lanka), Burma, and Malaya (Malaysia) in Asia, and Ghana in Africa achieved independence peacefully from the British Commonwealth, as did the Philippines from the United States. Other territories had to fight hard for their independence in bitter colonial wars, as in French Indochina (Vietnam, Laos, Cambodia) and French North Africa (Tunisia, Algeria). Communism recruited supporters from within the ranks of the new nationalist movements in Asia and Africa, first by helping them in their struggles against Western capitalist powers, and later, after independence was achieved, by competing with Western capitalism in extending financial and technical aid. Chinese nationalism under Chiang Kai-shek during World War II was diminished with the takeover of the Chinese communists. But Chinese communism soon began to drift away from supranational communism, as the European communist countries had earlier. By the late 1960s Russian and Chinese mutual recriminations revealed a Chinese nationalism in which Mao Zedong had risen to share the place of honour with Lenin. As Chinese communism turned further and further inward, its influence on new Asian and African nations waned.

Ambitions among new Asian and African nations clashed. The complex politics of the UN illustrated the problems of the new nationalism. The struggle with Dutch colonialism that brought the establishment of Indonesia continued with the UN mediation of the dispute over West Irian (Irian Jaya). In the Suez crisis of 1956, UN forces intervened between those of Egypt and Israel. Continuing troubles in the Middle East, beginning with the establishment of Israel and including inter-Arab state disputes brought on by the establishment of the United Arab Republic, concerned the UN. Other crises involving the UN included the India-Pakistan dispute over Jammu and Kashmir; the Korean partition and subsequent war; the four-year intervention in the Congo; the struggle of Greece and Turkey over newly independent Cyprus; and Indonesian and Philippine objection to the inclusion of Sarawak and Sabah (North Borneo) in newly formed Malaysia.

Even though these new nations shared a pride in their independence, many also faced difficulties. As a result of inadequate preparation for self-rule, the first five years of independence in the Congo passed with no semblance of a stable government. The problem of widely different peoples and languages was exemplified in Nigeria, where an uncounted population included an uncounted number of tribes (at least 150, with three major divisions) that used an uncounted number of languages (more than 100 language and dialect clusters). The question of whether the predominantly Muslim state of Jammu and Kashmir should go with Muslim Pakistan or Hindu India lasted for more than 20 years after the India Independence Act became effective in 1949. Desperate economic competition caused trouble, as in Israel where the much-needed waters of the Jordan River kept it in constant dispute with its water-hungry Arab neighbours.

REGIONAL VARIETIES OF NATIONALISM

Nationalist movements around the world have taken many different forms. While all include an element of pride in one's origins, various nationalist groups have coalesced around such themes as ethnicity, equality with other countries, modernization, independence, religion, civil rights, land rights, and language.

ETHNIC MOVEMENTS IN EUROPE

Many nationalist movements in Europe have been notable for their emphasis on ethnicity. Among the peoples that have agitated for political unity—and in some cases a separate state encompassing the members of their ethnic group—have been the Slavs, the Irish, and the Basques. An extreme and violent example of ethnic nationalism is the practice of ethnic cleansing, which occurred during the disintegration of the multiethnic republic of Yugoslavia (originally a political union of South Slavs) in the 1990s.

Pan-Slavism

Pan-Slavism was a 19th-century movement that recognized a common ethnic background among the various Slav peoples of eastern and east central Europe and sought to unite those peoples for the achievement of common cultural and political goals. The Pan-Slav movement originally was formed in the first half of the 19th century by West and South Slav intellectuals, scholars, and poets, whose peoples were at that time also developing their sense of national identity. The Pan-Slavists engaged in studying folk songs, folklore, and peasant vernaculars of the Slav peoples, in demonstrating the similarities among them, and in trying to stimulate a sense of Slav unity. As such activities were conducted mainly in Prague, that city became the first Pan-Slav centre for studying Slav antiquities and philology.

The Pan-Slavism movement soon took on political overtones, and in June 1848, while the Austrian Empire was weakened by revolution, the Czech historian František Palacký convened a Slav congress in Prague. Consisting of representatives of all Slav nationalities ruled by the Austrians, the congress was intended to organize coopera- tive efforts among them for the purpose of compelling the emperor to transform his monarchy into a federation of equal peoples under a democratic Habsburg rule.

Although the congress had little practical effect, the movement remained active, and by the 1860s it became particularly popular in Russia, to which many Pan-Slavs looked for leadership as well as for protection from Austro- Hungarian and Turkish rule. Russian Pan-Slavists, however, altered the theoretical bases of the movement. Adopting the Slavophile notion that Western Europe was spiritually and culturally bankrupt and that it was Russia's historic mission to rejuvenate Europe by gaining political domi- nance over it, the Pan-Slavists added the concept that Russia's mission could not be fulfilled without the support of other Slav peoples, who must be liberated from their Austrian and Turkish masters and united into a Russian- dominated Slav confederation.

Although the Russian government did not officially support this view, some important members of its foreign department, including its representatives at Constantinople and Belgrade, were ardent Pan-Slavists and succeeded in drawing both Serbia and Russia into wars against the Ottoman Empire in 1876–77.

When efforts were made in the early 20th century to call new Pan-Slav congresses and revive the movement,

ETHNIC CLEANSING

Ethnic cleansing refers to the attempt to create ethnically homogeneous geographic areas through the deportation or forcible displacement of persons belonging to particular ethnic groups. Ethnic cleansing sometimes involves the removal of all physical vestiges of the targeted group through the destruction of monuments, cemeteries, and houses of worship. The term, a literal translation of the Serbo-Croatian phrase *etnicko ciscenje*, was widely employed in the 1990s (though the term first appeared earlier) to describe the brutal treatment of various civilian groups in the conflicts that erupted upon the disintegration of the Federal Republic of Yugoslavia. These groups included Bosniacs (Bosnian Muslims) in Bosnia and Herzegovina, Serbs in the Krajina region of Croatia, and ethnic Albanians and later Serbs in the Serbian province of Kosovo. The term also has been attached to the treatment by Indonesian militants of the people of East Timor, many of whom were killed or forced to abandon their homes after citizens there voted in favour of independence in 1999, and to the plight of Chechens who fled Grozny and other areas of Chechnya following Russian military operations against Chechen separatists during the 1990s.

Ethnic cleansing as a concept has generated considerable controversy. Some critics see little difference between it and genocide. Defenders, however, argue that ethnic cleansing and genocide can be distinguished by the intent of the perpetrator: whereas the primary goal of genocide is the destruction of an ethnic, racial, or religious group, the main purpose of ethnic cleansing is the establishment of ethnically homogeneous lands, which may be achieved by any of a number of methods including genocide.

The precise legal definition of ethnic cleansing has been the subject of intense scrutiny within various international bodies, including the UN, the two ad hoc international tribunals created in the 1990s to prosecute violations of international humanitarian law in the former Yugoslavia and in Rwanda (the International Criminal Tribunal for the Former Yugoslavia and the International Criminal Tribunal for Rwanda, respectively), and the International Criminal Court (ICC), which began sittings in 2002. The establishment of the ICC reinforced the links between ethnic cleansing and other offenses such as genocide, crimes against humanity, and war crimes.

the nationalistic rivalries among the various Slav peoples prevented their effective collaboration.

Irish Republicanism: Sinn Féin

Sinn Féin (Irish: "We Ourselves" or "Ourselves Alone"), organized in both Northern Ireland and the Republic of Ireland, is a nationalist party in Northern Ireland, representing Roman Catholics who want to achieve a united Ireland. It is the political wing of the Provisional Irish Republican Army (IRA).

Sinn Féin was of little importance until the Easter Rising in Dublin (1916), after which it became the rallying point for extreme nationalist sentiment, referred to as Republicanism. The unequivocal demand by Sinn Féin's leader, Eamon de Valera, for a united and independent Ireland won the party 73 of the 105 Irish seats in the British Parliament in 1918. Sinn Féin members of Parliament met in Dublin in January 1919 and declared themselves the parliament of an Irish republic, setting up a provisional government to rival Ireland's British administration.

The ensuing Irish War of Independence (1919–21) between the IRA and the British army was ended by the Anglo-Irish Treaty (1921), which was negotiated by representatives of Sinn Féin—most notably Michael Collins—and British officials, including Prime Minister David Lloyd George. The treaty did not grant Ireland full independence, however. Twenty-six of the 32 counties of Ireland became the Irish Free State, which held dominion status within the British Empire until its withdrawal from the Commonwealth in 1949; the remaining six counties, sometimes referred to as the province of Ulster, continued to be part of the United Kingdom. The treaty split Sinn Féin into two factions, one supporting the treaty under the leadership of Collins and the other opposing the treaty under Eamon de Valera. The two sides fought against each other in the Irish Civil War (1922–23), which ended in the defeat of the anti-treaty forces.

Reacting to sectarian violence in Northern Ireland beginning in the late 1960s, local units of the IRA were organized to defend Catholic communities in the province. Following a party conference in Dublin in 1969, Sinn Féin split again over the question of whether to support the IRA's use of violence to protect Catholics in Northern Ireland and end British control there. Whereas the "Official" wing of the party, which was later renamed the Workers' Party, emphasized political and parliamentary tactics and rejected violence after 1972, the "Provisional" wing, or Provos, believed that violence—particularly terrorism—was necessary and justified. This split was paralleled in the IRA, which also divided into official and provisional factions.

In the early 1980s Sinn Féin began to emphasize political and parliamentary tactics, adopting a strategy later known as "the ballot and the Armalite" (rifle). In 1981 a series of dramatic hunger strikes by Republican prisoners in which 10 men died (7 of whom were IRA members) generated sympathy for the Republican cause and helped to increase Sinn Féin's popularity among Catholics in Northern Ireland. The election of IRA hunger striker Bobby Sands to the British Parliament demonstrated the popularity of Republicanism.

In 1983 Gerry Adams became leader of Sinn Féin. Three years later the party chose to take the seats it had won in the Dáil (Ireland's House of Representatives), though it continued to abstain from participation in the British Parliament. Two years later the party began sometimes secret negotiations with John Hume, leader of the Social Democratic and Labour Party (SDLP), Sinn Féin's chief rival as the voice of Irish nationalism, and in 1993 Adams and Hume issued a joint statement of principles for a peaceful settlement of the conflict in Northern Ireland. The statement presented Sinn Féin in a new light, though the party continued to be associated with high-profile acts of paramilitary violence. In 1997, after the IRA reinstated a cease-fire it had declared in 1994, Sinn Féin was permitted to join multiparty peace talks.

The talks resulted in the Good Friday Agreement (April 1998) on steps leading to a new power-sharing government in Northern Ireland. The IRA made some critical concessions, including its agreement that the Republic of Ireland should change its constitution to remove a territorial claim to Northern Ireland and that Northern Ireland should remain part of the United Kingdom for as long as the majority of its population so desired. Sinn Féin endorsed the agreement and campaigned aggressively for its acceptance in referenda that were passed in Northern Ireland and the republic in May. In elections to the new Northern Ireland Assembly, Sinn Féin won nearly 18 percent of the vote.

Basque Nationalism

The Basque Nationalist Party (Basque: Euzko Alderdi Jeltzalea [EAJ]; Spanish: Partido Nacionalist Vasco [PNV]), commonly known by the acronym EAJ-PNV, supports greater autonomy for the Basque Country (including Navarra) within Spain. The party was established in 1895 in Bilbao by journalist Sabino de Arana y Goiri to contest local elections. However, the party soon expanded to the rest of Vizcaya province and later to the entire country.

Since its founding, the EAJ-PNV has adopted a moderate Christian Democratic stance, endorsing a mixed economy and opposing unfettered capitalism. This centrism helped the EAJ-PNV achieve widespread support in the Basque Country, and from the 1910s to the '30s it captured some one-third of the vote and elected several members to the Spanish Cortes (legislature) in Madrid. After the Cortes passed legislation granting the Basque Country autonomy in October 1936, the EAJ-PNV formed an autonomous government and established an alliance with Republican forces against General Francisco Franco during the Spanish Civil War (1936–39).

Following the Republicans' defeat, Basque nationalism was suppressed, the Basque Country's statute of autonomy was abolished in 1939, and many of the party's leaders were forced into exile. With the restoration of democracy in the 1970s, the Basque Country's second statute of autonomy was approved in 1979, and the EAJ-PNV reestablished itself as the leading political party in the region. Unlike the Basque separatist ETA, the party eschews violence to achieve its goals and has condemned ETA's terrorist tactics; indeed, in 1989 the EAJ-PNV led mass demonstrations against ETA.

ETA

The nationalist movement in the Basque provinces before the Spanish Civil War was nonviolent. The inflexible centralism of the Franco regime and its repression of any expression of regional difference, however, were instrumental in stimulating the development of a more radical nationalism among Basque youth in the 1950s. Euzkadi Ta Azkatasuna (Basque Homeland and Liberty), best known by its Basque acronym, ETA, was created in 1959 and, influenced by anti-imperialist struggles in the developing world, quickly took up armed opposition. In December 1973 ETA assassinated Admiral Luis Carrero Blanco, Franco's hand-picked successor as head of the government.

So long as ETA was seen to be fighting against the Franco dictatorship, it received considerable sympathy both inside and outside the Basque provinces. Its continued use of violence during and after the transition to democracy cost it whatever support it had enjoyed in the rest of Spain. In the Basque Country itself the continuing use of terror led to much public revulsion and to demonstrations demanding the end to violence. Nevertheless, Batasuna, the political party generally considered to be the political wing of ETA, has continually won between 15 and 20 percent of the votes cast in the Basque Country in regional and national elections.

CHINESE NATIONALISM

Modern Chinese nationalism emerged in the early 20th century, most notably in the May Fourth Movement, an intellectual revolution and sociopolitical reform movement that occurred in 1917–21. The movement spurred the successful reorganization of the Nationalist Party

(Kuomintang), later ruled by Chiang Kai-shek, and stimulated the birth of the Chinese Communist Party as well.

May Fourth Movement

The May Fourth Movement was directed toward national independence, emancipation of the individual, and rebuilding society and culture. In 1915, in the face of Japanese encroachment on China, young intellectuals, inspired by "New Youth" (*Xin qingnian*), a monthly magazine edited by the iconoclastic intellectual revolutionary Chen Duxiu, began agitating for the reform and strengthening of Chinese society. As part of this New Culture movement, they attacked traditional Confucian ideas and exalted Western ideas, particularly science and democracy. Their inquiry into liberalism, pragmatism, nationalism, anarchism, and socialism provided a basis from which to criticize traditional Chinese ethics, philosophy, religion, and social and political institutions. Moreover, led by Chen and the American-educated scholar Hu Shi, they proposed a new naturalistic vernacular writing style (*baihua*), replacing the difficult 2,000-year-old classical style (*wenyan*).

These patriotic feelings and the zeal for reform culminated in an incident on May 4, 1919, from which the movement took its name. On that day, more than 3,000 students from 13 colleges in Beijing held a mass demonstration against the decision of the Versailles Peace Conference, which drew up the treaty officially ending World War I, to transfer the former German concessions in Shandong province to Japan. The Chinese government's acquiescence to the decision so enraged the students that they burned the house of the minister of communications and assaulted China's minister to Japan, both pro-Japanese officials. Over the following weeks, demonstrations occurred throughout the country; several students died or were wounded in these incidents, and more than 1,000 were arrested. In the big cities, strikes and boycotts against Japanese goods were begun by the students and lasted more than two months. For one week, beginning June 5, merchants and workers in Shanghai and other cities went on strike in support of the students. Faced with this growing tide of unfavourable public opinion, the government acquiesced; three pro-Japanese officials were dismissed, the cabinet resigned, and China refused to sign the peace treaty with Germany.

As a part of this movement, a campaign had been undertaken to reach the common people; mass meetings were held throughout the country, and more than 400 new publications were begun to spread the new thought. As a result, the decline of traditional ethics and the family system was accelerated, the emancipation of women gathered momentum, a vernacular literature emerged, and the modernized intelligentsia became a major factor in China's subsequent political developments.

Nationalist Party

China's Nationalist Party, also called Kuomintang (KMT; "National People's Party"), governed all or part of mainland China from 1928 to 1949 and subsequently ruled Taiwan under Chiang Kai-shek and his successors for most of the time since then. Originally a revolutionary league working for the overthrow of the Chinese monarchy, the Nationalists became a political party in the first year of the Chinese republic (1912). The party participated in the first Chinese parliament, which was soon dissolved by a coup d'état (1913). This defeat moved its leader, Sun Yat-sen, to organize it more tightly, first (1914) on the model of a Chinese secret society and, later (1923–24), under Soviet guidance, on that of the Bolshevik party. The Nationalist Party owed its early successes largely to Soviet aid and advice and to close collaboration with the Chinese communists (1924–27).

After Sun Yat-sen's death in 1925, leadership of the party passed gradually to Chiang Kai-shek, who brought most of China under its control by ending or limiting regional warlord autonomy (1926–28). Nationalist rule, inseparable from Chiang's, became increasingly conservative and dictatorial but never totalitarian. The party program rested on Sun's Three Principles of the People: nationalism, democracy, and people's livelihood. Nationalism demanded that China regain equality with other countries, but the Nationalists' resistance to the Japanese invasion of China (1931–45) was less rigorous than their determined attempts to suppress the Chinese Communist Party (CCP). The realization of democracy through successive constitutions (1936, 1946) was also largely a myth. Equally ineffective were attempts to improve the people's livelihood or eliminate corruption. The Nationalist Party's failure to effect such changes itself derived partly from weaknesses in leadership and partly from its unwillingness to radically reform China's age-old feudal social structure.

After the defeat of Japan in World War II (1939–45), civil war with the communists was renewed with greater vigour. In 1949–50, following the victories of the Chinese communists on the mainland, a stream of Nationalist troops, government officials, and other refugees estimated at some two million persons, led by Chiang, poured into Taiwan; a branch of the Nationalist Party that was opposed to Chiang's policies and aligned itself with the CCP still exists on the mainland. Taiwan became the effective territory, apart from a number of small islands off the mainland China coast, of the Republic of China. The Nationalists for many years constituted the only real political force, holding virtually all legislative, executive, and judicial

posts. The first legal opposition to the Nationalist Party
came in 1989, when the pro-independence Democratic
Progressive Party (DPP; established 1986) won one-fifth
of the seats in the Legislative Yuan.

The Nationalists remained in power throughout the
1990s, but in 2000 the DPP's presidential candidate, Chen
Shui-bian, defeated the Nationalists' candidate, Lien
Chan, who finished third. In legislative elections the following year the Nationalist Party not only lost its majority
in the legislature but its plurality in the number of seats
(to the DPP). However, in 2004 the Nationalists and their
allies regained control of the legislature, and in 2008 the
party captured nearly three-fourths of the legislative seats,
crushing the DPP. To resolve Taiwan's long-standing differences with China, the party endorsed the policy of the
"Three Nots": not unification, not independence, and not
military confrontation.

INDEPENDENCE MOVEMENTS IN SOUTH ASIA

Great Britain controlled much of South Asia, including
India and Sri Lanka (known as Ceylon until 1972), until the
mid-20th century. Nationalist sentiment inspired movements in both countries that resulted in independence.

The Indian National Congress dominated the Indian
movement for independence from Britain. As a broadly
based political party, the National Congress also has
formed most of India's governments from the time of
independence in 1947.

Sri Lanka gained its independence from Britain just
after India, in 1948. However, independence did not bring
peace. Growing tensions between the Tamil people of Sri
Lanka and the Sinhalese Buddhist majority prompted
Tamil militants to undertake a guerrilla war against the

central government in hopes of creating a separate Tamil state, Eelam, for themselves in the north and northeast.

Indian National Congress

The Indian National Congress first convened in December 1885, though the idea of an Indian nationalist movement opposed to British rule dated from the 1850s. During its first several decades, the Congress passed fairly moderate reform resolutions, though many within the organization were becoming radicalized by the increased poverty that accompanied British imperialism. In the early 20th century, elements within the party began to endorse a policy of *swadeshi* ("of our own country"), which called for the boycott of imported British goods and the promotion of Indian-made goods. By 1917 the group's "extremist" Home Rule wing, which was formed by Bal Gangadhar Tilak and Annie Besant the previous year, had begun to exert significant influence by appealing to India's diverse social classes.

In the 1920s and '30s the Congress, led by Mohandas Gandhi, promoted nonviolent noncooperation to protest the perceived feebleness of the constitutional reforms of 1919 and Britain's manner of carrying them out. Much of this civil disobedience was implemented through the All India Congress Committee, formed in 1929, which advocated tax avoidance to protest British rule. Another wing of the Congress Party, which believed in working within the existing system, contested general elections in 1923 and 1937 as the Swaraj (Home Rule) Party, with particular success in the latter year, winning 7 out of 11 provinces.

When World War II began in 1939, Britain made India a belligerent without consulting Indian elected councils. This angered Indian officials and prompted the Congress to declare that India would not support the war effort until it had been granted complete independence. In 1942 the organization sponsored mass civil disobedience to support the demand that the British "quit India." After the war the British government of Clement Attlee passed an independence bill (1947), and in January 1950 India's constitution as an independent state took effect.

SATYAGRAHA

Satyagraha (Hindi: "insistence on truth" or "zeal for truth") was a concept introduced in the early 20th century by Mahatma Gandhi to designate a determined but nonviolent resistance to evil. Gandhi's *satyagraha* became a major tool in the Indian struggle against British imperialism and has since been adopted by protest groups in other countries.

According to this philosophy, *satyagrahis*—practitioners of *satyagraha*—achieve correct insight into the real nature of an evil situation by observing a nonviolence of the mind, by seeking truth in a spirit of peace and love, and by undergoing a rigorous process of self-scrutiny. *Satyagraha* draws from the ancient Indian ideal of *ahimsa* ("noninjury"), which is pursued with particular rigour by Jains. In developing *ahimsa* into a modern concept with broad political consequences, as *satyagraha*, Gandhi also drew from the writings of Leo Tolstoy and Henry David Thoreau, from the Bible, and from the *Bhagavadgita*, the great Sanskrit epic. Gandhi first conceived *satyagraha* in 1906 in response to a law discriminating against Asians that was passed by the British colonial government of the Transvaal in South Africa. In 1917 the first *satyagraha* campaign in India was mounted in the indigo-growing district of Champaran. During the following years, fasting and economic boycotts were employed as methods of *satyagraha*, until the British left India in 1947.

The Tamil Tigers

Vellupillai Prabhakaran formed the Liberation Tigers of Tamil Eelam (LTTE), or Tamil Tigers, in 1972. During the 1970s the LTTE carried out a number of guerrilla attacks. In 1983, after the killing of 13 soldiers by Tamil guerrillas and retaliatory attacks by the Sri Lankan military, large-scale violence erupted between the government and the LTTE. By 1985 the group was in control of Jaffna and most of the Jaffna Peninsula in northern Sri Lanka. Under Prabhakaran's orders, the LTTE eliminated most of its rival Tamil groups by 1987. To fund its operations, the group engaged in bank robberies and drug smuggling.

The LTTE lost control of Jaffna in October 1987 to an Indian peacekeeping force (IPKF) that had been sent to Sri Lanka to assist in the implementation of a complete cease-fire. However, following the withdrawal of the IPKF in March 1990, the Tigers grew in strength and conducted several successful guerrilla operations and terrorist attacks. On May 21, 1991, a suicide bomber killed former Indian prime minister Rajiv Gandhi while he was campaigning in the Indian state of Tamil Nadu. Other attacks included an August 1992 land-mine explosion in Jaffna, which killed 10 senior military commanders; the May 1993 assassination of Sri Lankan Pres. Ranasinghe Premadasa; and a January 1996 suicide bomb attack on the central bank of Colombo that killed 100 people. An elite unit of the LTTE, the "Black Tigers," is responsible for carrying out suicide attacks. If faced with unavoidable capture by Sri Lankan authorities, Black Tigers purportedly commit suicide by swallowing cyanide capsules that they wear around their necks.

Negotiations between the LTTE and the government broke down in the mid-1990s. In December 2000 the

LTTE declared a unilateral cease-fire, which lasted only until April. Thereafter, fighting between the guerrillas and the government again intensified until February 2002, when the government and the LTTE signed a permanent cease-fire agreement. Sporadic violence continued, however, and in 2006 the European Union added the LTTE to its list of banned terrorist organizations. Soon after, heavy fighting erupted between the rebels and government forces; thousands were killed, bringing the number of civil-war-related deaths in Sri Lanka to nearly 70,000 since the bilateral outbreak of violence in the early 1980s. In January 2008 the government formally abandoned the 2002 cease-fire agreement, and authorities captured major strongholds of the LTTE over the following months. The town of Kilinochchi, the administrative centre of the LTTE, came under government control in January 2009. By late April, government troops had cornered the remaining LTTE fighters along a small stretch of the northeast coast, and in mid-May the government announced that its forces had occupied this last stronghold, defeating the rebels and killing Prabhakaran.

THE VIET MINH AND VIETNAMESE INDEPENDENCE

The Viet Minh (Viet Nam Doc Lap Dong Minh Hoi; "League for the Independence of Vietnam"), formed in China by Ho Chi Minh in May 1941, led the struggle for Vietnamese independence from French rule. Although it was led primarily by communists, the Viet Minh operated as a national front organization open to persons of various political persuasions.

In late 1943 members of the Viet Minh, led by Gen. Vo Nguyen Giap, began to infiltrate Vietnam to launch guerrilla operations against the Japanese, who occupied the country during World War II (1939–45). The Viet Minh forces liberated considerable portions of northern Vietnam, and after the Japanese surrender to the Allies, Viet Minh units seized control of Hanoi and proclaimed the independent Democratic Republic of Vietnam.

The French at first promised to recognize the new government as a free state but failed to do so. On Nov. 23, 1946, at least 6,000 Vietnamese civilians were killed in a French naval bombardment of the port city of Haiphong, and the first Indochina War began. The Viet Minh had popular support and was able to dominate the countryside, while the French strength lay in urban areas. As the war neared an end, the Viet Minh was succeeded by a new organization, the Lien Viet, or Vietnamese National Popular Front. In 1951 the majority of the Viet Minh leadership was absorbed into the Lao Dong, or Vietnamese Workers' Party (later Vietnamese Communist) Party, which remained the dominant force in North Vietnam.

Elements of the Viet Minh joined with the Viet Cong guerrilla force against the U.S.-supported government of South Vietnam and the United States in the Vietnam War (or Second Indochina War) of the late 1950s, '60s, and early '70s. After the reunification of the country (1976) under communist rule, Viet Minh leaders continued to take an active role in Vietnamese politics.

THE YOUNG TURKS AND TURKISH NATIONALISM

The Young Turks (Turkish: Jöntürkler) was a coalition of various reform groups in the Ottoman Empire (a Turkish empire, centred in what is now Turkey, that held power from the Middle Ages until 1922) that led a revolutionary movement against the authoritarian regime of Sultan Abdülhamid II. The movement culminated in the establishment of a constitutional government. After their rise to power, the Young Turks introduced programs that promoted the modernization of the Ottoman Empire and a new spirit of Turkish nationalism. Their handling of foreign affairs, however, resulted in the dissolution of the Ottoman state.

In 1889 a group of students in the Imperial Medical Academy in Istanbul initiated a conspiracy against Abdülhamid that spread rapidly to other colleges in the city. When the plot was uncovered, many of its leaders fled abroad, mainly to Paris, where they prepared the groundwork for a future revolution against Abdülhamid. Among the most notable of the liberal émigrés was Ahmed Rıza, who became a key spokesman for the influential Young Turk organization known as the Committee of Union and Progress (CUP), which advocated a program of orderly reform under a strong central government and the exclusion of all foreign influence. A major rival faction was formed by Prince Sabaheddin. His group, called the League of Private Initiative and Decentralization, espoused many of the same liberal principles as those propounded by the CUP, but, unlike the latter, it favoured administrative decentralization and European assistance to implement reforms.

Although the CUP and the League played a significant role in disseminating and stimulating liberal thought, the actual impetus for the Young Turk Revolution of 1908 came from groups within the empire, particularly from discontented members of the 3rd Army Corps in Macedonia. Many young officers of the corps garrisoned at Salonika (now Thessaloníka, Greece) organized to form the Ottoman Liberty Society in 1906. This secret revolutionary group merged with the CUP in Paris the following year, bringing to the Young Turk ideologists the command of the 3rd Army Corps. Later in 1907 the CUP and the League of Private Initiative and Decentralization agreed, though reluctantly, to work together to achieve their common goal.

On July 3, 1908, Maj. Ahmed Niyazi of the 3rd Corps led a revolt against the provincial authorities in Resna. Other conspirators soon followed his example, and the rebellion rapidly spread throughout the empire. Unable to rely on government troops, Abdülhamid announced on July 23 the restoration of the 1876 constitution and recalled parliament. The Young Turks had succeeded in establishing a constitutional government, but their deep-seated ideological differences resurfaced and prevented them from taking effective control of that government until 1913, when the CUP under new leaders—the triumvirate of Talât Paşa, Ahmed Cemal Paşa, and Enver Paşa—set itself up as the real arbiter of Ottoman politics.

While in power, the Young Turks carried out administrative reforms, especially of provincial administration, that led to more centralization. They were also the first Ottoman reformers to promote industrialization. In addition, the programs of the Young Turk regime effectuated greater secularization of the legal system and provided for the education of women and better state-operated primary schools. Such positive developments in domestic affairs, however, were largely overshadowed by the disastrous consequences of the regime's foreign policy decisions. An overly hasty appraisal of Germany's military capability by the Young Turk leaders led them to break neutrality and enter World War I (1914–18) on the side of the Central Powers. Upon the end of the war, with defeat imminent, the CUP Cabinet resigned on Oct. 9, 1918, less than a month before the Ottomans signed the Armistice of Mudros.

NATIONALISM IN THE MIDDLE EAST

Nationalism has been an especially powerful force in the Middle East since the country of Israel was created there in 1948. The establishment of Israel, itself the result of a Jewish nationalist movement called Zionism, prompted an increase in nationalism among the Arabs of the region, particularly the Palestinians. Palestinian nationalism, fueled by religious differences with the Jews of Israel (Arabs largely follow Islam), led to the formation of the groups known as the Palestine Liberation Organization and Ḥamās.

Zionism

Zionism is the Jewish nationalist movement that has had as its goal the creation and support of a Jewish national state in Palestine, the ancient homeland of the Jews (Hebrew: Eretz Yisra'el, "the Land of Israel"). Though Zionism originated in eastern and central Europe in the latter part of the 19th century, it is in many ways a continuation of the ancient nationalist attachment of the Jews and of the Jewish religion to the historical region of Palestine, where one of the hills of ancient Jerusalem was called Zion.

In the 16th and 17th centuries a number of "messiahs" came forward trying to persuade Jews to "return" to Palestine. The Haskala ("Enlightenment") movement of the late 18th century, however, urged Jews to assimilate into Western secular culture. In the early 19th century interest in a return of the Jews to Palestine was kept alive mostly by Christian millenarians. Despite the Haskala, eastern European Jews did not assimilate and in reaction to tsarist pogroms formed the Ḥovevei Ẓiyyon ("Lovers of Zion") to promote the settlement of Jewish farmers and artisans in Palestine.

A political turn was given to Zionism by Theodor Herzl, an Austrian journalist who regarded assimilation as most desirable but, in view of anti-Semitism, impossible to realize. Thus, he argued, if Jews were forced by external pressure to form a nation, they could lead a normal existence only through concentration in one territory. In 1897 Herzl convened the first Zionist Congress at Basel, Switz., which drew up the Basel program of the movement, stating that "Zionism strives to create for the Jewish people a home in Palestine secured by public law."

The centre of the movement was established in Vienna, where Herzl published the official weekly *Die Welt* ("The World"). Zionist congresses met yearly until 1901 and then every two years. When the Ottoman government refused Herzl's request for Palestinian autonomy, he found support in Great Britain. In 1903 the British government offered 6,000 square miles (15,500 square km) of uninhabited Uganda for settlement, but the Zionists held out for Palestine.

At the death of Herzl in 1904, the leadership moved from Vienna to Cologne, then to Berlin. Prior to World War I Zionism represented only a minority of Jews, mostly from Russia but led by Austrians and Germans. It developed propaganda through orators and pamphlets, created its own newspapers, and gave an impetus to what was called a "Jewish renaissance" in letters and arts. The development of the Modern Hebrew language largely took place during this period.

The failure of the Russian Revolution of 1905 and the wave of pogroms and repressions that followed caused growing numbers of Russian Jewish youth to emigrate to Palestine as pioneer settlers. By 1914 there were about 90,000 Jews in Palestine; 13,000 settlers lived in 43 Jewish agricultural settlements, many of them supported by the French Jewish philanthropist Baron Edmond de Rothschild.

Upon the outbreak of World War I political Zionism reasserted itself, and its leadership passed to Russian Jews living in England. Two such Zionists, Chaim Weizmann and Nahum Sokolow, were instrumental in obtaining the Balfour Declaration from Great Britain (Nov. 2, 1917), which promised British support for the creation of a Jewish national home in Palestine. The declaration was included in Britain's League of Nations mandate over Palestine (1922).

In the following years the Zionists built up the Jewish urban and rural settlements in Palestine, perfecting autonomous organizations and solidifying Jewish cultural life and Hebrew education. In March 1925 the Jewish population in Palestine was officially estimated at 108,000, and it had risen to about 238,000 (20 percent of the population) by 1933. Jewish immigration remained relatively slow, however, until the rise of Hitlerism in Europe. Nevertheless, the Arab population feared Palestine eventually would become a Jewish state and bitterly resisted Zionism and the British policy supporting it. Several Arab revolts, especially in 1929 and 1936–39, caused the British to devise schemes to reconcile the Arab and Zionist demands.

Hitlerism and the large-scale extermination of European Jews led many Jews to seek refuge in Palestine and many others, especially in the United States, to embrace Zionism. As tensions grew among Arabs and Zionists, Britain submitted the Palestine problem first to Anglo-U.S. discussion for solution and later to the UN, which on Nov. 29, 1947, proposed partition of the country into separate Arab and Jewish states and the internationalization of Jerusalem. The creation of the State of Israel on May 14, 1948, brought about the Arab-Israeli war of 1948–49, in the course of which Israel obtained more land than had been provided by the UN resolution, and drove out 800,000 Arabs who became displaced persons known as Palestinians. Thus 50 years after the first Zionist congress and 30 years after the Balfour Declaration, Zionism achieved its aim of establishing a Jewish state in Palestine, but at the same time it became an armed camp surrounded by hostile Arab nations and Palestinian "liberation" organizations engaged in terrorism in and outside of Israel.

Palestine Liberation Organization

The Palestine Liberation Organization (PLO) is an umbrella political organization claiming to represent the world's estimated eight million Palestinians — those Arabs, and their descendants, who lived in mandated Palestine before the creation there of the State of Israel in 1948. It was formed in 1964 to centralize the leadership of various Palestinian groups that previously had operated as clandestine resistance movements. It came into prominence only after the Arab-Israeli war of June 1967, however, and engaged in a protracted guerrilla war against Israel during the 1960s, '70s, and '80s before entering into peace negotiations with that country in the 1990s.

After 1967 the influence of the more militant and independent-minded groups within the PLO increased. Major PLO factions or those associated with it included Fatah (since 1968 the preeminent faction within the PLO), the Popular Front for the Liberation of Palestine (PFLP), the Democratic Front for the Liberation of Palestine (DFLP), and al-Ṣāʿiqah. Over the decades the PLO's membership has varied as its constituent bodies have reorganized and disagreed internally. The more radical factions have remained steadfast in their goals of the destruction of Israel and its replacement with a secular state in which Muslims, Jews, and Christians would, ostensibly, participate as equals. Moderate factions within the PLO, however, have proved willing to accept a negotiated settlement with Israel that would yield a Palestinian state, which at times has led to internecine violence.

In 1969 Yāsir 'Arafāt, leader of Fatah, was named the
PLO's chairman. From the late 1960s the PLO organized
and launched guerrilla attacks against Israel from its bases
in Jordan, which prompted significant Israeli reprisals and
led to instability within Jordan. This, in turn, brought the
PLO into growing conflict with the government of King
Hussein of Jordan in 1970, and in 1971 the PLO was forcibly expelled from the country by the Jordanian army.
Thereafter the PLO shifted its bases to Lebanon and continued its attacks on Israel. The PLO's relations with the
Lebanese were tumultuous, and the organization soon
became embroiled in Lebanon's sectarian disputes and
contributed to that country's eventual slide into civil war.
During that time, factions within the PLO shifted from
attacks on military targets to a strategy of terrorism—a
policy the organization fervently denied embracing—and
a number of high-profile attacks, including bombings and
aircraft hijackings, were staged by PLO operatives against
Israeli and Western targets.

Beginning in 1974, 'Arafāt advocated an end to the
PLO's attacks on targets outside of Israel and sought the
world community's acceptance of the PLO as the legitimate representative of the Palestinian people. In 1974 the
Arab heads of state recognized the PLO as the sole legitimate representative of all Palestinians, and the PLO was
admitted to full membership in the Arab League in 1976.
Yet the PLO was excluded from the negotiations between
Egypt and Israel that resulted in 1979 in a peace treaty that
returned the Israeli-occupied Sinai Peninsula to Egypt but
failed to win Israel's agreement to the establishment of a
Palestinian state in the occupied territories of the West
Bank and Gaza Strip.

Israel's desire to destroy the PLO and its bases in
Lebanon led Israel to invade that country in June 1982.
Israeli troops soon surrounded the Lebanese capital of

Yāsir 'Arafāt fought to change the Palestine Liberation Organization's image from violent entity to legitimate representative of the Palestinian nation. Getty Images

Beirut, which for several years had been the PLO's head-quarters. Following negotiations, PLO forces evacuated Beirut and were transported to sympathetic Arab countries.

Bereft of bases from which PLO forces might attack the Jewish state and encouraged by the success of a popular uprising, the *intifāḍah* (Arabic: "shaking off"), that began in 1987 in the occupied territories, the PLO leadership developed a more flexible and conciliatory policy toward peace with Israel. On Nov. 15, 1988, the PLO proclaimed the "State of Palestine," a kind of government-in-exile; and on April 2, 1989, the PNC elected 'Arafāt president of the new quasi-state. The PLO during this period also recognized UN Resolutions 242 and 338, thereby tacitly acknowledging Israel's right to exist. It thus abandoned its long-standing goal of replacing Israel with a secular, democratic state in Palestine in favour of a policy accepting separate Israeli and Palestinian states, with the latter occupying the West Bank and the Gaza Strip.

'Arafāt's decision to support Iraq during the 1990–91 Persian Gulf War alienated the PLO's key financial donors among the gulf oil states and contributed to a further softening of its position regarding peace with Israel. In April 1993 the PLO under 'Arafāt's leadership entered secret negotiations with Israel on a possible peace settlement between the two sides. The first document in a set of Israel-PLO agreements—generally termed the Oslo accords—was signed on Sept. 13, 1993, by 'Arafāt and the leaders of the Israeli government. The agreements called for mutual recognition between the two sides and set out conditions under which the West Bank and Gaza would be gradually handed over to the newly formed Palestinian Authority (PA), of which 'Arafāt was to become the first president. This transfer was originally to have taken place over a five-year interim period in which Israel and the Palestinians were to have negotiated a permanent settlement. Despite some success, however, negotiations faltered sporadically throughout the 1990s and collapsed completely amid increasing violence—dubbed Al-Aqṣā *intifādah*—in late 2000. This second uprising had a distinctly religious character, and Islamic groups such as Hamās, which had come to the fore during the first *intifādah*, attracted an ever-larger following and threatened the PLO's dominance within Palestinian society.

Hamās

Hamās (English: Islamic Resistance Movement) is a militant Palestinian Islamic movement in the West Bank and Gaza Strip that is dedicated to the destruction of Israel and the creation of an Islamic state in Palestine. Founded in 1987, Hamās opposed the 1993 peace accords between Israel and the Palestine Liberation Organization (PLO).

From the late 1970s, Islamic activists connected with the pan-Islamic Muslim Brotherhood established a network of charities, clinics, and schools and became active in the territories (the Gaza Strip and West Bank) occupied by Israel after the 1967 Six-Day War. In Gaza they were active in many mosques, while their activities in the West Bank generally were limited to the universities. The Muslim Brotherhood's activities in these areas were generally nonviolent, but a number of small groups in the occupied territories began to call for jihad, or holy war, against Israel. In December 1987, at the beginning of the Palestinian *intifādah* movement against Israeli occupation, Hamās (which also is an Arabic word meaning "zeal") was established by members of the Muslim Brotherhood and religious factions of the PLO, and the new organization quickly acquired a broad following. In its 1988 charter, Hamās maintained that Palestine is an Islamic homeland that can never be surrendered to non-Muslims and that

waging holy war to wrest control of Palestine from Israel
is a religious duty for Palestinian Muslims. This position
brought it into conflict with the PLO, which in 1988 recognized Israel's right to exist.

Ḥamās's armed wing, the 'Izz al-Dīn al-Qassām Forces,
began a campaign of terrorism against Israel. Israel
responded by imprisoning the founder of Ḥamās, Shaykh
Aḥmad Yāsīn, in 1991 and arresting and deporting hundreds of Ḥamās activists. Ḥamās denounced the 1993
peace agreement between Israel and the PLO and, along
with the Islamic Jihad group, subsequently intensified its
terror campaign using suicide bombers. The PLO and
Israel responded with harsh security and punitive measures, although PLO chairman Yāsir 'Arafāt, seeking to
include Ḥamās in the political process, appointed Ḥamās
members to leadership positions in the Palestinian
Authority (PA). The collapse of peace talks between
Israelis and Palestinians in September 2000 led to an
increase in violence that came to be known as the Aqṣā
intifādah. That conflict was marked by a degree of violence
unseen in the first *intifādah*, and Ḥamās activists further
escalated their attacks on Israelis and engaged in a number
of suicide bombings in Israel itself.

In early 2005 Mahmoud Abbas, president of the PA,
and Israeli prime minister Ariel Sharon announced a suspension of hostilities as Israel prepared to withdraw troops
from some Palestinian territories. After much negotiation, Ḥamās agreed to the cease-fire, although sporadic
violence continued. In the 2006 elections for the
Palestinian Legislative Council, Ḥamās won a surprise victory over Fatah, capturing the majority of seats. The two
groups eventually formed a coalition government, though
clashes between Ḥamās and Fatah forces in the Gaza Strip
intensified, prompting Abbas to dissolve the Ḥamās-led

government and declare a state of emergency in June 2007. Hamās was left in control of the Gaza Strip, while a Fatah-led emergency cabinet had control of the West Bank.

Later that year Israel declared the Gaza Strip under Hamās a hostile entity and approved a series of sanctions that included power cuts, heavily restricted imports, and border closures. Hamās attacks on Israel continued, as did Israeli attacks on the Gaza Strip. After months of negotiations, in June 2008 Israel and Hamās agreed to implement a truce scheduled to last six months; however, this was threatened shortly thereafter as each accused the other of violations, which escalated in the last months of the agreement. When the truce officially expired on December 19, Hamās announced that they did not intend to extend it. Broader hostilities erupted shortly thereafter as Israel, responding to sustained rocket fire, mounted a series of air strikes across the region—among the strongest in years—meant to target Hamās. After a week of air strikes, Israeli forces initiated a ground campaign into the Gaza Strip amid calls from the international community for a cease-fire. Following more than three weeks of hostilities—in which perhaps more than 1,000 were killed and tens of thousands left homeless—Israel and Hamās each declared a unilateral cease-fire.

ANTICOLONIALISM IN AFRICA

Anticolonial efforts gripped much of Africa during the 20th century. The struggles of various African peoples, which were often met with suppression—sometimes violent—by colonial governments, were long and arduous but ultimately brought independence to the continent. The Pan-African movement was an outstanding example of African peoples uniting against colonial control. With independence, however, many African countries experienced political turmoil. In South Africa, the African National Congress fought for the representation of black people in the white-controlled government, which was in a way a continuation of European colonialism. In northern Africa, the National Liberation Front of Algeria led the war for independence from France but then established itself as Algeria's sole political party. Similar movements for political change, many of them informed by the nationalist sentiments of diverse African groups, took place throughout Africa.

Pan-African Movement

The Pan-African movement was dedicated to establishing independence for African nations and cultivating unity among black people throughout the world. It originated in conferences held in London (1900, 1919, 1921, 1923) and other cities. W.E.B. Du Bois, an American civil rights activist and historian, was a principal early leader. The important sixth Pan-African conference (Manchester, 1945) included Jomo Kenyatta and Kwame Nkrumah. The first truly intergovernmental conference was held in Accra, Ghana, in 1958, where Patrice Lumumba was a key speaker. Founded by Robert M. Sobukwe and others in South Africa in 1959, the Pan-Africanist Congress (PAC) was a political alternative to the African National Congress, which was seen as contaminated by non-African influences. The founding of the Organization of African Unity (OAU; now the African Union) by Julius Nyerere and others in 1963 was a milestone, and the OAU soon became the most important Pan-Africanist organization.

African National Congress

The African National Congress (ANC) is a South African political party and black nationalist organization. Founded in 1912 as the South African Native National Congress, it had as its main goal the maintenance of voting rights for Coloureds (persons of mixed race) and black Africans in Cape Province. It was renamed the African National Congress in 1923. From the 1940s it spearheaded the fight to eliminate apartheid, the official South African policy of racial separation and discrimination. The ANC was banned from 1960 to 1990 by the white South African government; during these three decades it operated underground and outside South African territory. The ban was lifted in 1990, and Nelson Mandela, the president of the ANC, was elected in 1994 to head South Africa's first multiethnic government.

In the late 1920s the ANC's leaders split over the issue of cooperation with the Communist Party (founded in 1921), and the ensuing victory of the conservatives left the

Nelson Mandela was imprisoned because of his stance against apartheid in his native South Africa. Once freed, he rose to prominence as the first democratically elected president of the country. Walter Dhladhla/AFP/ Getty Images

party small and disorganized through the 1930s. In the
1940s, however, the ANC revived under younger leaders
who pressed for a more militant stance against segregation in South Africa. The ANC Youth League, founded in
1944, attracted such figures as Walter Sisulu, Oliver Tambo,
and Mandela, who galvanized the movement and challenged the moderate leadership. Under the presidency of
Albert Luthuli, the ANC after 1952 began sponsoring nonviolent protests, strikes, boycotts, and marches against
the apartheid policies that had been introduced by the
National Party government that came to power in 1948.
Party membership grew rapidly. A campaign against the
pass laws (blacks were required to carry passes indicating
their employment status) and other government policies
culminated in the Defiance Campaign of 1952. In the process ANC leaders became a target of police harassment: in
1956 many of its leaders were arrested and charged with
treason (known as the Treason Trial, 1956–59).

In 1960 the Pan-Africanist Congress (PAC), which had
broken away from the ANC in 1959, organized massive
demonstrations against the pass laws during which police
killed 69 unarmed demonstrators at Sharpeville (south of
Johannesburg). At this point the National Party outlawed
both the ANC and the PAC. Denied legal avenues for
political change, the ANC first turned to sabotage and
then began to organize outside of South Africa for guerrilla warfare. In 1961 an ANC military organization,
Umkhonto we Sizwe ("Spear of the Nation"), with Mandela
as its head, was formed to carry out acts of sabotage as
part of its campaign against apartheid. Mandela and other
ANC leaders were sentenced to life imprisonment in 1964
(the Rivonia Trial). Although the ANC's campaign of guerrilla warfare was basically ineffective because of stringent
South African internal security measures, surviving ANC

cadres kept the organization alive in Tanzania and Zambia under Tambo's leadership. The ANC began to revive inside South Africa toward the end of the 1970s, following the Soweto uprising in 1976, when the police and army killed more than 600 people, many of them children. About 1980 the banned black, green, and gold tricolour flag of the ANC began to be seen inside South Africa.

South Africa descended into virtual civil war during the 1980s. The administration of F.W. de Klerk lifted the ban on the ANC in 1990, and its leaders were released from prison or allowed to return to South Africa and conduct peaceful political activities. Mandela, the most important of the ANC's leaders, succeeded Oliver Tambo as president in 1991. Mandela led the ANC in negotiations (1992–93) with the government over transition to a government elected by universal suffrage. In April 1994 the party swept to power in the country's first such election, winning more than 60 percent of the vote for seats in the new National Assembly. Mandela, who headed a government of national unity, was inaugurated as South Africa's first black president on May 10, 1994. After the withdrawal of the National Party from the government in 1996, the ANC entered into an alliance with its previous rival, the Inkatha Freedom Party, led by Mangosuthu Buthelezi. Mandela stepped down as ANC president in 1997, and in June 1999 his successor, Thabo Mbeki, became the second black president of South Africa.

The party celebrated its 90th anniversary in 2002. While the ANC continued to dominate South African politics, discord within the party led some members to break away and establish a new party, Congress of the People (COPE), in December 2008. Despite the challenge from COPE and other parties, the ANC was victorious in the 2009 general election.

National Liberation Front

The National Liberation Front (French: Front de Libération Nationale; FLN) was the only constitutionally legal party in Algeria from 1962 to 1989. The party was a continuation of the revolutionary body that directed the Algerian war of independence against France (1954–62). The FLN was created by the Revolutionary Committee of Unity and Action (Comité Révolutionnaire d'Unité et d'Action, or CRUA), a group of young Algerian militants organized in March 1954. The CRUA sought to reconcile the warring factions of the nationalist movement and to wage war against the French colonial presence in Algeria. By the middle of 1956 almost all the Algerian nationalist organizations had joined the FLN, which was then reorganized so that it resembled a provisional government, including a five-member executive body and a legislative body, which consisted of all the district heads.

During the Algerian war for independence, the National Liberation Army (Armée de Libération Nationale [ALN]), under the command of Col. Houari Boumedienne, acted as the military arm of the FLN. From camps stationed behind Tunisian and Moroccan borders, the ALN's external contingent provided logistical support and weaponry to ALN forces within the country. The war for independence continued until March 18, 1962, when the French at last signed a cease-fire agreement with the FLN at Évian-les-Bains and made provisions for future economic and social cooperation. In a referendum held July 1, 1962, the Algerians voted overwhelmingly for self-determination and approved the Évian Agreement.

The proclamation of Algerian independence on July 3, 1962, was immediately followed by a power struggle within the FLN. A new constitution approved in February 1989 eliminated both the country's socialist ideology and its one-party political system, in effect signaling the further decline of the FLN. A number of parties subsequently emerged, several of which soon challenged the FLN. The FLN lost greater presence in the midst of the political turmoil and violence of the 1990s. In the early 21st century, however, despite a number of internal crises, a revived FLN performed well in parliamentary and regional elections. In addition, the election of FLN member Abdelaziz Bouteflika to the country's presidency in 1999, as well as his subsequent appointment to the largely honorary position as head of the FLN in 2005, laid the foundation for closer links between the party and the presidency.

PERONISM IN ARGENTINA

One of the most evident expressions of nationalism in South America was the Peronist movement in Argentina. Peronism refers to the nationalistic and populist policies espoused by Pres. Juan Perón. It has played an important part in Argentina's history since the mid-1940s.

The Peronist movement arose as the personal following of Col. Juan Perón. In 1943, after participating in a successful military coup, Perón became Argentina's minister of labour, a position through which he enacted various social measures to help the country's growing class of urban industrial workers. Gaining the admiration of the masses, Perón called for the state to take a leading role in the economy to ensure cooperation between businesses and labour. In 1946 he was elected to the presidency with the strong support of the workers and their labour unions; he also gained the support of many lower-middle-class citizens and of the country's industrialists. After Perón was overthrown and exiled in

1955 by the military, the leaderless Peronist movement was weakened by factional conflicts, since it was composed of many divergent elements, from left-wing trade unionists to right-wing authoritarian nationalists. Nonetheless, the movement remained the main civilian contender for power in Argentina.

Under the new name of the Justicialist Nationalist Movement (later the Justicialist Party), the Peronists swept back into power in 1973 when the military permitted the first general elections in 10 years. Perón returned from exile and became president. However, deep dissension between right-wing and left-wing Peronists erupted into terrorism and violence after Perón's death in 1974, and the military overthrew Perón's widow and successor as president, Isabel, in 1976. The Peronists lost the presidential election of 1983, but in 1989 their candidate, Carlos Saúl Menem, was elected to the presidency. Breaking with traditional Peronist policies, Menem implemented free-market-oriented policies, which expanded the party's base to include the wealthy and business classes. In 1999 the Peronists lost the presidency, but after massive rioting forced the resignation of Pres. Fernando de la Rúa in 2001, the Peronists recaptured the office.

INDIGENOUS PEOPLES' RIGHTS

The rights of indigenous peoples around the world were largely ignored until the 20th century, when a number of communities began demanding recognition of their legal, political, and land rights. Prominent among these groups were the Indians of the Indigenismo movement in Latin America (notably the Maya of Guatemala) and American Indians (Native Americans) in the United States, though the various peoples known as Scheduled Tribes in India, the Aboriginals of Australia, the Maori of New Zealand, and others were active as well. Some sought greater representation in politics; others fought for recognition as sovereign nations.

While most indigenous groups focused by necessity on local, regional, or national issues, in the late 20th and early 21st centuries many groups increasingly emphasized their interaction with the global community of aboriginal peoples. The quest for indigenous self-determination received international recognition in 1982, when the UN Economic and Social Council created the Working Group on Indigenous Populations. In 1985 this group began to draft an indigenous rights document. In 1995 the UN Commission on Human Rights received the draft Declaration of the Rights of Indigenous Peoples. The commission assigned a working group to review the declaration, and in 2006 the group submitted a final document to the Human Rights Council. Despite efforts by many members of the UN General Assembly to block a vote on the declaration, it was passed in 2007 by an overwhelming margin: 144 votes in favour, 11 abstentions, and 4 negative votes (Australia, Canada, New Zealand, and the United States).

Indigenismo

Indigenismo is a movement in Latin America advocating a dominant social and political role for Indians in countries where they constitute a majority of the population. A sharp distinction is drawn by its members between Indians and Europeans, or those of European ancestry, who have dominated the Indian majorities since the Spanish conquest in the early 16th century. In Mexico, beginning with the Revolution of 1911, the movement became very influential, particularly during the presidency of Lázaro Cárdenas (1934–40), when serious efforts were made to reconstitute the nation according to its Indian heritage. In Peru the Aprista movement was strongly influenced by Indigenismo, and its members even proposed that Latin America be renamed Indo-America.

One of the most renowned advocates of indigenous rights in Latin America is the Guatemalan activist Rigoberta Menchú (born in 1959). As a young woman, Menchú, of the Quiché Maya group, became an activist in the local women's rights movement and joined with the Catholic church to advocate for social reform. The activism of Menchú and her family led to persecution by Guatemala's military government. During Guatemala's ensuing civil war, her father died in a fire while protesting human rights abuses by the military. Menchú's younger brother was kidnapped, tortured, and killed by a military death squad in 1979, and her mother was kidnapped, raped, mutilated, and murdered by soldiers the following year. Menchú fled to Mexico in 1981 and was cared for there by members of a liberal Roman Catholic group. She soon joined international efforts to make the Guatemalan government cease its brutal counterinsurgency campaigns against Indian peasants, becoming a skilled public speaker and organizer in the course of her efforts.

Menchú gained international prominence in 1983 with her widely translated book *I, Rigoberta Menchú*. She received the Nobel Peace Prize in 1992 for her continuing efforts to achieve social justice and mutual reconciliation in Guatemala; she used the prize money to found the Rigoberta Menchú Tum Foundation, an Indian advocacy organization. In February 2007 Menchú created the Indian-led political movement Winaq (Mayan: "The Wholeness of the Human Being"). That September, as the candidate of a coalition between Winaq and the left-wing

Encounter for Guatemala party, she ran for president of Guatemala but earned less than 3 percent of the vote. The following year Menchú began the legal process of creating a formal Winaq political party. If formed, it would be the first Guatemalan political party to represent indigenous groups directly.

American Indian Movement

The American Indian Movement (AIM) is a militant American Indian civil rights organization, founded in Minneapolis, Minn., in 1968 by Dennis Banks, Clyde Bellecourt, Eddie Benton Banai, and George Mitchell. Later, Russell Means became a prominent spokesman for the group. Its original purpose was to help Indians in urban ghettos who had been displaced by government programs that had the effect of forcing them from the reservations. Its goals eventually encompassed the entire spectrum of Indian demands—economic independence, revitalization of traditional culture, protection of legal rights, and, most especially, autonomy over tribal areas and the restoration of lands that they believed had been illegally seized.

AIM was involved in many highly publicized protests. It was one of the Indian groups involved in the occupation (1969–71) of Alcatraz Island; the march (1972) on Washington, D.C., to protest violation of treaties (in which AIM members occupied the office of the Bureau of Indian Affairs); and the takeover (1973) of a site at Wounded Knee to protest the government's Indian policy. In the mid-1970s AIM's efforts were centred on the prevention of resource exploitation of Indian lands by the federal government. With many of its leaders in prison, and torn by internal dissension, the national leadership disbanded in 1978, although local groups continued to function. From 1981 an AIM group occupied part of the Black Hills (South

Dakota) to press its demands for return of the area to
Indian jurisdiction.

SEPARATISM IN QUEBEC

In Canada the issue of Quebec's autonomy dominated
politics for the last decades of the 20th century. Through
various historical constitutional guarantees, Quebec,
which is the sole Canadian province where citizens of
French origin are in the majority, has developed a distinctive culture that differs in many respects from that of the
rest of Canada—and, indeed, from the rest of North
America. Although there are many in Quebec who support the confederation with the English-speaking
provinces, many French Quebecois have endorsed separatism and secession from the rest of Canada as a means to
ensure not only material prosperity and liberty but also
ethnic survival. As a consequence, they have tended to act
as a cohesive unit in national matters and to support those
political parties most supportive of their claims. In 1976
Quebec's voters elected the Parti Québécois, whose major
policy platform was "sovereignty association," a form of
separation from Canada but with close economic ties, to
form its provincial government. In 1980, however, three-
fifths of Quebecois voted against outright separation; in
1995 a proposition aimed at separation—or at least a major
restructuring of Quebec's relationship with Canada—was
defeated again, though by a margin of only 1 percent. The
1995 referendum highlighted Quebec's internal divisions,
as nine-tenths of English speakers opposed separation
while three-fifths of French speakers supported it.

There have been several unsuccessful efforts to entice
Quebec to approve the constitution formally and to
develop a balance of powers acceptable to both Quebec
and the rest of Canada. For example, the Meech Lake

Accord (1987), which would have recognized Quebec's status as a distinct society and would have re-created a provincial veto power, failed to win support in Manitoba and Newfoundland, and the Charlottetown Accord (1992), which addressed greater autonomy for both Quebec and the aboriginal population, was rejected in a national referendum (it lost decisively in Quebec and the western provinces).

Meanwhile, the Bloc Québécois, which supports Quebec's independence and maintains links with the provincial Parti Québécois, was formed in 1990 to contest federal elections. It won 54 seats in Canada's House of Commons in 1993 and became the official opposition until 1997. Its federal representation dropped in 2000, to 38 seats, but in 2004 and 2006 the party's support rebounded, and it won more than 50 seats at each election. In the minority Conservative government of Stephen Harper, the Bloc was courted as a coalition partner, most notably with the 2006 motion that recognized the people of Quebec as a nation "within a united Canada."

AFROCENTRISM AND BLACK NATIONALISM

Afrocentrism is a cultural and political movement whose mainly African American adherents regard themselves and all other blacks as syncretic Africans and believe that their worldview should positively reflect traditional African values. Molefi Asante, an African American scholar and activist, coined the terms Afrocentrism, Afrocology, and Afrocentricity.

Afrocentrism was influenced by several earlier black nationalist movements, including Ethiopianism and Pan-Africanism. The latter became a major presence in the United States and elsewhere with the emergence of the Jamaican activist Marcus Garvey, who promoted the idea of an African diaspora and called for a separate African state for black Americans. Garvey's bitter enemy, W.E.B. Du Bois, who helped to found the integration-minded National Association for the Advancement of Colored People (NAACP) in 1909, was also interested in Pan-Africanism and organized world conferences on the subject from 1919 to 1927. Other antecedents included the Negritude literary movement, launched in France in the 1930s by Francophone African intellectuals such as Léopold Senghor, and the Nation of Islam, whose leaders—including Elijah Muhammad and Malcolm X—preached not only the need for a black homeland but also the cultural and genetic superiority of blacks.

Equally important to Afrocentrism were figures such as the African American scholar Maulana Karenga, whose work resulted in the creation of the Afrocentric holiday of Kwanzaa (honoring African heritage and culture) in 1966; the Senegalese scientist Cheikh Anta Diop, who wrote about the cultural unity of Africa, the African nature of Egyptian civilization, and the "theft" of African civilization by Europeans; and the African American historian Carter G. Woodson, who emphasized the teaching of African history as a way of counteracting feelings of inferiority inculcated in black Americans through centuries of subordination by whites.

Afrocentrism gained significant legitimacy in the United States from the 1960s as a result of the civil rights movement, the multicultural movement, and the immigration of large numbers of nonwhites. Its following increased dramatically during the 1980s, when many African Americans felt alienated from the "conservative revolution" of Pres. Ronald Reagan but were simultaneously attracted by the conservatives' call for a return to traditional values. The Afrocentrists' complicated reaction to the conservative revival both reflected and reinforced conservative elements in Afrocentric thinking.

Black nationalism was a political and social movement prominent in the 1960s and early '70s in the United States among some African Americans. The movement, which can be traced back to Marcus Garvey's Universal Negro Improvement Association of the 1920s, sought to acquire economic power and to infuse among blacks a sense of community and group feeling. Many adherents to black nationalism assumed the eventual creation of a separate black nation by African Americans. As an alternative to being assimilated by the American nation, which is predominantly white, black nationalists sought to maintain and promote their separate identity as a people of black ancestry. With such slogans as "black power" and "black is beautiful," they also sought to inculcate a sense of pride among blacks.

Chapter 9: Religio-Political Movements

I n the 20th century there arose a number of political movements related to their members' adherence to a particular religion. Christian and Islamic movements drew numerous followers and attracted widespread attention, but some political activity linked to Sikhism and Hinduism also emerged.

LIBERATION THEOLOGY

Liberation theology was a 20th-century Roman Catholic movement centred in Latin America that sought to apply religious faith by aiding the poor and oppressed through involvement in political and civic affairs. It stressed both heightened awareness of the socioeconomic structures that caused social inequities and active participation in changing those structures.

Liberation theologians believed that God speaks particularly through the poor and that the Bible can be understood only when seen from the perspective of the poor. They perceived that the Roman Catholic church in Latin America was fundamentally different from the church in Europe—i.e., that the church in Latin America was a church for and of the poor. In order to build this church, they established *communidades de base*, or base communities, local Christian groups composed of 10 to 30 members each, that both studied the Bible and attempted to meet their parishioners' immediate needs for food, water, sewage disposal, and electricity. A great number of base communities, led mostly by laypersons, sprang into being throughout Latin America.

The birth of the liberation theology movement is usually dated to the second Latin American Bishops' Conference, which was held in Medellín, Colombia, in 1968. At this conference the attending bishops issued a document affirming the rights of the poor and asserting that industrialized nations enriched themselves at the expense of Third World countries. The movement's seminal text, *Teología de la liberación* (1971; *A Theology of Liberation*), was written by Gustavo Gutiérrez, a Peruvian priest and theologian. Other leaders of the movement included Archbishop Oscar Arnulfo Romero of El Salvador (killed in 1980), Brazilian theologian Leonardo Boff, Jesuit scholar Jon Sobrino, and Archbishop Helder Câmara of Brazil.

The liberation theology movement gained strength in Latin America during the 1970s. Because of their insistence that ministry includes involvement in the political struggle of the poor against wealthy elites, liberation theologians were often criticized—both formally, from within the Roman Catholic church, and informally—as naive purveyors of Marxism and advocates of left-wing social activism. By the 1990s the Vatican, under Pope John Paul II, had begun trying to curb the movement's influence through the appointment of more conservative prelates in Brazil and elsewhere in Latin America.

THE CHRISTIAN RIGHT

In the United States in late 19th and early 20th centuries, Christian fundamentalists opposed the teaching of the theory of biological evolution in the public schools and supported the temperance movement against the sale and consumption of intoxicating liquor. Nevertheless, for much of the 20th century, Christian fundamentalism was not primarily a political movement. The Christian Right that emerged with the formation of Jerry Falwell's Moral Majority in 1979 was a response to transformations in American society and culture that took place in the 1960s and '70s. Fundamentalists were alarmed by a number of developments that, in their view, threatened to undermine the country's traditional moral values. These included the civil rights movement, the women's movement, and the gay rights movement; the relatively permissive sexual morality prevalent among young people; the teaching of evolution; and rulings by the U.S. Supreme Court that banned institutionally initiated group prayer and reading of the Bible in public schools and that affirmed the legal right to abortion. The federal government's attempts to revoke the tax-exempt status of many Christian schools founded to circumvent the federally mandated racial integration of public schools further galvanized many Christian fundamentalists in the South. Conservative Roman Catholics and Mormons, as well as a small number of Orthodox Jews, subsequently joined the fundamentalists in their political activism.

ISLAMIST MOVEMENTS

Because the term *fundamentalism* is Christian in origin, because it carries negative connotations, and because its use in an Islamic context emphasizes the religious roots of the phenomenon while neglecting the nationalistic and social grievances that underlie it, many scholars prefer to call Islamic fundamentalists "Islamists" and to speak of "Islamist movements" instead of Islamic fundamentalism. (The members of these movements refer to themselves simply as Muslims.) Nevertheless, the term *Islamic fundamentalism* has been current in both popular and scholarly literature since the late 20th century.

The subject of Islamic fundamentalism attracted a great deal of attention in the West after the Iranian Revolution of 1978–79—which deposed Iran's ruler, Mohammad Reza Shah Pahlavi (1919–80), and established an Islamic republic—and especially after the September 11 terrorist attacks on the United States in 2001 by al-Qaeda, an international Islamist terrorist network. The spectacular nature of these events may have lent plausibility to the common but mistaken belief in the West that Islam and Islamic fundamentalism are closely connected, if not identical. In fact, however, not all Muslims believe that the Qur'ān, the central religious text of Islam, is the literal and inerrant word of God, nor do all of them believe that Islam requires strict conformity to all the religious and moral precepts in the Qur'ān. More important, unlike genuine Islamic fundamentalists, most Muslims are not ideologically committed to the idea of a state and society based on Islamic religious law.

The character of Islamist movements varies greatly throughout the world. Some Islamists resort to terrorism, and some do not. Some espouse leftist political and economic programs, borrowing ideas from Marxism and other varieties of socialism, while others are more conservative. Most Islamists, however, insist on conformity to a code of conduct based on a literal interpretation of sacred scripture. They also insist that religion encompasses all aspects of life and hence that religion and politics cannot be separated. Like most fundamentalists, they generally have a Manichaean (dualistic) worldview: they believe that they are engaged in a holy war, or jihad, against their evil enemies.

To some extent, the Islamists' hostility toward the West is symptomatic of the rejection of modernity attributed to all fundamentalist movements, since much of what is modern is derived from the West. Another important factor is the Islamists' resentment of Western political and economic domination of the Middle East.

Among the Islamist movements that have attracted the most attention in the West is the Palestinian movement Ḥamās, which was founded in 1987. Ḥamās was created primarily to resist what most Palestinians viewed as the occupation of their land by Israel. There is thus a clearly nationalist dimension to this movement, though it is also committed to the creation of a strictly Islamic state. Ḥamās opposed the idea of a Palestinian state in the West Bank and Gaza and insisted on fighting a jihad to expel the Israelis from all of Palestine—from the Jordan River to the Mediterranean and from Lebanon to Egypt. It justified its terrorist attacks on Israelis as legitimate acts of war against an occupying power. Like some other Islamist movements in the Middle East, Ḥamās provides basic social services—including schools, clinics, and food for the unemployed—that are not provided, or are inadequately provided, by local authorities. These charitable activities are an important source of its appeal among the Palestinian population.

THE IRANIAN REVOLUTION

In January 1978, incensed by what they considered to be slanderous remarks made in a Tehrān newspaper against Ayatollah Ruhollah Khomeini, the exiled religious leader of the Shīʿite community in Iran, thousands of Iranian students took to the streets. They were followed by thousands more Iranian youth—mostly unemployed recent immigrants from the countryside—who began protesting the regime's excesses. The ruler of Iran, Mohammad Reza Shah Pahlavi, vacillated, assuming the protests to be part of an international conspiracy against him. Government

Religious beliefs clashed with politics to instigate the Iranian Revolution of the 1970s. Ayatollah Ruhollah Khomeini engineered the overthrow of the country's sitting government and named himself leader for life. Gabriel Duval/AFP/Getty Images

forces killed many people in the ensuing chaos, which only served to fuel the violence.

In exile, Khomeini coordinated this upsurge of opposition and demanded the shah's abdication. In January 1979, in what was officially described as a "vacation," the shah and his family fled Iran. The Regency Council established to run the country during the shah's absence proved unable to function, and Prime Minister Shahpur Bakhtiar, hastily appointed by the shah before his departure, was incapable of effecting compromise with Khomeini. Crowds in excess of a million demonstrated in Tehrān, proving the wide appeal of Khomeini, who arrived in Iran amid wild rejoicing on February 1. Khomeini, acclaimed as the religious leader of Iran's revolution, appointed a government four days later. In December a referendum on a new constitution created an Islamic republic in Iran, with Khomeini named Iran's political and religious leader for life.

HEZBOLLAH

Hezbollah (Arabic: Ḥizb Allāh; "Party of God") is a militia group and political party that first emerged as a faction in Lebanon following the Israeli invasion of that country in 1982. A group of Lebanese Shīʿite clerics formed Hezbollah with the goal of driving Israel from Lebanon and establishing an Islamic state there. Hezbollah was based in the predominately Shīʿite areas of the Biqāʿ Valley, southern Lebanon, and southern Beirut. It coordinated its efforts closely with Iran, from which it acquired substantial logistical support, and drew its manpower largely from disaffected younger, more radical members of Amal, a largely secular political movement. Throughout the 1980s Hezbollah engaged in increasingly sophisticated attacks against Israel and fought in Lebanon's civil war (1975–90), repeatedly coming to blows with Amal. During this time, Hezbollah allegedly engaged in terrorist attacks including kidnappings and car bombings, directed predominantly against Westerners, but also established a comprehensive social services network for its supporters.

Hezbollah was one of the few militia groups not disarmed by the Syrians at the end of the civil war, and they continued to fight a sustained guerrilla campaign against Israel in southern Lebanon until Israel's withdrawal in 2000. Hezbollah emerged as a leading political party in post–civil war Lebanon.

On July 12, 2006, Hezbollah, in an attempt to pressure Israel into releasing three Lebanese jailed in Israeli prisons, launched a military operation against Israel, killing a number of Israeli soldiers and abducting two as prisoners of war. This action led Israel to launch a major military offensive against Hezbollah. The 34-day war between Hezbollah and Israel resulted in the deaths of more than 1,000 Lebanese and the displacement of some 1,000,000. Fighting the Israeli Defense Forces to a standstill—a feat no other Arab militia had accomplished—Hezbollah and its leader, Hassan Nasrallah, emerged as heroes throughout much of the Arab world.

AL-QAEDA

Al-Qaeda (Arabic: al-Qā'idah; "the Base") is a broad-based militant Islamist organization founded by Osama bin Laden in the late 1980s. Al-Qaeda began as a logistical network to support Muslims fighting against the Soviet Union during the Afghan War; members were recruited throughout the Islamic world. When the Soviets withdrew from Afghanistan in 1989, the organization dispersed but continued to oppose what its leaders considered corrupt Islamic regimes and foreign (i.e., U.S.) presence in

Islamic lands. Based in The Sudan for a period in the early
1990s, the group eventually reestablished its headquarters in Afghanistan (c. 1996) under the patronage of the
Taliban militia.

Al-Qaeda merged with a number of other militant
Islamist organizations, including Egypt's Islamic Jihad
and the Islamic Group, and on several occasions its leaders declared jihad (holy war) against the United States.
The organization established camps for Muslim militants
from throughout the world, training tens of thousands in
paramilitary skills, and its agents engaged in numerous
terrorist attacks, including the destruction of the U.S.
embassies in Nairobi, Kenya, and Dar es Salaam, Tanzania
(1998), and a suicide bomb attack against the U.S. war-
ship *Cole* in Aden, Yemen (2000). In 2001, 19 militants
associated with al-Qaeda staged the September 11 attacks
against the United States. Within weeks the American
government responded by attacking Taliban and al-Qaeda
forces in Afghanistan. Thousands of militants were killed
or captured, among them several key members (including
the militant who allegedly planned and organized the
September 11 attacks), and the remainder and their leaders were driven into hiding.

The invasion of Afghanistan in 2001 challenged that
country's viability as an al-Qaeda sanctuary and training
ground and compromised communication, operational,
and financial linkages between al-Qaeda leadership and its
militants. Rather than significantly weakening al-Qaeda,
however, these realities prompted a structural evolution
and the growth of "franchising." Increasingly, attacks were
orchestrated not only from above by the centralized leadership (after the U.S. invasion of Afghanistan, based in the
Afghan-Pakistani border regions) but also by the local-
ized, relatively autonomous cells it encouraged. Such
grassroots independent groups—coalesced locally around

a common agenda but subscribing to the al-Qaeda name and its broader ideology—thus meant a diffuse form of militancy, and one far more difficult to confront.

TALIBAN

The Taliban (Persian: Ṭālebān; "Students") is an ultraconservative political and religious faction that emerged in Afghanistan in the mid-1990s following the withdrawal of Soviet troops, the collapse of Afghanistan's communist regime, and the subsequent breakdown in civil order. The faction took its name from its membership, which consisted largely of students trained in *madrasahs* (Islamic religious schools) that were established for Afghan refugees in the 1980s in northern Pakistan.

The Taliban emerged as a force for social order in 1994 in the southern Afghan province of Kandahār and quickly subdued the local warlords who controlled the south of the country. By late 1996 popular support for the Taliban among Afghanistan's southern Pashtun ethnic group, as well as assistance from conservative Islamic elements abroad, enabled the faction to seize the capital, Kabul, and gain effective control of the country. Resistance to the Taliban continued, however, particularly among non-Pashtun ethnic groups—namely the Tajik, Uzbek, and Hazāra—in the north, west, and central parts of the country, who saw the power of the predominantly Pashtun Taliban as a continuation of the traditional Pashtun hegemony of the country. By 2001 the Taliban controlled all but a small section of northern Afghanistan. World opinion, however, largely disapproved of the Taliban's social policies—including the near-total exclusion of women from public life (including employment and education), the systematic destruction of non-Islamic artistic relics (as occurred in the town of Bamiyan), and the implementation of harsh criminal punishments—and only a few countries recognized the regime. More significant was the fact that the Taliban allowed Afghanistan to be a haven for Islamic militants from throughout the world, including an exiled Saudi Arabian, Osama bin Laden, who, as leader of al-Qaeda, stood accused of organizing numerous terrorist attacks against American interests. The Taliban's refusal to extradite bin Laden to the United States following the attacks on the World Trade Center in New York City and the Pentagon outside Washington, D.C., on Sept. 11, 2001, prompted a military confrontation with the United States and allied powers. The Taliban was subsequently driven from power.

SIKH POLITICAL ACTIVISM

Sikh political activists of the late 20th and early 21st centuries sought to create an independent Sikh state in the Indian province of Punjab. Sikh activism first attracted attention in the West in 1978, when the fiery preacher Jarnail Singh Bhindranwale reportedly led a march to break up a gathering of the Sikh Nirankari movement, which orthodox Sikhs considered heretical. Bhindranwale, like other fundamentalists, stressed the need for conformity to a sacred text (the Adi Granth) and for the creation of a Sikh state governed according to sacred law. But such fundamentalist concerns were subordinated to nationalistic ones.

In June 1984, Indian troops stormed the Golden Temple in Amritsar and killed Bhindranwale and hundreds of his armed supporters. The assassination, as well as what Sikhs considered the desecration of their holiest shrine, infuriated the Sikh community and led to the assassination of Indira Gandhi, India's prime minister, by two of her Sikh bodyguards in October 1984. This in turn sparked riots in which Hindu mobs killed more than 2,000 Sikhs.

HINDU POLITICAL ACTIVISM

Hindu political activism in India actually has been influenced more by nationalism than by religion, in part because Hinduism does not have a specific sacred text to which conformity can be demanded. Moreover, conformity to a religious code has never been of particular importance to Hindu groups such as the Bharatiya Janata Party (BJP). For the members of such groups, Hinduism is above all a symbol of national identity rather than a set of rules to be obeyed.

The nationalistic orientation of the BJP is reflected in its name, which means "the Party of the Indian People." Similarly, the name of the Rashtriya Swayamesevak Sangh (RSS), a "self-defense" force associated with the BJP, means "National Volunteers Corps." Neither the BJP nor the RSS advocates the creation of a Hindu state. The principal concern of both groups is the danger posed to "the Hindu nation" by Islamic proselytization among untouchables and lower-caste Hindus; both groups have also vehemently opposed Christian proselytization in India for the same reason.

In a notorious incident in 1992, the Babri Mosjid ("Mosque of Bābur") at Ayodhya was demolished by a mob of militant Hindus; the subsequent rioting led to the deaths of more than 1,000 people. Although there was real religious fervour associated with the belief that the site of the mosque was the birthplace of the Hindu god Rama and the location of an ancient Hindu temple, the attack was above all a reflection of the Hindu nationalists' belief in the essentially Hindu character of India and their perception of Muslims as inherently alien.

Chapter 10:
Social and Ethical Movements

From the 19th century into the 21st, a variety of social and ethical movements have greatly influenced political developments in the United States, Europe, and around the world. Different movements have demanded equal rights for women, freedom and equal rights for people of African origin, an end to war, gay rights, and rights for animals. With their concern for individual rights and social justice, these movements share many of the tenets of modern liberalism.

WOMEN'S RIGHTS

The movement for women's rights, also known as the feminist movement, is based on the belief in the social, economic, and political equality of the sexes. Throughout most of Western history, however, women have not been viewed as men's equals. Women were long confined to the domestic sphere, while public life was reserved for men. In medieval Europe, women were denied the right to own property, to study, or to participate in public life. At the end of the 19th century in France, they were still compelled to cover their heads in public, and, in parts of Germany, a husband still had the right to sell his wife. Even as late as the early 20th century, women could neither vote nor hold elective office in Europe and in most of the United States (where several territories and states granted woman suffrage long before the federal government did so). Women were prevented from conducting business without a male representative, be it father, brother, husband, legal agent, or even son. Married women could not exercise control over their own children without the permission of their husbands. Moreover, women had little or no access to education and were barred from most professions. In some parts of the world, such restrictions on women continue today.

THE SUFFRAGE MOVEMENT AND AFTERMATH

The first women's rights convention in the United States was held in July 1848 in the small town of Seneca Falls, New York. Although Seneca Falls was followed by women's rights conventions in other states, the interest spurred by those first moments of organizing quickly faded. Concern in the United States turned to the pending Civil War, while, in Europe, the reformism of the 1840s gave way to the repression of the late 1850s. When the feminist movement rebounded, it became focused on a single issue, woman suffrage, a goal that would dominate international feminism for almost 70 years.

After the U.S. Civil War, American feminists assumed that woman suffrage would be included in the 15th Amendment to the U.S. Constitution, which prohibited disfranchisement on the basis of race. Yet leading abolitionists refused to support such inclusion, which prompted Elizabeth Cady Stanton, a leader of the Seneca Falls Convention, and Susan B. Anthony, a temperance activist, to form the National Woman Suffrage Association in 1869. At first, they based their demand for the vote on the Enlightenment principle of natural law, regularly invoking the concept of inalienable rights granted to all Americans by the Declaration of Independence. By 1900, however, the American passion for such principles as equality had been dampened by a flood of Eastern European immigrants and the growth of urban slums. Suffragist leaders, reflecting that shift in attitude, began appealing for the vote not

At the fore of the women's rights movement was the formidable team of Elizabeth Cady Stanton (left) *and Susan B. Anthony. The two waged battle to earn women the right to vote.* Kean Collection/Hulton Archive/ Getty Images

on the principle of justice or on the common humanity of men and women but on racist and nativist grounds. As early as 1894, in a speech, Carrie Chapman Catt declared that the votes of literate, American-born, middle-class women would balance the votes of foreigners.

This elitist inclination widened the divide between feminist organizers and the masses of American women who lived in those slums or spoke with foreign accents. As a result, working-class women—already more concerned with wages, hours, and protective legislation than with either the vote or issues such as women's property rights—threw themselves into the trade union movement rather than the feminists' ranks. Anthony, however, ceded no ground. In the 1890s, she asked for labour's support for woman suffrage but insisted that she and her movement would do nothing about the demands made by working women until her own battle had been won. Similarly, when asked to support the fight against Jim Crow segregation on the nation's railroads, she refused.

Alice Paul reignited the woman suffrage movement in the United States by copying English activists. Like the Americans, British suffragists, led by the National Union of Woman Suffrage Societies, had initially approached their struggle politely, with ladylike lobbying. But in 1903, a dissident faction led by Emmeline Pankhurst began a series of boycotts, bombings, and pickets. Their tactics ignited the nation, and, in 1918, the British Parliament extended the vote to women householders, householders' wives, and female university graduates over the age of 30.

Following the British lead, Paul's forces, the "shock troops" of the American suffrage crusade, organized mass demonstrations, parades, and confrontations with the police. In 1920, American feminism claimed its first major triumph with the passage of the Nineteenth Amendment to the Constitution, which gave women the right to vote.

Once the crucial goal of suffrage had been achieved, the feminist movement virtually collapsed in both Europe and the United States. Lacking an ideology beyond the achievement of the vote, feminism fractured into a dozen splinter groups. Each of these groups offered some civic contribution, but none was specifically feminist in nature. Filling the vacuum, the National Woman's Party, led by Paul, proposed a new initiative meant to remove discrimination from American laws and move women closer to equality through an Equal Rights Amendment (ERA) that would ban any government-sanctioned discrimination based on sex. Infighting began because many feminists were not looking for strict equality; they were fighting for laws that would directly benefit women. Paul, however, argued that protective legislation—such as laws mandating maximum eight-hour shifts for female factory workers— actually closed the door of opportunity on women by imposing costly rules on employers, who would then be inclined to hire fewer women.

The debate was not limited to the United States. Some proponents of women's rights, such as Aletta Jacobs of The Netherlands or Beatrice Webb of England, agreed with Paul's demand for equality and opposed protective legislation for women. Women members of trade unions, however, defended the need for laws that would help them. But this philosophical dispute was confined to relatively rarefied circles. Throughout the United States, as across Europe, Americans believed that women had achieved their liberation. Women were voting, although in small numbers and almost exactly like their male counterparts.

The Great Depression and World War II (1939–45) largely obliterated feminist activism on any continent. The war did open employment opportunities for women— from working in factories ("Rosie the Riveter" became an

American icon) to playing professional baseball—but these doors of opportunity were largely closed after the war, when women routinely lost their jobs to men discharged from military service. This turn of events angered many women, but few were willing to mount any organized protest. In the United States, women began marrying younger and having more children than they had in the 1920s. By 1960, the percentage of employed female professionals was down compared with figures for 1930.

THE SECOND WAVE OF FEMINISM

In 1961 Pres. John F. Kennedy created the President's Commission on the Status of Women and appointed Eleanor Roosevelt to lead it. Its report, issued in 1963, firmly supported the nuclear family and preparing women for motherhood. But it also documented a national pattern of employment discrimination, unequal pay, legal inequality, and meagre support services for working women that needed to be corrected through legislative guarantees of equal pay for equal work, equal job opportunities, and expanded child-care services. The Equal Pay Act of 1963 offered the first guarantee, and the Civil Rights Act of 1964 was amended to bar employers from discriminating on the basis of sex.

Some deemed these measures insufficient in a country where classified advertisements still segregated job openings by sex, where state laws restricted women's access to contraception, and where incidences of rape and domestic violence remained undisclosed. In the late 1960s, then, the notion of a women's rights movement—the so-called "second wave" of feminism—took root at the same time as the civil rights movement, and women of all ages and circumstances were swept up in debates about gender, discrimination, and the nature of equality.

Mainstream groups such as the National Organization for Women (NOW) launched a campaign for legal equity, while ad hoc groups staged sit-ins and marches for any number of reasons, from assailing college curricula that lacked female authors to promoting the use of the word *Ms.* as a neutral form of address—that is, one that did not refer to marital status. Health collectives and rape crisis centres were established. Children's books were rewritten to obviate sexual stereotypes. Women's studies departments were founded at colleges and universities. Protective labour laws were overturned. Employers found to have discriminated against female workers were required to compensate with back pay. Excluded from male-dominated occupations for decades, women began finding jobs as pilots, construction workers, soldiers, bankers, and bus drivers. Unlike the first wave, second-wave feminism also provoked extensive theoretical discussion about the origins of women's oppression, the nature of gender, and the role of the family.

By the end of the 20th century, European and American feminists had begun to interact with the nascent feminist movements of Asia, Africa, and Latin America. As this happened, women in developed countries, especially intellectuals, were horrified to discover that women in some countries were required to wear veils in public or to endure forced marriage, female infanticide, widow burning, or female genital cutting (FGC). Many Western feminists soon perceived themselves as saviours of Third World women, little realizing that their perceptions of and solutions to social problems were often at odds with the real lives and concerns of women in other regions. In many parts of Africa, for example, the status of women had begun to erode significantly only with the arrival of European colonialism. In those regions, then, the notion that patriarchy was the chief problem—rather than European imperialism—seemed absurd.

The conflicts between women in developed and developing nations played out most vividly at international conferences. After the 1980 World Conference of the United Nations Decade for Women: Equality, Development and Peace in Copenhagen, women from less-developed nations complained that the veil and FGC had been chosen as conference priorities without consulting the women most concerned. During the 1994 International Conference on Population and Development in Cairo, women from the Third World protested outside because they believed Europeans and Americans had hijacked the agenda. The protesters had expected to talk about ways that underdevelopment was holding women back. Instead, conference organizers chose to focus on contraception and abortion. In Beijing, at the Fourth World Conference on Women in 1995, Third World women again criticized the priority American and European women put on reproductive rights language and issues of discrimination on the basis of sexual orientation, and their disinterest in the platform proposal that was most important to less-developed nations—that of restructuring international debt.

Still, the close of the 20th century saw women around the world advancing their interests, although often in fits and starts. Feminism was derailed in countries such as Afghanistan, where the staunchly reactionary and antifeminist Taliban banned even the education of girls. Elsewhere, however, feminism achieved significant gains for women, as seen in the eradication of FGC in many African countries or government efforts to end widow burning in India. More generally, and especially in the West, feminism had influenced every aspect of contemporary life, communication, and debate, from the heightened concern over sexist language to the rise of academic fields such as women's studies and ecofeminism. Sports, divorce laws, sexual mores, organized religion—all had been affected, in many parts of the world, by feminism.

ABOLITIONISM

In Western Europe and the Americas, *c.* 1783–1888, the abolition movement was responsible for creating the emotional climate necessary for ending the transatlantic slave trade and slavery. Portuguese exploration of the west coast of Africa beginning in 1420 had created an interest in slavery in the recently formed colonies of North America, South America, and the West Indies, where the need for plantation labour generated an immense market for slaves. Between the 16th and 19th centuries, an estimated total of 12 million Africans were forcibly transported to the Americas.

Despite its brutality and inhumanity, the slave system aroused little protest until the 18th century, when rationalist thinkers of the Enlightenment began to criticize it for its violation of the rights of man, and Quaker and other evangelical religious groups condemned it for its un-Christian qualities. By the late 18th century, moral disapproval of slavery was widespread, and antislavery reformers won a number of deceptively easy victories during this period. In Britain, Granville Sharp secured a legal decision in 1772 that West Indian planters could not hold slaves in Britain, since slavery was contrary to English law. In the United States, all of the states north of Maryland abolished slavery between 1777 and 1804.

But antislavery sentiments had little effect on the centres of slavery themselves: the great plantations of the Deep South, the West Indies, and South America. Turning their attention to these areas, British and American abolitionists began working in the late 18th century to prohibit the importation of African slaves into the British colonies and the United States. Under the leadership of William Wilberforce and Thomas Clarkson, these forces succeeded in getting the slave trade to the British colonies abolished in 1807. The United States prohibited the importation of slaves that same year, though widespread smuggling continued until about 1862.

Antislavery forces then concentrated on winning the emancipation of those populations already in slavery. They were triumphant when slavery was abolished in the British West Indies by 1838 and in French possessions 10 years later.

The situation in the United States was more complex because slavery was a domestic rather than a colonial phenomenon, being the social and economic base of the plantations of 11 Southern states. Moreover, slavery had gained new vitality when an extremely profitable cotton-based agriculture developed in the South in the early 19th century. Reacting to abolitionist attacks that branded its "peculiar institution" as brutal and immoral, the South had intensified its system of slave control, particularly after the Nat Turner revolt of 1831. By that time, American abolitionists realized the failure of gradualism and persuasion, and they subsequently turned to a more militant policy, demanding immediate abolition by law.

Probably the best-known abolitionist was the aggressive agitator William Lloyd Garrison, founder of the American Anti-Slavery Society (1833–70). Others, drawn from the ranks of the clergy, included Theodore Dwight Weld and Theodore Parker; from the world of letters, John Greenleaf Whittier, James Russell Lowell, and Lydia Maria Child; and, from the free-black community, such articulate former slaves as Frederick Douglass and William Wells Brown.

American abolitionism laboured under the handicap that it threatened the harmony of North and South in the Union, and it also ran counter to the U.S. Constitution, which left the question of slavery to the individual states. Consequently, the Northern public remained unwilling to adopt abolitionist policy and was distrustful of abolitionist extremism. But a number of factors combined to give the movement increased momentum. Chief among these was the question of permitting or outlawing slavery in new Western territories, with Northerners and Southerners taking increasingly adamant stands on opposite sides of that issue throughout the 1840s and '50s. There was also revulsion at the ruthlessness of slave hunters under the Fugitive Slave Law (1850), and the far-reaching emotional response to Harriet Beecher Stowe's antislavery novel *Uncle Tom's Cabin* (1852) further strengthened the abolitionist cause.

Jolted by the raid (1859) of the abolitionist extremist John Brown on Harpers Ferry, the South became convinced that its entire way of life, based on the cheap labour provided by slaves, was irretrievably threatened by the election to the presidency of Abraham Lincoln (November 1860), who was opposed to the spread of slavery into the Western territories. The ensuing secession of the Southern states led to the American Civil War (1861–65). The war, which began as a sectional power struggle to preserve the Union, in turn led Lincoln (who had never been an abolitionist) to emancipate the slaves in areas of the rebellion by the Emancipation Proclamation (1863) and led further to the freeing of all other slaves in the United States by the Thirteenth Amendment to the Constitution in 1865.

Under the pressure of worldwide public opinion, slavery was completely abolished in its last remaining Latin American strongholds, Cuba and Brazil, in 1880–86 and 1883–88, respectively, and thus the system of African slavery as a Western phenomenon ceased to exist.

CIVIL RIGHTS MOVEMENT

In the United States starting in the late 1950s, a mass movement demanding civil rights for African Americans broke the pattern of racially segregated public facilities in the South and achieved the most important breakthrough in equal-rights legislation for blacks since the Reconstruction period (1865–77). The movement was based on nonviolent protest action.

Denied constitutional guarantees (1787) because of their mainly slave status at the founding of the republic, black Americans were first promised fundamental citizenship rights in the thirteenth–fifteenth constitutional amendments (1865–70). The Civil Rights Act of 1875 required equal accommodations for blacks with whites in public facilities (other than schools), but in 1883 the Supreme Court effectively voided this legislation. By 1900, 18 states of the North and West had legislated public policies against racial discrimination, but in the South new laws eroded the franchise and reinforced segregation practices, while the U.S. Supreme Court upheld "separate but equal" facilities for the races in *Plessy* v. *Ferguson* (1896), thus legitimizing the segregation of blacks from whites.

During World War II (1939–45), progress was made in outlawing discrimination in defense industries (1941) and after the war in desegregating the armed forces (1948). During the late 1940s and early 1950s, lawyers for the National Association for the Advancement of Colored People (NAACP) pressed a series of important cases before the Supreme Court in which they argued that segregation meant inherently unequal (and inadequate) educational and other public facilities for blacks. These cases culminated in the Court's landmark decision in *Brown* v. *Board of Education of Topeka* (May 17, 1954), in which it declared that separate educational facilities were inherently unequal and therefore unconstitutional. This historic decision was to stimulate a mass movement on the part of blacks and white sympathizers to try to end the segregationist practices and racial inequalities that were firmly entrenched across the nation and particularly in the South. The movement was strongly resisted by many whites in the South and elsewhere.

After a black woman, Rosa Parks, was arrested for refusing to move to the African American section of a bus in Montgomery, Alabama (Dec. 1, 1955), blacks staged a one-day local boycott of the bus system to protest her arrest. Fusing these protest elements with the historic force of African American churches, a local Baptist minister, Martin Luther King, Jr., succeeded in transforming a spontaneous racial protest into a massive resistance movement, led from 1957 by his Southern Christian Leadership Conference (SCLC). After a protracted boycott of the Montgomery bus company forced it to desegregate its facilities, picketing and boycotting spread rapidly to other communities. During the period from 1955 to 1960, some progress was made toward integrating schools and other public facilities in the upper South and the region's border states, but the Deep South remained adamant in its opposition to most desegregation measures.

In 1960 the sit-in movement, largely under the auspices of the newly formed Student Nonviolent Coordinating Committee (SNCC), was launched at Greensboro, North Carolina, when black college students insisted on service at a local segregated lunch counter. Patterning its techniques on the nonviolent methods of Indian leader Mohandas Gandhi, the movement spread across the nation, forcing the desegregation of department stores, supermarkets, libraries, and movie theatres. In May 1961 the Congress of Racial Equality (CORE) sent "Freedom Riders" of both races through the South and elsewhere

Participants in the March on Washington, D.C., in August 1963. Library of Congress, Washington, D.C. (digital file no. 04297u); photograph, Warren K. Leffler

to test and break down segregated accommodations in interstate transportation. By September it was estimated that more than 70,000 students had participated in the movement, with approximately 3,600 arrested; more than 100 cities in 20 states had been affected. The movement reached its climax in August 1963 with the massive March on Washington, D.C., to protest racial discrimination and demonstrate support for major civil rights legislation that was pending in Congress.

The federal government under presidents Dwight D. Eisenhower (1953–61) and John F. Kennedy had been reluctant to vigorously enforce the *Brown* decision when this entailed directly confronting the resistance of Southern whites. In 1961–63 President Kennedy won a following in the black community by encouraging the movement's leaders, but Kennedy's administration lacked the political capacity to persuade Congress to pass new legislation guaranteeing integration and equal rights. After President Kennedy's assassination (November 1963), Congress, under the prodding of Pres. Lyndon B. Johnson, in 1964 passed the Civil Rights Act. This was the most far-reaching civil rights bill in the nation's history (indeed, in world history), forbidding discrimination in public accommodations and threatening to withhold federal funds from communities that persisted in maintaining segregated schools. It was followed in 1965 by the passage of the Voting Rights Act, the enforcement of which eradicated the tactics previously used in the South to disenfranchise black voters. This act led to drastic increases in the numbers of black registered voters in the South, with a comparable increase in the numbers of blacks holding elective offices there.

Up until 1966 the civil rights movement had united widely disparate elements in the black community along with their white supporters and sympathizers, but in that year signs of radicalism began to appear in the movement as younger blacks became impatient with the rate of change and dissatisfied with purely nonviolent methods of protest. This new militancy split the ranks of the movement's leaders and also alienated some white sympathizers, a process that was accelerated by a wave of rioting in the black ghettos of several major cities in 1965–67. After the assassination of Martin Luther King, Jr. (April 1968) and further black rioting in the cities, the movement as a cohesive effort disintegrated, with a broad spectrum of leadership advocating different approaches and varying degrees of militancy.

In the decades that followed, many civil rights leaders sought to achieve greater direct political power through elective office, and they sought to achieve more substantive economic and educational gains through affirmative-action

Soldiers stand guard in Washington, D.C., during the riots that occurred after the assassination of Martin Luther King, Jr., April 1968. Library of Congress, Washington, D.C. (digital file no. 04301u)

programs that compensated for past discrimination in job hiring and college admissions. Although the civil rights movement was less militant, it was still persevering.

PACIFISM

Pacifism renounces war and violence as a means of settling disputes, and pacifists believe that the waging of war by a state and the participation in war by an individual are absolutely wrong, under any circumstances. Since the Renaissance, concepts of pacifism have been developed with varying degrees of political influence. A great deal of pacifist thought in the 17th and 18th centuries was based on the idea that a transfer of political power from the sovereigns to the public was a crucial step toward world peace, since wars were thought of as arising from the dynastic ambitions and power politics of kings and princes. Thus was propagated the illusion that monarchies tended toward wars because the sovereigns regarded their states as their personal property and that compared to this, a republic would be peaceful. The offshoot of these theories was the creation of pacifist organizations in 19th-century Europe in which such ideas as general disarmament and the instigation of special courts to hear international conflicts were entertained. The theme of pacifism thereby caught the public interest and inspired an extensive literature.

Some of these ideas were later realized in the Court of Arbitration in The Hague, the League of Nations, the UN, and temporary disarmament conferences, but their overall effect was limited. In the 19th century, for instance, the real maintenance of a relative peace resulted from the statesmanlike political establishment of a balance of power among the great European states. The succeeding century, with its two world wars, its nuclear stalemate, and its unending succession of conflicts among developed and developing nations, has been notable chiefly for the utter irrelevance of pacifist principles and practices.

There are two general approaches or varieties of pacifist behaviour and aspirations. The one rests on the advocacy of pacifism and the complete renunciation of war as a policy to be adopted by a nation; the other stems from the conviction of an individual that his personal conscience forbids him to participate in any act of war and perhaps in any act of violence whatsoever.

The arguments for pacifism as a possible national policy run on familiar lines. The obvious and admitted evils of war are stressed — the human suffering and loss of life, the economic damage, and perhaps above all, the moral and spiritual degradation war brings. Since World War II

(1939–45) increasing emphasis has also been laid on the terrible powers of destruction latent in nuclear weapons. Pacifist advocates often assume that the abandonment of war as an instrument of national policy will not be possible until the world community has become so organized that it can enforce justice among its members. Nonpacifists would, in general, accept what pacifists say about the evils of war and the need for international organization. But they would claim that the pacifists have not faced squarely the possible evils that would result from the alternative policy of a nation's nonresistance in the face of external aggression: the possible mass deportations and even mass exterminations and the subjection of conquered peoples to totalitarian regimes that would suppress just those values which the pacifist stands for.

Personal pacifism is a relatively common phenomenon compared to national pacifism. Members of several small Christian sects who try to literally follow the precepts of Jesus Christ have refused to participate in military service in many nations and have been willing to suffer the criminal or civil penalties that followed. Not all of these and other conscientious objectors are pacifists, but the great majority of conscientious objectors base their refusal to serve on their pacifist convictions. There are, moreover, wide differences of opinion among pacifists themselves about their attitude toward a community at war, ranging from the very small minority who would refuse to do anything that could help the national effort to those prepared to offer any kind of service short of actual fighting.

An examination of two organizations in the United States, the Women's International League for Peace and Freedom (WILPF) and Students for a Democratic Society (SDS), demonstrates two vastly different approaches to antiwar activism. The WILPF has tended to employ moderate techniques, such as raising public awareness of the perils of war; SDS, on the other hand, used radical and sometimes illegal tactics.

The WILPF is the oldest continuously active peace organization in the United States. It encompasses some 100 branches in the United States and has other branches in approximately 50 countries. Philadelphia is the site of the U.S. headquarters, and Geneva is the home of the international headquarters. Officially, the WILPF came into being in 1919 at the end of World War I (1914–18), but it evolved from the Women's Peace Party, a pacifist organization founded by Jane Addams and others who attended the International Congress of Women at The Hague in April 1915. At the time, speaking out against the war was considered radical and unpatriotic, and some members of the Women's Peace Party paid a high price for their sentiments. The economist Emily Greene Balch lost her professorship at Wellesley College, and Addams was declared "the most dangerous woman in America." Eventually, the pacifist work of Addams and Balch was recognized—both won Nobel Peace Prizes (in 1931 and 1946, respectively). Throughout the 20th century, the WILPF persisted in its mission of opposing war and striving for political, economic, social, and psychological freedoms for all and remained firm in the belief that such freedoms are always severely compromised by the threat of war. Currently, the WILPF has identified as its main priorities disarmament, racial justice, and women's rights. The organization formed alliances with such other activist organizations as the Nuclear Weapons Freeze Campaign and the Women's Speaking Tour on Central America to increase support and publicity for its objectives.

SDS flourished in the United States in the mid- to late 1960s; while not strictly a pacifist group, it was known for its activism against the Vietnam War. SDS, founded in 1959, had its origins in the student branch of the League for Industrial Democracy, a social-democratic educational organization. An organizational meeting was held in Ann Arbor, Mich., in 1960, and Robert Alan Haber was elected president of SDS. Initially SDS chapters throughout the nation were involved in the civil rights movement. Operating under the principles of the "Port Huron Statement," a manifesto written by Tom Hayden and Haber and issued in 1962, the organization grew slowly until the escalation of U.S. involvement in Vietnam (1965). SDS organized a national march on Washington, D.C., in April 1965, and, from about that period, SDS grew increasingly militant, especially about issues relating to the war, such as the drafting of students. Tactics included the occupation of university and college administration buildings on campuses across the country. By 1969 the organization had split into several factions, the most notorious of which was the "Weathermen," or "Weather Underground," which employed terrorist tactics in its activities. Other factions turned their attention to the Third World or to the efforts of black revolutionaries. Increasing factionalism within the ranks of SDS and the winding down of the Vietnam War were but two of the reasons for the dissolution of SDS. By the mid-1970s the organization was defunct.

GAY RIGHTS

Before the end of the 19th century there were scarcely any "movements" for the rights of gay, lesbian, bisexual, or transgendered individuals, collectively known as gay rights. Homosexual men and women were given voice in 1897 with the founding of the Scientific-Humanitarian Committee in Berlin. The committee published emancipation literature, sponsored rallies, and campaigned for legal reform throughout Germany, as well as in The Netherlands and Austria, developing some 25 local chapters by 1922. Its founder was Magnus Hirschfeld, who in 1919 opened the Institute for Sexual Science (Institut für Sexualwissenschaft), which anticipated by decades other scientific centres (such as the Kinsey Institute for Research in Sex, Gender, and Reproduction, in the United States) that specialized in sex research. He also helped sponsor the World League of Sexual Reform, which was established in 1928 at a conference in Copenhagen.

Outside Germany, other organizations were also created. For example, in 1914 Edward Carpenter and Havelock Ellis founded the British Society for the Study of Sex Psychology for both promotional and educational purposes, and in the United States in 1924 Henry Gerber, an immigrant from Germany, founded the Society for Human Rights, which was chartered by the state of Illinois.

Despite the formation of such groups, political activity by homosexuals was generally not very visible. Gays were often harassed by the police wherever they congregated. World War II and its aftermath began to change that. The war brought many young people to cities and brought visibility to the gay community.

Beginning in the mid-20th century, an increasing number of organizations were formed. The Cultuur en Ontspannings Centrum ("Culture and Recreation Centre"), or COC, was founded in 1946 in Amsterdam. In the United States the first major male organization, founded in 1950–51 by Harry Hay, was the Mattachine Society, while the Daughters of Bilitis, founded in 1955 by Phyllis Lyon and Del Martin in San Francisco, was a leading group for women. In addition, the United States saw the publication of a national gay periodical, *One*, which in 1958 won a U.S. Supreme Court ruling that enabled it to mail the magazine through the postal service. In Britain a commission chaired by Sir John Wolfenden issued a groundbreaking report in 1957, which recommended that private homosexual liaisons between consenting adults be removed from the domain of criminal law; a decade later the recommendation was implemented by Parliament in the Sexual Offences Act, effectively decriminalizing homosexual relations for men age 21 or older (further legislation lowered the age of consent first to 18 [1994] and then to 16 [2001]).

The gay rights movement was beginning to win victories for legal reform, particularly in Western Europe, but perhaps the single defining event of gay activism occurred in the United States. In the early morning hours of June 28, 1969, police raided the Stonewall Inn, a gay bar located in New York City's Greenwich Village. Nearly 400 people joined a riot that lasted 45 minutes and resumed on succeeding nights. "Stonewall" came to be commemorated annually in June by Gay and Lesbian Pride Week, not only in U.S. cities but also in several other countries.

In the 1970s and '80s gay political organizations proliferated, particularly in the United States and Europe, and spread to other parts of the globe, though their relative size, strength, and success—and toleration by authorities—varied significantly. Groups such as the Human Rights Campaign, the National Gay and Lesbian Task Force, and Act-Up in the United States and Stonewall and Outrage! in the United Kingdom—and dozens and dozens of similar organizations in Europe and elsewhere—began agitating for legal and social reforms. In addition, the transnational International Lesbian and Gay Association was founded in Coventry, Eng., in 1978; now headquartered in Brussels, it plays a significant role in coordinating international efforts to promote human rights and fight discrimination against lesbian, gay, bisexual, and transgendered persons.

In the United States, gay activists won support from the Democratic Party in 1980, when the party added to its platform nondiscrimination clause a plank including sexual orientation. This support, along with campaigns by gay activists urging gay men and women to "come out of the closet" (indeed, in the late 1980s, National Coming Out Day was established and is now celebrated on October 11 in most countries), encouraged gay men and women to enter the political arena as candidates. The first openly gay government officials in the United States were Jerry DeGrieck and Nancy Wechsler, in Ann Arbor, Mich. DeGrieck and Wechsler both were elected in 1972 and came out while serving on the city council. In 1977 American gay rights activist Harvey Milk was elected to the San Francisco Board of Supervisors; Milk was assassinated the following year. In 1983 Gerry Studds, a sitting representative from Massachusetts, became the first member of the United States Congress to announce his homosexuality. In 1998 Tammy Baldwin, from Wisconsin, became the first openly gay politician to be elected to the U.S. House of Representatives.

Outside the United States, openly gay politicians also scored successes. In Canada in 1998 Glen Murray became the mayor of Winnipeg, Man.—the first openly gay politician to lead a large city. Large cities in Europe also were fertile grounds for success for openly gay politicians— for example, Bertrand Delanoë in Paris and Klaus Wowereit in Berlin, both elected mayor in 2001. At the local and national levels, the number of openly gay politicians increased dramatically during the 1990s and 2000s, and in 2009 Jóhanna Sigurðardóttir became prime minister of Iceland—the world's first openly gay head of government.

The issues that gay rights groups emphasized have varied since the 1970s by time and place, with different national organizations promoting policies specifically tailored to their country's milieu. In the United States, with its strong federal tradition, the battle for the repeal of sodomy laws initially was fought at the state level. In 1986 the U.S. Supreme Court upheld Georgia's antisodomy law in *Bowers* v. *Hardwick*; 17 years later, however, in *Lawrence* v. *Texas*, the Supreme Court reversed itself, effectively overturning the antisodomy law in Texas and in 12 other states. Other issues of primary importance for the gay rights movement since the 1970s include combating the HIV/AIDS epidemic and promoting disease prevention and funding for research; lobbying government for non-discriminatory policies in employment, housing, and other aspects of civil society; ending bans on military service for gay individuals; and expanding hate crimes legislation to include protection for gay, lesbian, and transgendered individuals.

At the turn of the 21st century, one of the movement's most prominent causes was the fight to secure marriage rights for gay and lesbian couples. The acceptance of same-sex partnerships was particularly apparent in northern Europe and in countries with cultural ties to that region. In 1989 Denmark became the first country to establish registered partnerships—an attenuated version of marriage—for same-sex couples. Soon thereafter Norway (1993), Sweden (1994), Greenland (1994), Iceland (1996), The Netherlands (1997), and Finland (2001) established similar laws, generally using specific vocabulary (e.g., civil union, civil partnership, domestic partnership, registered partnership) to differentiate same-sex unions from heterosexual marriages. By the early 21st century other European countries with such legislation included Croatia, France, Germany, Great Britain, Hungary, Luxembourg, Portugal, and Switzerland. Outside Europe, some jurisdictions also adopted some form of same-sex partnership rights; Israel recognized common-law same-sex marriage in the mid-1990s, while same-sex civil unions were legalized in New

Zealand in 2004, in the Brazilian state of Rio Grande do Sul also in 2004, and in Mexico City in 2006. In 2007 Uruguay became the first Latin American country to legalize same-sex civil unions.

Some jurisdictions opted to specifically apply the honorific of "marriage" to same-sex as well as heterosexual unions. In 2001 The Netherlands revised its same-sex partnership law and became the first country to replace civil unions with marriages. Countries that subsequently legalized gay marriage included Belgium (2003), Spain (2005), Canada (2005), South Africa (2006), Norway (2009), and Sweden (2009). In 2003 the European Union mandated that all of its members pass laws recognizing the same-sex marriages of fellow EU countries.

In the United States the question of whether couples of the same sex should be allowed to marry has roiled politics since the 1990s. In 1996 the U.S. Congress enacted the Defense of Marriage Act. This legislation declared that same-sex marriages would not be recognized for federal purposes, such as the award of Social Security benefits normally afforded to a surviving spouse or employment-based benefits for the partners of federal employees. The act also restated existing law by providing that no U.S. state or territory was required to recognize marriages from elsewhere when it had strong policies to the contrary.

Nonetheless, some states moved toward the legal recognition of same-sex partnerships. In 1999 the Vermont Supreme Court declared that same-sex couples were entitled under the state constitution to the same legal rights as married heterosexual couples; shortly thereafter the state legislature enacted a law creating "civil unions," which conferred all the rights and responsibilities of marriage but not the name. Several other states, including New Jersey, later established same-sex civil unions, while other states adopted policies that accorded some spousal rights to same-sex couples. In 2003 California enacted a similar statute, calling the relationships "domestic partnerships."

A handful of states—Massachusetts (2004), Connecticut (2008), Iowa, Vermont, Maine, and New Hampshire (all 2009)—allow same-sex marriage.

ANIMAL RIGHTS

The fundamental principle of the modern animal rights movement is that many nonhuman animals have basic interests that deserve recognition, consideration, and protection. In the view of animal rights advocates, these basic interests give the animals that have them both moral and legal rights.

It has been said that the modern animal rights movement is the first social reform movement initiated by philosophers. The Australian philosopher Peter Singer and the American philosopher Tom Regan deserve special mention, not just because their work has been influential but because they represent two major currents of philosophical thought regarding the moral rights of animals. Singer, whose book *Animal Liberation* (1972) is considered one of the movement's foundational documents, argues that the interests of humans and the interests of animals should be given equal consideration. A utilitarian, Singer holds that actions are morally right to the extent that they maximize pleasure or minimize pain; the key consideration is whether an animal is sentient and can therefore suffer pain or experience pleasure. This point was emphasized by the founder of modern utilitarianism, Jeremy Bentham, who wrote of animals, "The question is not, Can they *reason*?, nor, Can they *talk*? but, Can they *suffer*?" Given that animals can suffer, Singer argues that humans have a moral obligation to minimize or avoid causing such suffering, just as they have an obligation to minimize or avoid causing the suffering of other humans. Regan, who is not a utilitarian, argues that at least some animals have basic moral rights because they possess the same advanced cognitive abilities that justify the attribution of basic moral rights to humans. By virtue of these abilities, these animals have not just instrumental but inherent value. In Regan's words, they are "the subject of a life."

Regan, Singer, and other philosophical proponents of animal rights have encountered resistance. Some religious authors argue that animals are not as deserving of moral consideration as humans are because only humans possess an immortal soul. Others claim, as did the Stoics, that because animals are irrational, humans have no duties toward them. Still others locate the morally relevant difference between humans and animals in the ability to talk, the possession of free will, or membership in a moral community (a community whose members are capable of acting morally or immorally). The problem with these counterarguments is that, with the exception of the theological argument—which cannot be demonstrated—none differentiates all humans from all animals.

While philosophers catalyzed the modern animal rights movement, physicians, writers, scientists, academics, lawyers, theologians, psychologists, nurses, veterinarians, and other professionals worked within their own fields to promote animal rights. Many professional organizations were established to educate colleagues and the general public regarding the exploitation of animals.

At the beginning of the 21st century, lawsuits in the interests of nonhuman animals, sometimes with nonhuman animals named as plaintiffs, became common. Given the key positions that lawyers hold in the creation of public policy and the protection of rights, their increasing interest in animal rights and animal-protection issues was significant. Dozens of law schools in Europe, the United States, and elsewhere offered courses in animal law and animal rights; the Animal Legal Defense Fund had created an even greater number of law-student chapters in the United States; and at least three legal journals—*Animal Law*, *Journal of Animal Law*, and *Journal of Animal Law and Ethics*—had been established. Legal scholars were devising and evaluating theories by which nonhuman animals would possess basic legal rights, often for the same reasons as humans do and on the basis of the same legal principles and values. These arguments were powerfully assisted by increasingly sophisticated scientific investigations into the cognitive, emotional, and social capacities of animals and by advances in genetics, neuroscience, physiology, linguistics, psychology, evolution, and ethology, many of which have demonstrated that humans and animals share a broad range of behaviours, capacities, and genetic material.

Meanwhile, the increasingly systemic and brutal abuses of animals in modern society—by the billions on factory farms and by the tens of millions in biomedical-research laboratories—spawned thousands of animal rights groups. Some consisted of a mere handful of people interested in local, and more traditional, animal-protection issues, such as animal shelters that care for stray dogs and cats. Others became large national and international organizations, such as PETA (People for the Ethical Treatment of Animals) and the Humane Society of the United States, which in the early 21st century had millions of members and a multimillion-dollar annual budget. In all their manifestations, animal rights groups began to inundate legislatures with demands for regulation and reform.

ENVIRONMENTALISM

Environmentalism is a political and ethical movement that seeks to improve and protect the quality of the natural environment through changes to environmentally harmful human activities; through the adoption of forms of political, economic, and social organization that are thought to be necessary for, or at least conducive to, the benign treatment of the environment by humans; and through a reassessment of humanity's relationship with nature. In various ways, environmentalism claims that living things other than humans, and the natural environment as a whole, are deserving of consideration in reasoning about the morality of political, economic, and social policies.

The contemporary environmental movement arose primarily from concerns in the late 19th century about the protection of the countryside in Europe and the wilderness in the United States and the health consequences of pollution during the Industrial Revolution. In opposition to the dominant political philosophy of the time, liberalism—which held that all social problems, including environmental ones, could and should be solved through the free market—most early environmentalists believed that government rather than the market should be charged with protecting the environment and ensuring the conservation of resources. An early philosophy of resource conservation was developed by Gifford Pinchot (1865–1946), the first chief of the U.S. Forest Service, for whom conservation represented the wise and efficient use of resources. Also in the United States at about the same time, a more strongly biocentric approach arose in the preservationist philosophy of John Muir (1838–1914), founder of the Sierra Club, and Aldo Leopold (1887–1948), a professor of wildlife management who was pivotal in the designation of Gila National Forest in New Mexico in 1924 as America's first national wilderness area. Leopold introduced the concept of a land ethic, arguing that humans should transform themselves from conquerors of nature into citizens of it; his essays, compiled posthumously in *A Sand County Almanac* (1949), had a significant influence on later biocentric environmentalists.

Environmental organizations established from the late 19th to the mid-20th century were primarily middle-class lobbying groups concerned with nature conservation, wildlife protection, and the pollution that arose from industrial development and urbanization. There were also scientific organizations concerned with natural history and with biological aspects of conservation efforts.

Beginning in the 1960s the various philosophical strands of environmentalism were given political expression through the establishment of "green" political movements in the form of activist nongovernmental organizations and environmentalist political parties. Despite the diversity of the environmental movement, four pillars provided a unifying theme to the broad goals of political ecology: protection of the environment, grassroots democracy, social justice, and nonviolence. However, for a small number of environmental groups and individual activists who engaged in ecoterrorism, violence was viewed as a justified response to what they considered the violent treatment of nature by some interests, particularly the logging and mining industries. The political goals of the contemporary green movement in the industrialized West focused on changing government policy and promoting environmental social values. In the less-industrialized or developing world, environmentalism has been more closely involved in "emancipatory" politics and grassroots activism on issues such as poverty, democratization, and

ECOTERRORISM

The sometimes violent activities of some groups of environmental activists have been described as ecoterrorism. They include criminal trespass on the property of logging companies and other firms and obstruction of their operations, sometimes through the sabotage of company equipment or the environmentally harmless modification of natural resources in order to make them inaccessible or unsuitable for commercial use. Examples of this practice, known as "monkey-wrenching," are the plugging of factory waste outlets and driving spikes into trees so that they cannot be logged and milled. Other activities described as ecoterrorist include protest actions by animal rights groups, which have included the destruction of property in stores that sell products made of fur and the bombing of laboratories that perform experiments on animals.

political and human rights, including the rights of women and indigenous peoples. Examples of such movements include the Chipko movement in India, which linked forest protection with the rights of women, and the Assembly of the Poor in Thailand, a coalition of movements fighting for the right to participate in environmental and development policies.

The early strategies of the contemporary environmental movement were self-consciously activist and unconventional, involving direct-protest actions designed to obstruct and to draw attention to environmentally harmful policies and projects. Other strategies included public-education and media campaigns, community-directed activities, and conventional lobbying of policy makers and political representatives. The movement also attempted to set public examples in order to increase awareness of and sensitivity to environmental issues. Such projects included recycling, green consumerism (also known as "buying green"), and the establishment of alternative communities, including self-sufficient farms, workers' cooperatives, and cooperative-housing projects.

The electoral strategies of the environmental movement included the nomination of environmental candidates and the registration of green political parties. These parties were conceived of as a new kind of political organization that would bring the influence of the grassroots environmental movement directly to bear on the machinery of government, make the environment a central concern of public policy, and render the institutions of the state more democratic, transparent, and accountable. The world's first green parties—the Values Party, a nationally based party in New Zealand, and the United Tasmania Group, organized in the Australian state of Tasmania—were founded in the early 1970s. The first explicitly green member of a national legislature was elected in Switzerland in 1979; later, in 1981, four greens won legislative seats in Belgium. Green parties also have been formed in the former Soviet bloc, where they were instrumental in the collapse of some communist regimes, and in some developing countries in Asia, South America, and Africa, though they have achieved little electoral success there.

The most successful environmental party has been the German Green Party (die Grünen), which entered the Bundestag (parliament) in 1983. In 1998 it formed a governing coalition with the Social Democratic Party, and the party's leader, Joschka Fischer, was appointed as the country's foreign minister. Throughout the last two decades of

THE GREENS

The Greens are any of various environmentalist or eco-logical-oriented political parties formed in European countries and various countries elsewhere beginning in 1979. An umbrella organization known as the European Greens was founded in Brussels, Belg., in January 1984 to coordinate the activities of the various European parties, and Green representatives in the European Parliament sit in the Greens/European Free Alliance group.

The first and most successful party known as the Greens (die Grünen) was founded in West Germany by Herbert Gruhl, Petra Kelly, and others in 1979 and arose out of the merger of about 250 ecological and environ-mentalist groups. The party sought to organize public support for the control of nuclear energy and of air and water pollution. The Greens became a national party in 1980. The program that they adopted called for the dis-mantling of both the Warsaw Pact and NATO, the demilitarization of Europe, and the breaking up of large economic enterprises into smaller units, among other proposals. This program attracted many members of the left wing of the Social Democratic Party into the Greens' ranks. The Greens won a sprinkling of seats in various Land (state) elections from 1979 on, and in 1983 they won a 5.6 percent share of the vote in national elections to the Bundestag (Federal Diet), thereby achieving their first representation in that legislative chamber.

By the end of the 1980s almost every country in western and northern Europe had a party known as the Greens or by some similar name (e.g., Green List in Italy, Green Alliance in Ireland and Finland, Green Alternatives in Austria, Green Ecology Party in Sweden, Ecologist Party in Belgium). Green parties developed also overseas in such countries as Canada, Australia, New Zealand, Argentina, and Chile. After the revolutions of 1989, Green parties or groups also began to emerge in Eastern Europe.

the 20th century, green parties won national representation in a number of countries and even claimed the office of mayor in European capital cities such as Dublin and Rome in the mid-1990s.

By this time green parties had become broad political vehicles, though they continued to focus on the environment. In developing party policy, they attempted to apply the values of environmental philosophy to all issues facing their countries, including foreign policy, defense, and social and economic policies.

Despite the success of some environmental parties, environmentalists remained divided over the ultimate value of electoral politics. For some, participation in elections is essential because it increases the public's awareness of environmental issues and encourages traditional political parties to address them. Others, however, have argued that the compromises necessary for electoral success invariably undermine the ethos of grassroots democracy and direct action. This tension was perhaps most pronounced in the German Green Party. The party's Realos (realists) accepted the need for coalitions and compromise with other political parties, including traditional parties with views sometimes contrary to that of the Green Party. By contrast, the Fundis (fundamentalists) maintained that direct action should remain the major form of political action and that no pacts or alliances should be formed with other parties. Likewise, in Britain, where the Green Party achieved success in some local elections but failed to win representation at the national level (though it did win 15 percent of the vote in the 1989 European Parliament elections), this tension was evidenced in disputes between so-called "electoralists" and "radicals."

By the late 1980s environmentalism had become a global as well as a national political force. Some environmental nongovernmental organizations (e.g., Greenpeace, Friends of the Earth, and the World Wildlife Fund) established a significant international presence, with offices throughout the world and centralized international headquarters to coordinate lobbying campaigns and to serve as campaign centres and information clearinghouses for their national affiliate organizations. Transnational coalition building was and remains another important strategy for environmental organizations and for grassroots movements in developing countries, primarily because it facilitates the exchange of information and expertise but also because it strengthens lobbying and direct-action campaigns at the international level.

Through its international activism, the environmental movement has influenced the agenda of international politics. Although a small number of bilateral and multilateral international environmental agreements were in force before the 1960s, since the 1972 United Nations Conference on the Human Environment in Stockholm, the variety of multilateral environmental agreements has increased to cover most aspects of environmental protection as well as many practices with environmental consequences, such as the trade in endangered species, the management of hazardous waste, especially nuclear waste, and armed conflict. The changing nature of public debate on the environment was reflected also in the organization of the 1992 United

GREENPEACE

Greenpeace is an international organization dedicated to preserving endangered species of animals, preventing environmental abuses, and heightening environmental awareness through direct confrontations with polluting corporations and governmental authorities. Greenpeace was founded in 1971 in British Columbia to oppose U.S. nuclear testing at Amchitka Island in Alaska. The loose-knit organization quickly attracted support from ecologically minded individuals and began undertaking campaigns seeking, among other goals, the protection of endangered whales and seals from hunting, the cessation of the dumping of toxic chemical and radioactive wastes at sea, and the end of nuclear-weapons testing. The primary tactic of Greenpeace has been such "direct, nonviolent actions" as steering small inflatable craft between the harpoon guns of whalers and their cetacean

Members of Greenpeace let their concerns be known in India, 2009. The organization has a history of taking nonviolent but direct action against environmental threats. Prakash Singh/AFP/Getty Images

prey and the plugging of industrial pipes discharging toxic wastes into the oceans and the atmosphere. Such dangerous and dramatic actions brought Greenpeace wide media exposure and helped mobilize public opinion against environmentally destructive practices. Greenpeace also actively sought favourable rulings from national and international regulatory bodies on the control of environmental abuses, sometimes with considerable success. The organization has a small staff and relies largely on voluntary staffing and funding.

Nations Conference on Environment and Development (the Earth Summit) in Rio de Janeiro, Brazil, which was attended by some 180 countries and various business groups, nongovernmental organizations, and the media. In the 21st century, the environmental movement has combined the traditional concerns of conservation, preservation, and pollution with more contemporary concerns with the environmental consequences of economic practices as diverse as tourism, trade, financial investment, and the conduct of war. Environmentalists are likely to intensify the trends of the late 20th century, during which some environmental groups increasingly worked in coalition not just with other emancipatory organizations, such as human rights and indigenous-peoples groups, but also with corporations and other businesses.

Glossary

abolition The act of destroying or doing away with.

absolutism A political theory that states all power should be held by one ruler or authority.

acquiescence Being passive, or agreeing without any argument or dissent.

apartheid A former policy of segregation and political and economic discrimination against non-European groups in the Republic of South Africa.

aristocracy A government in which power is vested in a minority consisting of those believed to be best qualified.

autonomous Not controlled by outside forces; independent.

billeting Providing housing or lodging for military troops.

bourgeoisie The members of the middle class.

colony A new territory that retains ties with the parent state.

conscription Required enrollment in a group, particularly as it pertains to the military; the draft.

conservative A person who tends to maintain existing views, conditions, or institutions.

coup d'état The violent overthrow or alteration of an existing government by a small group.

democracy A government by the people.

doctrine A statement of fundamental government policy, especially in international relations.

egalitarianism The belief in equal rights for all people.

fascism A tendency toward strong autocratic or dictatorial control of a nation.

feminism The theory of political, economic, and social equality between the sexes.

fundamentalism A movement or attitude stressing strict and literal adherence to a set of basic principles.

hinterland A remote area located far away from a city or metropolis.

impressments The taking of people or property for public service or use.

indemnity Exemption from having to pay for damages.

indigenous Originating or living naturally in a particular region or environment.

laissez-faire A doctrine opposing governmental interference in economic affairs beyond the minimum necessary for the maintenance of peace and property rights.

Levelers A group of radicals arising during the English Civil Wars and advocating equality before the law and religious toleration.

leviathan An animal or object that is much larger than usual.

liberal One who is open minded or not strict in the observance of orthodox, traditional, or established forms or ways.

majoritarianism The practice of letting the majority make decisions for a group.

Marxism The political, economic, and social principles and policies advocated by Karl Marx.

metaphysical Based on abstract thought or theory.

monarchy The undivided rule or absolute sovereignty of a nation by a single person.

neoclassical A renewed interest or belief in classical (traditional) concepts or ideas.

neofascist One who has a specific admiration for Benito Mussolini and Italian fascism or any other fascist leader or state.

oligarchy Government by the few.

philosophes The philosophical, political, and social writers of 18th-century France.

populist Someone who supports the rights of the common people.

prelate A high-ranking member of the clergy.

propaganda Information disseminated to sway others toward a cause.

referendum The practice of submitting to popular vote a measure passed on or proposed by a legislative body or by popular initiative.

royalist One who supports a country's monarch.

sansculottes Militant supporters of the French Revolution.

suffrage The right to vote.

supremacist One who believes that a certain group is superior to all other groups.

tariff A tax on imported and exported goods and services.

transient Something that does not occur or stay in one place for very long.

treatise Extensive, well-considered writing on a particular subject.

For Further Reading

Bosworth, R.J.B. *Mussolini's Italy: Life Under the Fascist Dictatorship, 1915–1945*. New York, NY: Penguin, 2007.

Buckner Armstrong, Julie. *The Civil Rights Reader: American Literature from Jim Crow to Reconciliation*. Athens, GA: University of Georgia Press, 2009.

D'Amato, Paul. *The Meaning of Marxism*. Chicago, IL: Haymarket Books, 2006.

Dawn, Karen. *Thanking the Monkey: Rethinking the Way We Treat Animals*. New York, NY: Harper Paperbacks, 2008.

Eltzbacher, Paul. *The Great Anarchists: Ideas and Teachings of Seven Major Thinkers*. Mineola, NY: Dover Publications, 2004.

Encyclopædia Britannica. *The Founding Fathers*. Hoboken, NJ: John Wiley & Sons, 2007.

Formisano, Ronald P. *For the People: American Populist Movements from the Revolution to the 1850s*. Chapel Hill, NC: University of North Carolina Press, 2007.

Gellner, Ernest. *Nations and Nationalism*. Oxford, UK: Blackwell Publishing, 2006.

Hobbes, Thomas. *Leviathan*. London, UK: Oxford University Press, 2009.

Jacai, Fens. *Ten Years of Madness: Oral Histories of China's Cultural Revolution*. South San Francisco, CA: China Books and Periodicals, 2007.

Locke, John. *The Selected Political Writings of John Locke* (Norton Critical Editions). New York, NY: W.W. Norton & Co., 2005.

Neely, Sylvia. *A Concise History of the French Revolution*. Latham, MD: Rowman & Littlefield Publishers, 2008.

Newman, Michael. *Socialism: A Very Short Introduction.* New York, NY: Oxford University Press, 2005.

Purkiss, Diane. *The English Civil War: Papists, Gentlewomen, Soldiers, and Witchfinders in the Birth of Modern Britain.* Jackson, TN: Basic Books, 2007.

Rapport, Mike. *1848: Year of Revolution.* Jackson, TN: Basic Books, 2009.

Schmemann, Serge. *When the Wall Came Down: The Berlin Wall and the Fall of Soviet Communism.* Boston, MA: Kingfisher (Houghton Mifflin), 2007.

Smith, Miriam. *Political Institutions and Lesbian and Gay Rights in the United States and Canada.* New York, NY: Routledge, 2008.

Taylor, Lewis. *Shining Path: Guerrilla War in Peru's Northern Highlands.* Liverpool, UK: Liverpool University Press, 2006.

Weyler, Rex. *Greenpeace: How a Group of Ecologists, Journalists, and Visionaries Changed the World.* Vancouver, BC: Raincoast Books, 2004.

Wolfe, Alan. *The Future of Liberalism.* New York, NY: Alfred A. Knopf, 2009.

*I*ndex

D